Read This First

The information in this book is as up to date and accurate as we can make it. But it's important to realize that the law changes frequently, as do fees, forms and procedures. If you handle your own legal matters, it's up to you to be sure that all information you use—including the information in this book—is accurate. Here are some suggestions to help you:

First, make sure you've got the most recent edition of this book. To learn whether a later edition is available, check the edition number on the book's spine and then go to Nolo's online Law Store at www.nolo.com or call Nolo's Customer Service Department at 800-728-3555.

Next, even if you have a current edition, you need to be sure it's fully up to date. The law can change overnight. At www.nolo.com, we post notices of major legal and practical changes that affect the latest edition of a book. To check for updates, find your book in the Law Store on Nolo's website (you can use the "A to Z Product List" and click the book's title). If you see an "Updates" link on the left side of the page, click it. If you don't see a link, that means we haven't posted any updates. (But check back regularly.)

Finally, we believe accurate and current legal information should help you solve many of your own legal problems on a cost-efficient basis. But this text is not a substitute for personalized advice from a knowledgeable lawyer. If you want the help of a trained professional, consult an attorney licensed to practice in your state.

4th edition

Hiring Independent Contractors

The Employers' Legal Guide

by attorney Stephen Fishman

Edited by attorney Amy DelPo

CPL

NOLO

Law for All

Fourth Edition	MAY 2003
Editor	AMY DELPO
Cover Design	TONI IHARA
Illustrations	MARI STEIN
Book Design	TERRI HEARSH
	STEPHANIE HAROLDE
Proofreading	ROBERT WELLS
CD-ROM Preparation	JENYA CHERNOFF & ANDRÉ ZIVKOVICH
Index	JANET PERLMAN
Printing	ARVATO SERVICES, INC.

Fishman, Stephen.
  Hiring independent contractors : the employers' legal guide / by Stephen Fishman.— 4th ed.
    p. cm.
  Includes index.
  ISBN 0-87337-918-7
    1. Independent contractors—Legal status, laws, etc.—United States—Popular works. 2.
  Witholding tax—Law and legislation—United States—Popular works. I. Title.

  KF898.F57 2003
  346.7302'4—dc21

                                                                    2003041281

For information on bulk purchases or corporate premium sales, please contact the Special Sales Department. For academic sales or textbook adoptions, ask for Academic Sales. Call 800-955-4775 or write to Nolo, 950 Parker Street, Berkeley, CA 94710.

Acknowledgments

Many thanks to:

Barbara Kate Repa and Amy DelPo for their superb editing.

Jake Warner for his editorial contributions.

Fred Daily for many helpful comments on federal tax law.

Terri Hearsh for the outstanding book design and Margaret Livingston for her good-natured and meticulous production work.

Jenya Chernoff and André Zivkovich for CD-ROM preparation.

Janet Perlman for the helpful index.

Bob Wells for thorough proofreading.

About the Author

Stephen Fishman received his law degree from the University of Southern California in 1979. After stints in government and private practice, he became a full-time legal writer in 1983. He has helped write and edit over a dozen reference books for attorneys. Among the books he has written for Nolo are *Working for Yourself: Law & Taxes for Independent Contractors, Freelancers & Consultants*.

Table of Contents

Index

Why You Need This Book

This is a book about the legal ins and outs of hiring and working with independent contractors (ICs)—people who contract to work for others without having the legal status of an employee.

You need this book if you work with or plan to work with independent contractors. This book serves as a complete legal guide to safely hiring and using independent contractors. It explains how to determine whether a worker should be classified as an independent contractor or employee, how to document your classification decision and how to reduce the chances of being subject to or losing an IRS or other government audit.

This book is for business owners, top management and personnel managers. But they are not the only ones who need to know how to hire and deal with independent contractors. For a worker to qualify as an IC, he or she must be treated like one. Business managers at all levels must understand how to treat independent contractors, or risk inadvertently converting them into employees. Other workers who come into daily contact with independent contractors should have a basic understanding of the issues involved as well.

While not specifically written for independent contractors, many of them will find much of the information in this book useful, too.

A. What Are Independent Contractors?

An independent contractor is a person who contracts to perform services for others, but who does not have the legal status of an employee. Most people who qualify as independent contractors follow their own trade, business or profession—that is, they are in business for themselves. This is why they are called "independent" contractors. They earn their livelihoods from their own independent businesses instead of depending upon an employer to earn a living.

Good examples of ICs are professionals with their own practices—for example, doctors, lawyers, dentists and accountants. You may have many choice names for your dentist, but "employee" is probably not one of them. If your dentist has his or her own practice, he or she is an independent businessperson offering dental services to the public, not your employee.

However, a worker doesn't have to be a highly educated professional to be an IC. The person you hire to paint your office or mow your lawn can also be a businessperson and qualify as an IC.

B. Why Hire Independent Contractors?

There are numerous reasons why you might choose to hire an independent contractor for a job. These are discussed in more detail in Chapter 2. Often the biggest reason that a company wants to classify a worker as an independent contractor rather than as an employee, however, is that independent contractors tend to be less expensive than employees. To use an independent contractor, companies simply need to pay whatever the IC charges them for the job. With employees, however, there are a number of additional costs. Employers must withhold federal and state income taxes from their employees' paychecks, and they must pay to the government fees and taxes for Social Security, Medicare, unemployment insurance and workers' compensation insurance. In addition, an employer might choose to provide certain benefits to employees, such as health insurance, stock options, retirement benefits, paid sick leave and paid vacation time.

ICs also offer flexibility. A company can hire them for specific, limited tasks and gain their specialized expertise, without the cost and obligations associated with full-time employees. ICs allow companies to expand or contract the workforce quickly and cheaply, without the headaches and costs of layoffs or firings.

C. Who Decides Whether a Worker Is an Independent Contractor?

Initially, it's up to you to decide whether to classify a worker as an IC or employee. But your decision is subject to review by the Internal Revenue Service (IRS) and other state and federal government agencies. Unfortunately, there is no single test used to determine when workers are and are not ICs. Instead, different, although often similar, legal tests are used by various government agencies and courts to determine worker status.

These government agencies include:

- the IRS (see Chapter 4 for information on how the IRS classifies workers)
- your state's unemployment compensation insurance agency (see Chapter 6 for information on various state rules)
- your state's workers' compensation insurance agency (see Chapter 7 for information on state workers' compensation rules)
- your state's tax department (see Chapter 6 for more about this), and
- the U.S. Labor Department (see Chapter 9 for information on the Labor Department rules).

Each of these agencies is concerned with classifying workers for different reasons, and each has different biases and practices. Each agency normally makes its worker classification decision on its own and does not have to consider what other agencies have done, though they are often strongly influenced by other decisions. It's possible for one agency to find that a worker is an IC and another to find that he or she is an employee. It's equally possible for a worker to be deemed an IC in one state and an employee in another. These conflicts in classification are rare, but they happen.

The result is a legal morass that confuses and frightens many hiring firms. The only way to successfully wade through this legal thicket is to spend some time and effort learning how these government agencies go about classifying workers. If you fail to do so, you leave yourself vulnerable to government auditors who like nothing better than to reclassify ICs as employees and impose assessments, penalties and fines on hapless business owners.

D. Questions to Answer Before Hiring Any Worker

As you may have guessed by now, whether a worker is an IC or employee is not one question, but many. Before you hire any worker, you should answer all the questions listed below. Rest assured that this book gives detailed explanations and guidance in answering each question for your work situation.

- Will the IRS consider the worker an IC? If so, you won't need to withhold and pay federal payroll taxes for the worker, including Social Security taxes, federal disability taxes and federal income tax withholding. If the worker is an employee, you will. (See Chapter 4 for information on the IRS rules.)
- Will your state unemployment compensation agency consider the worker an IC? If so, you won't need to pay for state unemployment compensation coverage. Otherwise, you will. (See Chapter 6 for state unemployment compensation rules.)
- If your state has income taxes, will your state tax department consider the worker an IC? If so, you won't need to withhold state income taxes from the worker's paychecks. Otherwise, you will. (See Chapter 6 for information on state tax rules.)
- Will your state workers' compensation insurance agency consider the worker an IC? If so, you won't need to provide workers' compensation coverage for the worker. Otherwise, you probably will. (See Chapter 7 for information on workers' compensation rules.)
- Will the U.S. Labor Department consider the worker an IC? If so, you won't need to pay the worker time-and-a-half for overtime. If the worker is an employee, you might have

to pay it. (See Chapter 9 for information about the Labor Department test.)

- Will the worker be considered an IC under federal and state laws outlawing workplace discrimination? If so, you're protected from many types of discrimination lawsuits. (See Chapter 9 for information about anti-discrimination laws.)

- Will the worker be an IC for intellectual property ownership purposes? If so, you need to take steps to obtain ownership of any intellectual property the worker creates on your behalf. (See Chapter 10 for information about intellectual property ownership.)

Your goal should be to ensure that a worker qualifies as an IC for all these purposes. While it is possible for a worker to have a hybrid status—that is, to be an IC for some purposes and an employee for others—in practice, this can be difficult. Most government agencies want workers to be employees, not ICs. If an agency discovers that you're treating a worker as an employee for any purpose, the chances go up that it will conclude that the worker is an employee for its purposes as well. Similarly, a finding by one agency that an IC is really an employee can lead others to reclassify the worker.

Icons Used in This Book

 Caution: A potential problem.

 See an Expert: An instance when you may need the advice of an attorney or other expert.

 Resources: Suggests books, websites or other resources that may be of use.

 Document: Signals that you can find a particular resource in one of the appendixes at the back of the book.

 CD-ROM/Document: Signals that you can find a particular resource in one of the appendixes and/or at a named agency and/or on the CD-ROM at the back of the book.

 Tip: Provides ideas and strategies for dealing with certain situations.

Benefits and Risks of Hiring Independent Contractors

There are many benefits to hiring ICs, but there are serious risks as well. No book can decide for you whether to use ICs in your business. But this chapter helps you make your own informed decision by summarizing the benefits and risks that may be involved.

A. Benefits of Using Independent Contractors

It can cost less to use ICs instead of employees because you don't have to pay employment taxes and various other employee expenses. In addition, you will be less vulnerable to some kinds of lawsuits. Perhaps most importantly, however, hiring ICs gives hiring firms greater flexibility in expanding and contracting the workforce.

1. Financial Savings

It usually costs more to hire employees than ICs because, in addition to employee salaries or other compensation, you usually have to pay a number of employee expenses. These expenses add at least 20% to 30% to your payroll costs, often more. For example, if you pay an employee $10 per hour, you must pay an additional $2 to $3 or more per hour in employee expenses.

You incur none of these expenses when you hire an IC. Even though ICs are often paid more

per hour than employees doing the same work, you can still save money by adding them to your workforce.

In addition to the costs of payroll processing, the most common employee expenses include:

- federal payroll taxes
- unemployment compensation insurance
- workers' compensation insurance
- office space and equipment, and
- employee benefits such as vacation and health insurance.

a. Federal payroll taxes

Employers must withhold and pay federal payroll taxes for employees. They must pay a 7.65% Social Security tax and a small—usually .08%—federal unemployment tax out of their own pockets. Employees' own Social Security taxes and federal income taxes must also be withheld from their paychecks by their employers and paid to the IRS. (See Chapter 4.)

No federal payroll taxes need be withheld or paid for ICs. This not only saves hiring firms money, but accounting and bookkeeping costs as well.

b. Unemployment compensation

Employers in every state are required to contribute to a state unemployment insurance fund on behalf of most types of employees. The unemployment tax rate is usually somewhere between 2% to 5% of employee wages—up to the maximum amount of wages that are taxable under the state's unemployment compensation law. (See Chapter 6.)

c. Workers' compensation insurance

Employers must provide workers' compensation insurance coverage for most types of employees in case the employees become injured on the job. Workers' compensation insurance is obtained from either private insurers or state workers' compensation funds. Premiums can range from a few hundred dollars per year to thousands, depending upon the employee's occupation and a company's claims history. Workers' compensation insurance need not be provided for ICs. (See Chapter 7 for information about state workers' compensation laws.)

d.   Office space and equipment

Employers normally provide their employees with workspace and whatever equipment they need to do the job. This is not necessary for ICs, who normally provide their own workplaces and equipment. Office space is usually a hiring firm's second biggest expense; only employee salaries and benefits cost more.

e.   Employee benefits

Although not required by law, employers usually provide their employees with benefits such as health insurance, paid vacations, sick leave, retirement benefits and life or disability insurance. You need not and should not provide ICs with such benefits.

Health insurance costs, in particular, can be enormous. Many employers are cutting back on health insurance benefits for employees in attempts to save money. But these kinds of cutbacks can have high costs in employee discontent.

2.   Reduced Exposure to Lawsuits

When you hire employees, you may be subject to some types of lawsuits for which you aren't liable when you hire ICs.

a.   Labor and anti-discrimination laws

Employees have a wide array of rights under state and federal labor and anti-discrimination laws. Among other things, these laws:

- impose a minimum wage and require many employees to be paid time-and-a-half for overtime
- make it illegal for employers to discriminate against employees on the basis of race, color, religion, gender and national origin
- protect employees who wish to unionize, and
- make it unlawful for employers to knowingly hire illegal aliens.

In recent years, a growing number of employees have brought lawsuits against employers alleging violations of these laws. Some employers have had to pay hefty damages to their employees. In addition, various watchdog agencies, such as the U.S. Department of Labor and the U.S. Equal Employment Opportunity Commission, have authority to take administrative or court action against employers they claim have violated these laws.

Few of these anti-discrimination and employment laws apply to ICs. So you have much less exposure to these kinds of employee claims and lawsuits when you have ICs as workers. (See Chapter 9.)

b.   Wrongful termination liability

Another type of lawsuit employees can potentially file against you is for wrongful termination. In these legal actions, an employee claims that his or her firing was illegal or constitutes a breach of contract. Wrongful termination laws vary from state to state. Under some circumstances, for example, it might be a breach of contract for you to fire an employee without good cause. To guard against wrongful termination claims, hiring firms must carefully document the reasons for firing an employee.

ICs are not employees and so cannot bring wrongful termination lawsuits. However, there usually are contractual restrictions on when you can fire an IC. (See Section B5.)

c. Liability for workers' actions

When you hire an employee, you're liable for anything he or she does within the scope of employment. For example, if an employee gets into an auto accident while making a delivery, you may be liable for the damages.

Subject to several important exceptions, this is not the case with ICs. You are not liable for an IC's actions, work-related or not, unless:

- the IC you hired was not qualified to do the job and you were negligent in hiring him or her
- an injury occurs because you gave the IC bad directions
- you know the IC is violating the law in working for you—for example, you hire an unlicensed IC to perform work that requires a construction contractor license, or
- you hire an IC to do work that is inherently dangerous—for example, building demolition.

3. Flexibility in Hiring

What is most important for many hiring firms is that working with ICs provides a level of flexibility that can't be obtained with employees. An IC can be hired to accomplish a specific task and then forgotten, enabling a business to obtain specialized expertise for a short period. You need not go through the trauma and potential severance costs and lawsuits brought on by laying off or firing an employee. And an experienced IC can usually be productive immediately, eliminating the time and expense involved in training employees. By using ICs, you can expand and contract your workforce as needed, quickly and inexpensively.

B. Risks of Using Independent Contractors

After reading about the possible benefits you can get from ICs, you might be thinking: "I'll never hire an employee again; I'll just use independent contractors." But be aware that there are some substantial risks involved in classifying workers as ICs.

1. Federal Audits

The IRS wants to see as many workers as possible classified as employees, not ICs, so that it can immediately collect taxes based on payroll withholding. Being pegged as employees also makes it far more difficult for workers to under-report their income or otherwise evade taxes. In recent years, the IRS has mounted an aggressive attack on employers who, in its view, misclassify employees as ICs.

If the IRS audits your business and determines that you have misclassified employees as ICs, it may impose substantial interest and penalties. Such assessments can easily put a small company out of business. The owners of an unincorporated business may be held personally liable for such assessments and penalties. But, even if your business is a corporation, you could still be held personally liable for the tax, interest and penalties.

Federal audits don't end with the IRS. Other agencies can also get into the act. These include the Department of Labor, which enforces the federal minimum wage and hours laws; the National Labor Relations Board, which enforces employees' federal right to unionize, and the Occupational Safety and Health Administration, which enforces workplace safety laws. (See Chapter 9 for information about labor and anti-discrimination laws.)

2. State Audits

Audits by state agencies are even more common than federal audits. State audits most frequently occur when workers classified as ICs apply for unemployment compensation after their services are terminated. Your state unemployment compensation agency will begin an investigation, and you may be subject to fines and penalties if it is determined that workers should have been classified as employees for unemployment compensation purposes.

If workers classified as ICs are injured on the job and apply for workers' compensation benefits, you can expect an audit by your state workers' compensation agency, because workers' compensation benefits are for employees only. Very substantial penalties can be imposed on hiring firms that misclassify employees as ICs for workers' compensation purposes. These include fines, penalties and court orders preventing you from doing business until you obtain workers' compensation insurance. (See Chapter 7 for more about state workers' compensation laws.)

Although not as common as unemployment insurance or workers' compensation audits, your state tax agency may also conduct audits to ensure that your workers are properly classified for purposes of your state income tax law. Again, fines and penalties may be imposed for misclassification of employees as ICs. (See Chapter 6 for more information about state tax laws.)

3. Loss of Control

Another possible drawback to classifying workers as ICs is that you lose control over the worker. Unlike employees, whom you can closely supervise and micromanage, independent contractors must be left alone to do the job you are paying them to do. If you help them too much or interfere too much in their performance, you risk turning them into employees. (See Chapter 3 for more about this control issue.)

Some business owners can't stand not being in charge of everything and everybody involved with their business. They particularly want to be able to closely supervise their workers. If you want to control how a worker performs, classify him or her as an employee.

4. Loss of Continuity

Generally, employers use a particular IC only as needed for short-term projects. They should spread their hiring around and not rely too much on one IC. Having workers constantly coming and going can be inconvenient and disruptive for any workplace. And the quality of work you get from various ICs may be uneven. One reason businesses hire employees is to be able to depend on having the same workers available day after day.

5. Restrictions on Right to Fire

You do not have an unrestricted right to fire an IC as you do with most employees. Your right to terminate an IC's services is limited by the terms of your agreement. If you terminate an IC who performs adequately and otherwise satisfies the terms of the agreement, you'll be liable to the IC for breaking the agreement. In other words, the IC can sue you and get an order requiring you to pay a substantial amount of money in damages.

6.   Liability for Injuries

Employees covered by workers' compensation who are injured on the job cannot sue you for damages. They are allowed only to file workers' compensation claims and receive workers' compensation benefits. This is not the case with ICs. They can sue you for damages if they claim they were injured because of your negligence, such as your failure to provide a safe workplace. If the injuries are substantial and your negligence clear, you may end up being liable for large amounts of damages. When you hire ICs, you should have liability insurance to cover the costs of such lawsuits. This may or may not be cheaper than obtaining workers' compensation insurance.

7.   Possible Loss of Copyright Ownership

If you hire ICs to create works that can be copyrighted—for example, book chapters or photographs—you can pay for the work and yet not be considered the owner unless you use written agreements transferring copyright ownership in advance. This is not the case with employees. (See Chapter 10 for information about intellectual property issues.) ■

The Common Law Test

A worker is not an independent contractor simply because you say so. Courts and government agencies will determine the worker's status by applying a legal worker classification test. There are all sorts of classification tests, and we will introduce you to all of them in this book. In this chapter, however, we take a close look at the most frequently used test—the common law test. As you read through this book, you may see that one agency or another in your state uses this test or some form of it. Although each agency that uses the common law test puts its own spin on it, they all apply essentially the same criteria and theories.

One of the most well-known agencies that uses the common law test is the IRS. Because the IRS test is so important and crucial to worker classification, we devote an entire chapter—Chapter 4—to that particular use of the common law test. If you are looking for guidance on applying the IRS test or on classifying a worker for federal payroll tax purposes, skip ahead to Chapter 4.

A. The Need for a Legal Test to Determine Worker Status

As discussed in Chapter 1, ICs are people who are in business for themselves. Sometimes it's very easy to tell if workers are in business for themselves. This means it's easy to tell whether they are independent contractors.

EXAMPLE: You start a restaurant and contract with IBM to install a computer system for your business. There is no way IBM will be viewed as your employee. You need not worry about paying employment taxes for IBM's workers. That's IBM's problem. IBM is clearly an established independent business. Not even the most hard-nosed IRS auditor would question this.

EXAMPLE: You hire several people to wait tables in your restaurant and pay them sala-

ries, benefits and so forth. It is clear that a typical waitperson in a restaurant is not in business for himself. He is an employee of the restaurant. The restaurant owner—that is, you—are the one in business.

In cases like these, it's so clear that the worker is—or is not—in a separate business that there really is no need to apply any specific legal test to determine the worker's status. In many other cases, however, the issue is not quite so clear. Things can be especially foggy when workers perform specialized services by themselves—that is, without the help of assistants.

EXAMPLE: Instead of hiring IBM, you hire a computer consultant named Mike to install your computers. Mike has no employees and performs all the work for you personally. He ends up spending several months working on your computers. It's difficult to say for sure that Mike was in business for himself while he worked for you.

It may be helpful to view every worker in America as being somewhere in a continuum. At one end are workers who are clearly employees; at the other end are those who are clearly ICs. But in between these two extremes, there is a vast middle ground where work relationships have some elements of employment and some elements of independence. It is where workers fall into this uncertain middle ground that problems with the IRS, state tax authorities, unemployment compensation authorities and other agencies can develop.

It's to deal with cases falling within this middle ground that the courts and agencies have developed detailed legal tests to determine worker status. The purpose of these tests is to give both hiring firms and government agencies some objective and understandable basis for classifying workers. Unfortunately, these tests often do not provide a clear answer about how to classify a worker.

The common law test is the legal test most frequently used to determine worker status. It is also called the right of control test. This is the test used by:

- the IRS (see Chapter 4 for a detailed examination of how the IRS applies the common law test)
- unemployment compensation insurance agencies in many states (see Chapter 6 to find out which states use the common law test)
- workers' compensation insurance agencies in many states (see Chapter 7 to find out which state's workers' compensation agencies use the common law test), and
- courts, to determine copyright ownership disputes (see Chapter 10 for more information about intellectual property issues).

OTHER TESTS FOR IC STATUS

The common law test isn't the only test used to determine worker status. Two other types of tests are used by some government agencies:

- **The Economic Reality Test:** Under this test, workers are employees if they are economically dependent upon the businesses for which they render services. Economic dependence equals an employment relationship. (See Chapter 6, Section B4, for a detailed discussion of this test.)
- **ABC Test:** About half the states use a special statutory test, also called the ABC test, to determine if workers are ICs or employees for purposes of unemployment compensation. This test focuses on just a few factors. (See Chapter 6 for a detailed discussion of this test.)

B. The Right of Control Is Key

The common law test is based on a very simple notion: Employers have the right to tell their employees what to do. The employer may not always exercise this right—for example, if an employee is experienced and well trained, the employer may not feel the need to closely supervise him or her—but the employer has the right to do so anyway.

Under the common law test, workers are employees if the people for whom they work have the right to direct and control them in the way they do their jobs—both as to the final results and as to the details of when, where and how the work is performed.

> EXAMPLE: Mary takes a job as a hamburger cook at the local AcmeBurger. AcmeBurger personnel carefully train her in how to make an AcmeBurger hamburger, including the type and amount of ingredients to use, the temperature at which the hamburger should be cooked and so forth. Once Mary starts work, AcmeBurger managers closely supervise how she does her job.
>
> Virtually every aspect of Mary's behavior on the job is under AcmeBurger control—including what time she arrives at and leaves work, when she takes her lunch break, what she wears and the sequence of the tasks she must perform. If Mary proves to be an able and conscientious worker, her supervisors may not look over her shoulder very often, but they have the right to do so at any time. Mary is AcmeBurger's employee.

In contrast, when you hire an IC, you hire an independent businessperson. A hiring firm normally does not have the right to control the way an independent businessperson—an IC—performs agreed-upon services. Its control is limited to accepting or rejecting the final results.

EXAMPLE: AcmeBurger develops a serious plumbing problem. AcmeBurger does not have any plumbers on its staff, so it hires Plumbing by Jake, an independent plumbing repair business owned by Jake. Jake looks at the problem and gives an estimate of how much it will cost to fix. The manager agrees and Jake and his assistant commence work. The manager doesn't give Jake any instructions on how to fix the plumbing problem—the manager just wants the problems resolved

In a relationship of this kind where Jake is clearly running his own business, it's virtually certain that AcmeBurger does not have the right to control the way Jake performs his plumbing services. Its control is limited to accepting or rejecting the final result. If AcmeBurger doesn't like the work Jake has done, it can refuse to pay him.

C. Factors for Measuring Control

The difficulty in applying the common law test is deciding whether a hiring firm has the right to control its workers. The government agencies you have to deal with can't look into your mind to see whether the right to control exists. They must rely primarily on indirect or circumstantial evidence indicating control or lack of it—for example, whether you provide a worker with tools and equipment, pay by the hour or have the right to fire the worker. This is what government auditors will be asking you about if you're audited.

To evaluate whether a worker passes muster as an IC, you need to examine these factors. The fact that you may know in your heart that you do not control a worker is not sufficient. What matters is how your relationship with the worker appears to a government auditor who doesn't know you or the worker.

Government auditors examine a number of different factors to determine whether a hiring firm has the right to control a worker. The following list of 25 factor includes virtually every factor any au-

ditor might consider. No agency uses all 25 factors; instead an agency may use anywhere from four to 20 from this list. Which factors are used by which agency is discussed in later chapters.

You don't need to memorize this list. It's included so that you can refer to it if you need it. There's no magic number of factors that you need to make a worker an IC or an employee. You need to look at the totality of the circumstances. In many cases, you will look at the list and so many factors will weigh in favor of IC status or employee status that you can feel secure in your classification. In other cases, you make go through the list and still feel like you don't know how to classify the worker. When that happens, consider consulting an expert, such as an accountant or an attorney, for assistance.

1. Making a Profit or Loss

Employees are typically paid for their time and labor and have no liability for business expenses. They will earn the same salary regardless of how the work is performed.

In contrast, ICs can earn a profit or suffer a loss as a result of the services being performed. They make money if their businesses succeed, but risk going broke if they fail. Whether ICs make money depends on how well they use their ingenuity, initiative and judgment in conducting their business.

Thus, if a worker has an opportunity to make a profit or suffer a loss based on the work being performed, then that fact makes the worker look more like an independent contractor.

2. Working on Specific Premises

Employees must work where their employers tell them, usually on the employer's premises. ICs are usually able to choose where to perform their services. Thus, work at a location specified by a hiring firm implies control by the firm, especially where the work could be done elsewhere. A person working at a hiring firm's place of business is physically within the firm's direction and supervision. If the person can choose to work off the premises, the firm obviously has less control. If a worker performs the work on your premises, that's a check in the independent contractor side of the column.

3. Offering Services to the General Public

Employees offer their services solely to their employers; ICs normally make their services available to the public. Thus, if the worker advertises his services or works for people other than the hiring firm, this tends to show that the worker is an IC.

4. Right to Fire

Unless the employee has an employment contract, the employee typically can be fired by the employer at any time, for any reason that is not illegal. An IC's relationship with a hiring firm can be terminated only according to the terms of their agreement. If you have a right to fire a worker at any time for any reason or for no reason at all, government auditors may conclude that you have the right to control that worker. The ever-present threat of dismissal must inevitably cause a worker to follow your instructions and otherwise do your bidding. Thus, the right to fire weighs in favor of employee status.

5. Furnishing Tools and Materials

Employees are typically furnished all the tools and materials necessary to do their jobs by their employers. ICs typically furnish their own tools and materials.

The fact that a hiring firm furnishes tools and materials, such as computers and construction equipment, tends to show control because the firm can determine which tools the worker is to use and, at least to some extent, in what order and how they will be used. In most circumstances, then, the furnishing of tools and materials by the hiring firm weighs in favor of IC status.

Sometimes, Tools Don't Matter

Sometimes ICs have to use a hiring firm's tools or materials. For example, a computer consultant may have to perform work on the hiring firm's computers. In such a situation, the fact that the tools are provided should be irrelevant.

6. Method of Payment

Employees are usually paid by unit of time—for example, by the hour, week or month. In such a situation, the hiring firm assumes the risk that the services provided will be worth what the worker is paid. To protect its investment, the hiring firm demands the right to direct and control the worker's performance. In this way, the hiring firm makes sure it gets a day's work for a day's pay.

ICs typically earn a flat rate for a project. The IC assumes the risk that the estimate for the rate will compensate for the time and expense spent on the project. The IC, then, will control how he does the work.

Thus, payment by the job or on a straight commission generally weighs in favor of IC status.

In many professions and trades, however, payment is customarily made by unit of time. For example, lawyers, accountants and psychiatrists typically charge by the hour. Where this is the general practice, the method of payment factor will not be given great weight.

7. Working for More Than One Firm

Many employees have more than one job at a time. However, employees owe a duty of loyalty toward their employers—that is, employees cannot engage in activities that harm or disrupt the employer's business. This restricts employees' outside activities. For example, an employee ordinarily wouldn't be permitted to take a second job with a competitor of the first employer. An employee who did so would be subject to dismissal.

ICs are generally subject to no such restrictions. They can work for as many clients or customers as they want. Having more than one client or customer at a time is very strong evidence of IC status. People who work for several firms at the same time are generally ICs because they're usually free from control by any one of the firms.

8. Continuing Relationship

Although employees can be hired for short-term projects, this type of relationship is more typical of ICs. An employee usually works for the same employer month after month, year after year, sometimes decade after decade. Such a continuing relationship is one of the hallmarks of employment. Indeed, one of the main reasons businesses hire employees is to have workers available on a long-term basis.

ICs, on the other hand, come and go. A firm hires them for a project, and then the relationship ends.

Thus, a continuing relationship is evidence of employee status.

9. Investment in Equipment or Facilities

A worker who makes a significant investment in the equipment and facilities to perform services is more likely to be considered an IC. By making such a financial investment, the worker risks losing it if the business is not profitable. Also, the worker is not dependent upon a hiring firm for the tools and facilities needed to do the work. Owning the tools and facilities also implies that the worker has the right to control their use.

On the other hand, lack of investment indicates dependence on the hiring firm for tools and facilities and is another hallmark of an employer-employee relationship.

This factor includes equipment and premises necessary for the work, such as office space, furniture and machinery. It does not include tools, instruments and clothing commonly provided by employees in their trade—for example, uniforms that are commonly provided by the employees themselves. Nor does it include education, experience or training.

Some types of workers typically provide their own inexpensive tools. For example, carpenters may use their own hammers and accountants their own calculators. Providing such inexpensive tools doesn't show that a worker is an IC. But a worker who provides his or her own $3,000 computer or $10,000 lathe is more likely to be an IC.

10. Business or Traveling Expenses

If the hiring firm pays a worker's business and traveling expenses, that fact points to employee status. To be able to control such expenses, the employer must retain the right to regulate and direct the worker's actions.

On the other hand, a person who is paid per project and who has to pay expenses out of pocket is more likely to be viewed as an IC. Any worker who is accountable only to himself or herself for expenses is free to work according to individual methods and means.

Of course, some ICs typically bill their clients for certain expenses. For example, accountants normally bill clients for travel, photocopying and other incidental expenses. This does not make them employees, since their clients do not control them.

11. Right to Quit

Employees normally work "at will." This means they can quit whenever they want to without incurring liability, even if it costs the employer substantial money and inconvenience.

ICs usually agree to complete a specific job. If they don't, they are liable to the hiring firm to make good any losses caused.

12. Instructions

Employers have the right to give their employees oral or written instructions that the employees must obey about when, where and how they are to work. Hiring firms generally do not give independent contractors these sorts of instructions.

This can be a difficult factor to evaluate because there is no requirement that instructions actually be given. Instead, the focus is on whether the hiring firm has the right to give them.

If a worker is running an independent business and you are just one client or customer among many, it's likely you don't have the right to give the worker instructions about how to perform the services. Your right is usually limited to accepting or rejecting the final results.

EXAMPLE: Art goes to Joe's Tailor Shop and hires Joe to make him a suit. Art chooses the fabric and style of the suit, but it's up to Joe to decide how to make the suit. When the suit is finished, Art can refuse to pay for it if he thinks it isn't made well. Joe is an independent contractor. If Art had presumed to tell Joe how to go about cutting the fabric and stitching the suit together, Joe would probably have kicked him out of his shop and gone on to his next customer.

On the other hand, you probably will have the right to give instructions to workers who are not running an independent business and are largely or solely dependent upon you for their livelihood.

EXAMPLE: Joe the tailor abandons his own tailor shop when he's hired to perform full-time tailoring services for Acme Suits, a large haberdashery chain. Joe is completely dependent upon Acme for his livelihood. Acme managers undoubtedly have the right to give Joe instructions, even if they don't feel the need to do so because Joe is such a good tailor.

A hiring firm may give an IC detailed guidelines as to the end results to be achieved. For example, a software programmer may be given highly detailed specifications describing the software programs to develop; or a building contractor may be given detailed blueprints showing precisely what the finished building should look like. Since these relate only to the end results to be achieved, not how to achieve them, they do not make the programmer or building contractor employees.

13. Sequence of Work

Employees may be required to perform services in the order or sequence set for them by the employer. ICs decide for themselves the order or sequence in which they work.

This factor is closely related to the right to give instructions. If a person must perform services in the order or sequence set by the hiring firm, it shows that the worker is not free to use discretion in working, but must follow established routines and schedules.

Often, because of the nature of the occupation, the hiring firm either does not set the order of the services or sets them infrequently. It is sufficient to show control, however, if the hiring firm retains the right to do so. For example, a salesperson who works on commission is usually permitted latitude in mapping out work activities. But one who hires such a salesperson normally has the discretion to

require him or her to report to the office at specified times, follow up on leads and perform certain
tasks at certain times. Such requirements interfere
with and take precedence over the salesperson's
own routines or plans. They indicate control by
the hiring firm and employee status for the salesperson.

14. Training

Employees may receive training from their employers. ICs ordinarily receive no training from those
who purchase their services.

Training may be done by teaming a new
worker with a more experienced one, by requiring
attendance at meetings or seminars or even by correspondence. Training shows control because it
indicates that the employer wants the services performed a particular way. This is especially true if
the training is given periodically or at frequent in-
tervals.

ICs are usually hired precisely because they
don't need any training. They possess special skills
or proficiencies that the hiring firm's employees do
not.

15. Services Performed Personally

Employees are required to perform their services
on their own—that is, they can't get someone else
to do their jobs for them. ICs ordinarily are not required to render services personally; for example,
they can hire their own employees or even other
ICs to do the work.

Ordinarily, when you hire an IC, he or she has
the right to delegate all or part of the work to others
without your permission. This is part and parcel of
running a business. For example, if you hire an accountant to prepare your tax return, the accountant
normally has the right to have assistants do all or
part of the work under his or her supervision.

Requiring someone you hire to perform the services personally indicates that you want to control
how the work is done, not just the end results. If
you were just interested in end results, you

wouldn't care who did the work; you'd just make
sure the work was done right when it was finished.

16. Hiring Assistants

Employees hire, supervise and pay assistants only
at the direction of the employer. ICs, on the other
hand, hire, supervise and pay their own assistants
without input from the hiring firm.

Government auditors are usually impressed by
the fact that a worker hires and pays his or her
own assistants. This is something employees simply do not do and is strong evidence of IC status
because it shows risk of loss if the worker's income does not match payroll expenses.

17. Set Working Hours

Employees ordinarily have set hours of work. ICs
are masters of their own time; they ordinarily set
their own work hours.

18. Working Full Time

An employer might require an employee to work
full time. ICs are free to work when and for whom
they choose—and usually have the right to work
for more than one client or customer at a time.

19. Oral or Written Reports

Employees may be required to submit regular oral
or written reports to the employer regarding the
progress of their work. ICs are generally not required to submit regular reports; they are responsible only for end results.

Submitting reports shows that the worker is
compelled to account for individual actions. Reports are an important control device for an employer. They help determine whether directions
are being followed and whether new instructions
should be issued.

This requirement focuses on regular reports that
enable an employer to keep track of employees'

day-to-day performance. It's quite common for ICs to make infrequent interim reports to hiring firms when they are working on long or complex projects. Such reports are typically tied to specific completion dates, timelines or milestones written into the contract. For example, a building contractor may be contractually required to report to the hiring firm when each phase of a complex building project is completed.

20. Integration Into Business

Employees typically provide services that are an integral part of the employer's day-to-day operations. In contrast, an independent contractor's services are usually outside the operation.

Integration in this context has nothing to do with race relations. It simply asks whether the worker is a regular part of the hiring firm's overall operations. According to most government auditors, the hiring firm would likely exercise control over integrated workers because they are so important to the success of the business.

> EXAMPLE: Fry King is a fast food outlet. It employs 15 workers per shift who prepare and sell the food. Jean is one of the workers on the night shift. Her job is to prepare all the French fries for the shift. Fry King would likely go out of business if it didn't have someone to prepare the French fries. French fry preparation is a regular or integral part of Fry King's daily business operations.

On the other hand, ICs generally have special skills that the hiring firm calls upon only sporadically.

> EXAMPLE: Over the course of a year, Fry King hires a painter to paint its business premises, a lawyer to handle a lawsuit by a customer who suffered from food poisoning and an accountant to prepare a tax return. All of these things may be important or even essential to Fry King—otherwise it wouldn't have them done—

but they are not a part of Fry King's normal overall daily operations of selling fast food.

21. Skill Required

Workers whose jobs require a low level of skill and experience are more likely to be employees. Workers with jobs requiring high skills are more likely to be ICs.

The skill required to do a job is a good indicator of whether the hiring firm has the right to control a worker. This is because you are far more likely to have control over the way low-skill workers do their jobs than you do over the way high-skill workers do their jobs.

For example, if you hire a highly skilled repair person to maintain an expensive and complex photocopier, it's doubtful that you know enough about photocopiers to supervise the work or even tell the repair person what to do. All you are able to know is whether the results the repair person achieves meet your requirements—that is, whether the photocopier works or not.

This is not the case, however, when you hire a person to do a job that does not require high skills or training, such as answering telephones. You are likely to spell out the details of how the work should be done and are certainly capable of supervising the worker. Workers in such occupations generally expect to be controlled by the person who pays them—that is, they expect to be given specific instructions as to how to work, be required to work during set hours, be provided with tools and equipment and so forth.

For these reasons, highly skilled workers are far more likely to be ICs than low-skill workers. However, not all high-skill workers are ICs. Corporate officers, doctors and lawyers, for example, can be employees just like janitors and other manual laborers if they are subject to a hiring firm's control.

> EXAMPLE: Dr. Smith leaves his lucrative solo medical practice to take a salaried position teaching medicine at the local medical school.

When Smith ran his own practice, he was an IC in business for himself. He paid all the expenses for his medical practice and collected all the fees. If the expenses exceeded the fees, he lost money. As soon as Smith took the teaching job, he became an employee of the medical school. The school pays him a regular salary and provides him with employee benefits, so he has no risk of loss as he did when he was in private practice. The school also has the right to exercise control over Smith's work activities—for example, requiring him to teach certain classes. It also supplies an office and all the equipment Smith needs. He is no longer in business for himself.

22.   Worker Benefits

Employees usually receive benefits such as health insurance, sick leave, pension benefits and paid vacation. ICs ordinarily receive no similar workplace benefits.

If you provide a worker with employee benefits such as health insurance, sick leave, pension benefits and paid vacation, it's only logical for courts and government agencies to assume that you consider the worker to be your employee subject to your control. To keep the benefits, it's likely that the worker would obey your orders. You'll have a very hard time convincing anyone that a person you provide with employee benefits is not your employee.

23.   Tax Treatment of the Worker

Employees have federal and state payroll taxes withheld by their employers and remitted to the government. ICs pay their own taxes.

Treating a worker as an employee for tax purposes—that is, remitting federal and state payroll taxes for the worker—is very strong evidence that you believe the worker to be your employee and

that you have the right to exercise control over him or her. Indeed, one court has ruled that paying federal and state payroll taxes for a worker is a virtual admission that the worker is an employee under the common law test. (*Aymes v. Bonelli*, 980 F.2d 857 (2d Cir. 1992).)

24.   Intent of the Hiring Firm and Worker

If it appears that the hiring firm and the worker honestly intended to create an IC relationship, it's likely that the hiring firm would not believe it had control, nor attempt to exercise control, over the worker. One way to establish intent to create an IC relationship is for the hiring firm and IC to sign an independent contractor agreement. (See Chapter 13 for guidance on creating such an agreement.)

On the other hand, if it appears that you never intended to create a true IC relationship and merely classified the worker as an IC to avoid an employer's legal obligations, the worker will likely be considered an employee.

25.   Custom in the Trade or Industry

The custom of classification in the trade or industry involved is an important part of the analysis. If the occupation is usually performed by employees, employee status is indicated.

> **EXAMPLE:** The longstanding custom among logging companies in the Pacific Northwest is to treat tree fellers—people who cut down trees—as ICs. They are customarily paid by the tree, receive no employee benefits and are free to work for many logging companies, not just one. None of the logging companies withhold or pay federal or state payroll taxes for tree fellers. The fellers pay their own self-employment taxes. This longstanding custom (among other factors) is strong evidence that the workers are ICs. ∎

Federal Taxes and the IRS Rules

P erhaps the most important reason to classify workers correctly is to make sure you abide by federal payroll tax rules. These are by far the biggest taxes that you will have to pay for a worker who is an employee—and they will carry the biggest fine if you misclassify a worker as an independent contractor.

The heavy hand in all of this is the U.S. Internal Revenue Service. This is the agency that enforces the federal payroll tax rules, and it is the agency that will audit you and levy fines against you if you go astray of those rules. If you learn only one set of rules for determining who is and who is not

an independent contractor in your workforce, the IRS set of rules should be the one.

In this chapter, we explain to you how to determine whether a worker is an independent contractor or employee under the IRS rules. For state tests, see Chapters 6 and 7.

The IRS provides detailed information about federal payroll taxes and its employee/independent classification rules in Publication 15 and Publication 15-A, respectively. You can find copies of both publications on the CD-ROM at the back of this book.

FEDERAL PAYROLL TAXES: THE BANE OF HAVING EMPLOYEES

Federal payroll taxes are one of the chief reasons that employees are more expensive than independent contractors. You must pay these taxes for each employee on your payroll. These taxes include the following:

- **Social Security and Medicare taxes:** Also called employment or FICA taxes, they pay for the Social Security and Medicare systems. These consist of a 12.4 % Social Security tax up to a ceiling amount that is adjusted each year for inflation. In 2003, the ceiling was $87,000. The 2.9% Medicare tax must be paid on all employee wages. Employers must pay half of these taxes themselves and deduct the other half from their employees' pay and send all the money to the IRS.

- **Federal unemployment tax:** Also called FUTA, this is ordinarily a 0.8% tax on the first $7,000 employees are paid annually, or $56 per year per employee. Employers must pay FUTA taxes out of their own pockets. This tax must be paid if an employer (1) pays wages to employees total-

ing $1,500 or more in any three-month period, or (2) has at least one employee during any day of a week during 20 weeks in a calendar year (the 20 weeks need not be consecutive).

- **Income tax withholding:** Employers don't have to contribute to their employees' income taxes, but they do have to withhold them from employees' paychecks and pay them to the IRS on their behalf—in effect, acting as unpaid tax collectors for the IRS.

You do not have to pay or withhold these taxes for independent contractors, who pay their own Social Security and Medicare taxes in the form of self-employment taxes and who pay income taxes directly to the IRS, usually in the form of quarterly estimated taxes.

IRS Circular E, Employer's Tax Guide, provides detailed information on federal payroll taxes. It is an outstanding resource that every employer should have. You can get a copy by calling the IRS at: 800-TAX-FORM (829-3676) or by calling or visiting your local IRS office. You can also download a copy of the guide off the IRS website at www.irs.gov.

A. Four Steps to Classification Under the IRS Rules

To determine whether a worker is an employee or independent contractor in the eyes of the IRS, you must go through the following four steps:

- **Step One:** Check to see if the worker is a statutory independent contractor—that is, someone who is an IC simply because the law says so. Three categories of workers can be statutory ICs: direct sellers, licensed real estate agents and companion sitters. (See Section B, below, for more information about statutory ICs.) If the worker is not a statutory independent contractor, go on to Step Two. If the worker is a statutory IC, do not proceed to Step Two. You can treat the worker as an IC, and you don't have to pay or withhold federal payroll taxes.

- **Step Two:** Apply the IRS common law test to determine whether the worker is an IC or employee. (See Section C, below, for information about the IRS common law test.) If you are certain the worker should be classified as an IC under these rules, proceed to Step Three. If you think the worker should be classified as an employee under the common law test, go to Step Four.

- **Step Three:** Check to see if the worker is a statutory employee. (Section D walks you through this process in more detail.) If the worker is not a statutory employee, and you determined that the worker could be classified as an independent contractor in Step Two, then you can stop. The worker is an IC, and you don't have to pay federal payroll taxes. If the worker is a statutory employee, go on to Step Four.

- **Step Four:** If you think the worker should be classified as an employee under the common law test or if the worker is a statutory employee, check to see if the worker fits into the Safe Harbor rules. (See Section E, below, for guidance on applying those rules.) If so, you can treat the worker as an independent contractor. You don't have to pay or withhold federal payroll taxes. If the worker does not fit into the Safe Harbor rules, then the worker is an employee and you must pay federal payroll taxes.

This Discussion Applies Only to Federal Payroll Taxes
In this chapter, we are only examining whether the employee is an IC for purposes of federal payroll taxes. Once you've come to a conclusion in this arena, your job is only half done. You must still determine whether the worker is an IC for purposes of state payroll taxes, unemployment insurance and workers' compensation insurance. We discuss these issues in more detail in later chapters.

Although the IRS is in charge of collecting federal payroll taxes, it's up to you to make the initial decision as to whether you must withhold and pay such taxes for workers. That is, you must look at each of your workers and decide who is an employee and who is an independent contractor and then pay your federal taxes accordingly.

Eventually, the IRS, may review and audit your classifications. The IRS takes this enforcement task very seriously. If it determines that you wrongly classified workers as ICs, it will impose charges and penalties. (See Chapter 5 for more about IRS audits.)

THE PERILS OF ASKING FOR AN IRS DETERMINATION

Given the confusing morass of classification rules, it might seem like a godsend to be told that you can find out how to classify a worker simply by filing a form with the IRS. Although you can indeed do this by filing IRS Form SS-8, it's not the panacea that it might seem at first blush.

Nearly 90% of all IRS rulings in response to SS-8 forms is a determination that the worker is an IC, not an employee. This undoubtedly reflects the IRS's bias in favor of classifying as many workers as possible as employees. In addition, the questions on the form tend to be slanted in favor of finding employee status.

Thus, we recommend the morass over the form. If you choose to go the form route, however, you can find a copy of Form SS-8 in the Appendix and on the CD-ROM.

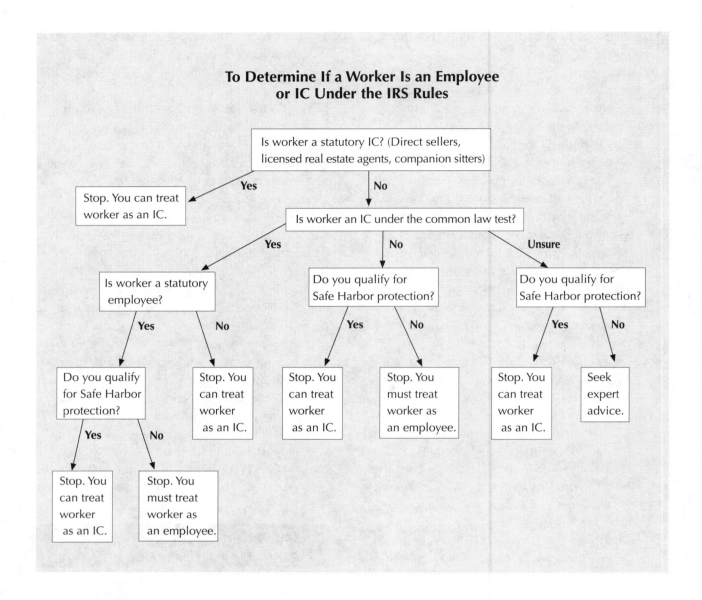

To Determine If a Worker Is an Employee or IC Under the IRS Rules

Is worker a statutory IC? (Direct sellers, licensed real estate agents, companion sitters)

Yes → Stop. You can treat worker as an IC.

No → Is worker an IC under the common law test?

Yes → Is worker a statutory employee?

    Yes → Do you qualify for Safe Harbor protection?

        Yes → Stop. You can treat worker as an IC.

        No → Stop. You must treat worker as an employee.

    No → Stop. You can treat worker as an IC.

No → Do you qualify for Safe Harbor protection?

    Yes → Stop. You can treat worker as an IC.

    No → Stop. You must treat worker as an employee.

Unsure → Do you qualify for Safe Harbor protection?

    Yes → Stop. You can treat worker as an IC.

    No → Seek expert advice.

⚠ Get Help If You Need It

Because IRS penalties for misclassifying employees as ICs can be substantial, it's important to classify all workers correctly. If you're not sure how to classify a worker after reading this book, seek assistance from a tax expert.

B. Step One: Check Statutory Independent Contractor Rules

To be a statutory IC, the worker must fall into one of the categories discussed below and must meet the following two threshold requirements:

- the worker's pay must be based on sales commissions and not on the number of hours worked, and
- there must be a written contract with the hiring firm providing that the worker will not be treated as an employee for federal tax purposes. (See Chapter 13 for guidance on creating a written independent contractor agreement.)

The IRS calls these workers "statutory non-employees," which is bureaucratese for ICs. The fortunate employers of these workers need not pay FICA or FUTA taxes or withhold federal income taxes.

Don't Forget State Taxes

These rules apply only to federal taxes—Social Security (FICA), Federal Unemployment Tax (FUTA) and federal income tax withholding. You may still have to pay state payroll taxes and provide workers' compensation coverage depending on how those tests classify the worker. See Chapter 6 for information on state payroll taxes. See Chapter 7 for information on state workers' compensation issues.

1. Direct Sellers

Direct sellers (commonly referred to as door-to-door salespeople) sell consumer products to people in their homes or at a place other than an established retail store—for example, at swap meets. The products they sell include tangible personal property that is used for personal, family or household purposes. These products include such things as vacuum cleaners, cosmetics, encyclopedias, gardening equipment and other similar products. They also include intangible consumer services or products such as home study courses and cable television services.

> **EXAMPLE:** Larry is a Mavon Guy. He sells men's toiletries door to door. He is paid a 20% commission on all his sales. This is his only remuneration from Mavon. He has a written contract with Mavon that provides that he will not be treated as an employee for federal tax purposes. Larry is a statutory independent contractor. Mavon need not pay FICA, FUTA or withhold federal income taxes for Larry. It's up to Larry to pay his own self-employment taxes. This is so whether or not Larry would qualify as an IC under the common law test.

Direct sellers can also include people who sell or distribute newspapers or shopping news. This is true whether they are paid by the publisher based on the number of papers delivered, or they purchase newspapers from the publisher and then sell them and keep the money.

2. Licensed Real Estate Agents

Most states require that real estate agents—called real estate sales people in some states—be licensed and work for a licensed real estate broker who is legally responsible for their actions. Real estate agents are usually paid on a straight commission basis. Whether they pay their own expenses and how much control the broker exercises over them varies from firm to firm.

Some real estate agents would probably qualify as employees under the common law test, while others would probably be ICs. Regardless of the common law test, however, they are statutory ICs if they meet the threshold requirements that we described above.

The broker need not pay FICA, FUTA or withhold federal income taxes.

> **EXAMPLE:** Mary is a licensed real estate agent who works for the Boldwell Canker real estate brokerage firm. Art, the real estate broker for whom she works, provides her with office space, pays most of her expenses and exercises a good deal of control over her actions. However, Mary's pay is based solely on commission fees from properties she lists and sells. Boldwell Canker has a written agreement with Mary providing that she will not be treated as an employee for federal tax purposes.
>
> Mary would probably qualify as Boldwell's employee under the common law test, but this doesn't matter because she is a statutory independent contractor. Boldwell need not pay FICA, FUTA or withhold federal income taxes for Mary.

C. Step Two: Analyze the Worker Under the Common Law Test

In cases other than statutory ICs (see Section B, above) and statutory employees (see Section D, below), the IRS uses a test called the common law test to determine a worker's status for federal pay-

PRIMARY **IRS** COMMON LAW FACTORS

	A worker will more likely be considered an IC if you:	A worker will more likely be considered an employee if you:
BEHAVIORAL CONTROL Factors that show whether a hiring firm has the right to control how a worker performs the specific tasks he or she has been hired to do	• do not provide training • do not give him or her instructions how to work, or • do not evaluate how the worker performs	• provide instructions that the worker must follow about how to work • give the worker detailed training • evaluate how the worker does the job
	A worker will more likely be considered an IC if he or she:	**A worker will more likely be considered an employee if:**
FINANCIAL CONTROL Factors showing whether a hiring firm has a right to control a worker's financial life	• has a significant investment in equipment and facilities • pays business or travel expenses himself or herself • makes his or her services available to the public • is paid by the job, and • has opportunity for profit or loss	• you provide equipment and facilities free of charge • you reimburse the worker's business or traveling expenses • the worker makes no effort to market his or her services to the public • you pay the worker by the hour or other unit of time, and • the worker has no opportunity for profit or loss—for example, because you pay by the hour and reimburse all expenses
	A worker will more likely be considered an IC if:	**A worker will more likely be considered an employee if:**
RELATIONSHIP OF THE WORKER AND HIRING FIRM Factors showing whether you and the worker believe he or she is an IC or employee	• you don't provide employee benefits such as health insurance • you sign an IC agreement with the worker • the worker performs services that are not a part of your regular business activities	• you provide employee benefits • you have no written IC agreement, and • the worker performs services that are part of your core business

roll tax purposes. This test is also called the right of control test because the goal of this test is to determine whether the hiring firm has the right to control the worker on the job. If so, the worker is an employee; if not, the worker is an IC.

The IRS looks at three areas to determine whether a hiring firm has the right to control a worker. These are:

• behavioral control on the job
• financial control, and
• the firm's relationship with the worker.

The following chart shows the primary factors the IRS looks at for each area.

We take a closer look at these three areas below. Be warned, however, that in close cases the analysis can be tricky. It is not necessary for all or even a majority of the factors to indicate IC status for a worker to be classified that way. All that is required is that the factors showing lack of control outweigh those showing control. There are no magic number of factors and no one factor alone is enough to make a worker an employee or an IC. It can be difficult to decide which way the scales tip because not all the factors are always equally important, and their importance can vary from case to case. In Section 4, below, we take a close look at how to apply this test.

1. Behavioral Control

Behavioral control means how you and your workers deal with each other on the job. Giving instructions, providing training and using evaluation systems are all strong evidence that you have the right to control a worker on the job and make the worker look like an employee in the IRS's eyes.

a. Instructions

The single most important factor in the common law test is instructions. In the worker classification context, instructions means telling—or having the right to tell even if you don't exercise that right—a worker how to get the job done. Instructions include telling a worker:

- when to do the work
- where to do the work
- what tools or equipment to use
- what workers to use to assist with the work
- where to purchase supplies or services
- what work must be performed by a specified person
- what routines or work patterns the worker must follow, and
- what order or sequence to follow in doing the work.

The more detailed the instructions the worker is required to follow, the more control the hiring firm exercises over the worker, and the more the worker looks like an employee. Requiring a worker to obtain prior approval before taking an action also constitutes instructions.

> **EXAMPLE:** Tanya is a truck driver who makes local deliveries for Zebra, Inc. She reports to the warehouse every morning. The warehouse manager tells Tanya what deliveries have to be made, how to load the cargo in the truck, what route to take and the order in which various elements of the cargo are to be delivered. These are instructions on how the work is to be done and strongly indicate that Tanya is Zebra's employee.

In contrast with the instructions listed above that tell a worker how to do the job, instructions about the end results a worker must achieve are perfectly consistent with IC status. Indeed, virtually every hiring firm instructs its ICs about what must done—for example, when the work must be completed and what form the finished work product should take.

> **EXAMPLE:** John, a self-employed truck driver, receives a call from Acme, Inc., to make a delivery run from the Gulf Coast to the Texas Panhandle. John accepts the job and agrees to pick up the cargo the next morning. Upon arriving at the warehouse, John is given an address to which to deliver the cargo and is told that the delivery must be completed in two days. These instructions concern what must be done, not how it is to be done, and are therefore consistent with IC status.

The IRS distinguishes between giving instructions on how to work and giving suggestions. A suggestion about how work is to be performed does not constitute the right to control. For example, a dispatcher may suggest that an IC truck driver avoid a particular highway because of traffic congestion. If the worker is free to ignore the advice and use the highway anyway, then the dispatcher's comment is merely a suggestion and consistent with IC status. If complying with the comment is mandatory or if the worker would suffer adverse consequences for noncompliance, however, then the comment is, in fact, an instruction and consistent with employee status.

Similarly, hiring firms can require ICs to comply with government or industry body rules and regulations. However, if the firm establishes more stringent guidelines than those required by the government or industry body, the IRS will view them as instructions indicating employee status.

Highly skilled professionals such as doctors, lawyers, accountants, engineers and computer specialists usually receive few, if any, instructions about how to perform their services. Firms that hire such workers frequently lack the knowledge necessary to give them such instructions. For this reason, in analyzing the status of professional workers, the IRS focuses more on the other two areas that we describe in this section: financial details of how the work is performed and evidence concerning the relationship of the parties.

Company Uniforms and Logos

In the past, the IRS viewed a firm's edict that workers wear company uniforms or put company logos on their vehicles as indicating employee status. Not any more. The IRS now recognizes that concerns about safety cause many businesses to tell their customers that the workers will be in a company uniform or have a company logo on their vehicles. Requiring a worker to don a uniform or logo for security purposes is now not viewed as an indicator of employee status.

b. Training

Providing a worker with periodic or ongoing training about procedures to be followed or methods to be used on a job is a strong indicator of employee status. However, the IRS now recognizes that not all training rises to this level. You may provide an IC with a short orientation or information session about your company policies, new product line or new government regulations without jeopardizing the worker's IC status. Moreover, workers who at-

tend training programs that are voluntary and for which they are not paid do not automatically lose their status as ICs.

c. Evaluations

Like instructions, evaluation systems are used by virtually all businesses to monitor the quality of work performed by workers. It is permissible to evaluate the quality of an IC's final work product. However, you should not use an evaluation system to measure compliance with performance standards concerning the details of how the work is performed. This shows you're trying to control how the worker does his or her job, which indicates employee status.

2. Financial Control

The second area of the IRS common law test looks for evidence of financial control—that is, whether the hiring firm has the right to control how the worker conducts business. The factors that usually need to be explored are whether the worker:

- has a significant investment in equipment or facilities
- is not reimbursed for expenses
- makes his or her services available to the public
- is paid by the job or by some other method, and
- has an opportunity for profit or loss.

a. Significant investment

Having a significant investment in equipment or facilities is a good indication that a worker is an IC. The IRS has not set any precise dollar amounts on what constitutes a significant investment. It says only that the investment must have substance.

An IC doesn't necessarily have to purchase costly equipment to have a significant investment—he or she may rent or lease it instead of buying it. Indeed, an IC can even lease equipment from the hiring firm. So long as the worker pays fair rental value, the lease may constitute a significant investment.

> **EXAMPLE:** Charlene is a backhoe operator for the Yippee Distributing Company. Charlene rents a $75,000 backhoe from Yippee for $1,000 per month—its fair rental value—and pays for liability insurance and regular maintenance on the backhoe. This is clearly a significant investment and helps establish that Charlene is an IC.

The IRS recognizes that many ICs do work that does not require large expenditures for equipment. For example, an IC consultant or salesperson may only require a telephone and home office. For this reason, a significant investment in equipment or facilities is not required for IC status.

b. Business expenses

The more expenses a worker has that a hiring firm does not reimburse, the more opportunity for profit or loss exists and the more control the worker has over his or her financial life—all of which strongly indicate IC status. Typical expenses for people who work for themselves include the following:

- rent and utilities
- advertising
- training
- wages of assistants
- licensing and professional dues
- insurance
- postage and delivery
- repairs and maintenance
- supplies
- travel, and
- inventory.

Of course, many ICs have many or all of their expenses reimbursed by their clients. The IRS recognizes this and does not view it as strong evidence of employee status.

IRS auditors are particularly impressed by fixed ongoing costs that a worker incurs regardless of whether work is currently being performed—for example, office rent and salaries for assistants.

c. Making services available to the public

Unlike employees, ICs' economic prosperity usually depends on their ability to get new business. To do so, ICs often advertise, maintain a visible business location and generally make themselves available for work in the relevant market. Evidence of such things—for example, a copy of a Yellow Pages ad—indicates IC status.

The IRS recognizes that not all ICs need to advertise or make themselves available to new clients, however. For example, many ICs obtain work by word of mouth without the need for advertising. Moreover, an IC who has negotiated a long-term contract may find advertising unnecessary and may be unavailable to work for others for the duration of the contract. For these reasons, the fact that a worker does not advertise, have a visible business location or make himself or herself available to new clients does not necessarily indicate employee status.

d. Method of payment

Paying a worker a flat fee for an entire job is a very strong evidence he or she is an IC, especially if the worker's expenses are not reimbursed. The worker runs the risk of losing money if the job takes longer or expenses are higher than anticipated. But he or she can also earn a windfall if the work can be done quickly with lower expenses than anticipated. Such an opportunity to earn a profit or suffer a loss is a hallmark of IC status.

Unfortunately, many ICs refuse to be paid by the job. Many insist on hourly, daily or weekly payment. A worker who is compensated in this manner is guaranteed a return for his or her labor and has little risk of loss. This is generally evidence of an employee status.

The IRS does recognize that some ICs—lawyers, for example—are typically paid by the hour instead of a flat fee. It's still better not to pay an IC an hourly wage, but it seems clear you can get away with it if it's a common practice in the IC's line of business.

Paying a worker on a commission basis is a neutral factor.

e.   Realization of profit or loss

The IRS believes that the ability to realize a profit or incur a loss is the strongest evidence there is that a worker controls the business aspects of the services he or she renders. All the factors discussed above are relevant in determining whether a worker can earn a profit or suffer a loss. In addition, the IRS considers whether a worker is free to make business decisions that affect profit or loss

3.   Relationship of the Parties

The IRS lumps several other factors under the rubric of relationship of the parties. What it's basically looking for is how you and the worker perceive your relationship with one another. The IRS figures that if you and a worker intended to create an IC relationship instead of an employee relationship, you likely will not have the right to control the worker. The IRS can't read your mind, so it looks for concrete evidence of your intent. We look at that issue more closely in this section.

a.   Use of written IC agreements

A written agreement describing the worker as an IC is good evidence that you and the worker intended to create an IC relationship. A written IC agreement, by itself, can never make a worker an IC, but it can be particularly helpful in close cases. If the evidence is so evenly balanced that it is difficult or impossible for an IRS auditor to decide whether a worker is an IC or employee, the existence of a written IC agreement can tip the balance in favor of IC status. This makes it important to use these agreements. (See Chapter 13 for guidance on creating your own independent contractor agreement.)

b.   Employee benefits

Providing a worker with employee-type benefits such as health insurance, sick leave, paid vacation leave or pension benefits is evidence that you intended to create an employment relationship.

c.   IRS W-2 form

In the eyes of the IRS, filing an IRS W-2 form for a worker shows that you consider the worker to be an employee.

d.   Duration of relationship

Employees are typically hired for an indefinite period; they continue to work as long as their employers need and/or want their services. For this reason, if you hire a worker with the expectation that the relationship will continue indefinitely, the IRS believes you probably intended to create an employment relationship.

However, the IRS recognizes that an IC can perform services for the same hiring firm for a long time. The relationship between a hiring firm and IC may be long term because:
- the IC has signed a long-term contract, or
- the IC's contracts are regularly renewed by the hiring firm because the IC does a good job, prices his or her services reasonably or no one else is readily available to do the work. As long as your contract with an IC is not open-ended, it can last for as long as needed. Just make sure that each contract has a definite end date.

e.   Performing key services

Another important factor for the IRS is whether the services a worker performs are key to the hiring firm's regular business. The IRS figures that if the services an IC performs are vital to your regular business, you will be more likely to control how the IC does the job.

For example, a law firm is less likely to supervise and control a painter it hires to paint its of-

FACTORS THAT ARE NO LONGER IMPORTANT

Recognizing the changing nature of work in modern America, the IRS now de-emphasizes several factors that it used to consider crucial in determining worker status.

Working full time. It used to be considered the kiss of death for an IC to work full time for a client. IRS auditors saw this as very strong evidence of employee status. However, the IRS now recognizes that an independent contractor may work full time for one business either because other contracts are lacking, because this is the way time is allocated or because the contract requires exclusive effort.

Having multiple clients. The IRS used to view having multiple clients as strong evidence of IC status. Indeed, hiring firms would often encourage their ICs to work for others. It now says that having multiple clients is no longer useful evidence of IC status because many employees moonlight by working for a second employer.

Place of performance. Working on a hiring firm's premises used to be regarded as important evidence of employee status. No longer. The IRS now says that where the work is performed is largely irrelevant. However, this factor is still important in many state audits. For example, in half the states, you may be considered an employer for unemployment compensation purposes if a worker works at your place of business or another place you designate. (See Chapter 6 for information about state tests.)

Hours of work. The fact that a worker performed his or her services during hours the hiring firm chose used to be viewed as an indicator of employee status. Again, the IRS has changed its view. Some work must, by its nature, be performed at a specific time. On the other hand, the fact that a worker has flexible hours is not considered evidence of IC status because many employees now work flexible hours.

Right to fire, Right to quit. The IRS no longer views an unfettered right to quit or fire as strong evidence of an employee relationship.

fices than a paralegal it hires to work on its regular legal business. However, it is still possible for the paralegal to be classified as an IC. The IRS will examine all the facts and circumstances; this one factor alone does not make a worker an employee. A paralegal hired by a law firm could very well be an IC if, for example, he or she was a specialist hired to help with especially difficult or unusual legal work.

4. Applying the Test

When you examine your relationship with any worker, you will probably find some facts that support IC status and other facts that support employee status. This is because ICs are rarely totally unconstrained in performing their contracts, while employees almost always have some degree of autonomy.

You need to weigh all the evidence to determine whether, looking at the relationship as a whole, evidence of control (indicating the worker is an employee) or autonomy (indicating the worker is an IC) predominates. A good way to do this is to draw up a simple chart with those factors that indicate IC status on one side and those that show employee status on the other.

The following examples are taken directly from the IRS manual on how to classify workers and are being used to train IRS auditors. They illustrate that the IRS expects to find a mix of facts and that not all factors need to point to IC status for a worker to be classified that way.

EXAMPLE: An attorney is a sole practitioner who rents office space and pays for the following items: telephone, computer, online legal research linkup, fax machine and photocopier. The attorney buys office supplies and pays bar dues and membership dues for three other professional organizations. The attorney has a part-time receptionist who also does the bookkeeping. The attorney pays the receptionist, withholds and pays federal and state employment taxes and files a Form W-2 each year. For the past two years, the attorney has had only one client—a corporation with which there has been a longstanding relationship. The attorney charges the corporation an hourly rate for services and sends monthly bills detailing the work performed for the prior month. The bills include charges for long distance calls, online research time, fax charges, photocopies, mailing costs and travel costs for which the corporation has agreed to reimburse.

Analysis: There are factors here that show control and factors that show autonomy. The attorney has a number of ongoing business expenses that give him a risk of loss—he pays for an office, supplies, professional dues and an employee receptionist. The fact that he has an employee is very strong evidence of IC status. On the other side of the ledger, he has only one client and is paid by the hour and reimbursed for certain expenses. However, hourly payment and expense reimbursement are common among attorneys, so these factors probably would not be viewed as very important by the IRS. Having a long relationship with a single client points to employee status, but this factor is probably outweighed by the factors showing IC status.

EXAMPLE: A manufacturer's representative is the sole proprietor of a building supplies business and has an exclusive contract with a building supplies manufacturer. The representative has the sole right to the territory covered and sells only that manufacturer's products, but did not pay anything for the right to the territory. The representative has a bachelor's degree in civil engineering and belongs to several professional associations, paying membership dues. The representative has an office and a secretary, but the manufacturer does not reimburse for these expenses. The representative's name appears in the Yellow Page advertisements under both the representative's sole proprietorship name and the name of the manufacturer represented. The representative is required to provide regular trip reports to the manufacturer and attend sales meetings and trade shows conducted in the representative's territory.

The representative bids on portions of major commercial construction contracts. These jobs require engineering skills and design work to adapt the building materials to the project plans. All bids are subject to the manufacturer's review. Upon winning a bid, the representative engages and pays the workers who will install the building materials, providing the necessary construction bonds. The representative submits invoices to the general contractor for payment directly to the representative on forms prescribed by the manufacturer. If the general contractor fails to pay, the representative is responsible for collecting and is liable to the manufacturer for payment.

Analysis: This complex example has a real mix of factors. However, although several factors point to employee status, it's likely the representative would be classified as an IC because he has such a strong risk of loss. He is personally responsible for hiring and paying the workers who install the manufacturer's building materials. He is also responsible for collecting the amounts due from the building contractor customers. If the contractors fail to pay, the representative must pay the manufacturer out of his own pocket. The representative could easily lose his shirt if he can't collect from a contractor. This enormous financial risk points strongly to IC status and likely outweighs the employee factors.

5. IRS and Court Rulings for Specific Occupations

This section examines IRS rulings, court decisions and IRS guidelines that give detailed guidance on how to classify particular workers in nine occupations:

- architects
- attorneys
- beauty salon and barbershop workers
- limousine drivers
- van operators
- taxi drivers
- television commercial and professional video workers
- truck drivers, and
- companion sitters.

Following these guidelines will give you persuasive ammunition if the IRS ever decides to audit your business and to question how you've classified your workers.

Useful for Safe Harbor Protection

Using this information may also help qualify your business for Safe Harbor protection should the need ever arise. (See Section E, below, for a detailed discussion about the Safe Harbor rules.)

a. Architects

An architect who performs services for a variety of clients and who assumes professional liability for his or her work product will almost certainly be viewed as an IC by the IRS.

However, the IRS has ruled that an ostensibly independent architect could be classified as an employee when circumstantial evidence suggests that the architect is a de facto employee, such as when an architectural firm gives the architect an office,

staff support, expense accounts and instruction on how the project is to be completed. In other words, the firm might be calling the architect an IC, but treating the architect just like an employee.

Therefore, firms using self-employed architects need to be very careful. It's best that the architect performs his or her services from an outside office without any supervision by the firm. The firm's control over the architect should be limited to accepting or rejecting the architect's final work product.

Draftspeople Treated Differently

Licensed architects are not the only people who work in the architectural design field. For example, there are also thousands of architectural draftspeople. The IRS generally classifies such workers as employees. These workers are relatively low-skilled and unlicensed. As you may recall, the IRS is more likely to classify low-skill workers as employees because companies generally supervise and direct their work.

b. Attorneys

A lawyer who holds himself or herself out to the public and who is hired by a company or individual to litigate or defend a particular lawsuit is an IC. This remains true even when the lawyer spends most or all of his or her time on the case. And this rule applies even where a lawyer who has a variety of clients is paid an annual retainer to defend any suit brought against the client.

There is a different, rule, however, for attorneys who work as associates in law firms. The IRS will deem an attorney to be an employee of a law firm when the law firm pays the attorney a salary, provides the attorney with office space and secretarial help and requires the attorney to work a specified number of hours. This is so even if the firm allows the associate to retain all the fees the firm earns from some of its cases.

In-house corporate counsel—lawyers who work full-time representing a single company and who do not offer their services to the public—are almost always company employees and are ordinarily classified as such.

Contract attorneys are lawyers hired by law firms to help out on a per project basis. Some contract attorneys are hired through employment agencies and others are hired directly. Unlike associates, they are not considered members of the firm. Whether they should be classified as ICs or employees depends on how they are treated on the job.

c.   Beauty salon and barber shop workers

Beauty salons and barbershops are often staffed by ICs. The owner of the shop will typically rent or lease a chair or booth to a barber, beautician, hair stylist or manicurist—and all of these people can be considered ICs by the IRS in the right circumstances. When deciding whether to classify these people as ICs or as employees, the IRS is predominantly interested in how these workers are paid (see below). The IRS has a list of questions that it generally asks the owners of barber shops and beauty shops when it is trying to determine whether a worker is an employee or independent contractor. These questions can be quite instructive for shop owners who want to ensure that they establish IC relationships with their workers:

- How does the worker pay the shop owner for the space he or she uses? Workers who pay a flat fee rather than a percentage of their earnings are usually found to be ICs by the IRS because this shows they have a risk of loss.
- How much is the weekly/monthly rate? The higher the rate, the greater the risk of loss and the more likely the worker is an IC.
- Does the worker rent a particular space? In the case of a barber or hair stylist, renting a particular space—as opposed to simply working anywhere the shopkeeper wants—indicates IC status because it shows that the owner does not control where the worker does his or her work.
- Who is responsible for damage to the chair? If the barber or stylist is responsible, he or she will have a greater risk of loss, which will indicate IC status.
- Who maintains the worker's appointment book? The worker should maintain his or her own book. If the owner maintains the book, it shows control over the worker and indicates employee status.
- Who collects the money earned by the worker? If the worker collects the money he or she earns, this will indicate IC status.
- Who pays for the worker's supplies? Generally, if a worker pays for his or her own supplies, this fact will indicate IC status.
- Who maintains the books and records of the individual? If the worker maintains his or her own books and records, this fact will point to IC status.
- How are assistants compensated? ICs pay for their own assistants; shop owners pay for assistants for their employees.

To ensure that the IRS classifies a worker as an IC, the shop owner should not supervise or otherwise control the worker. However, the shop can require the worker to comply with some basic work rules, including the following:

- maintaining a clean work area
- maintaining his or her own tools, and
- providing and maintaining his or her own uniforms.

In most states, barbers and beauticians must also have a license. If they are not licensed, these workers will look more like employees to the IRS.

The following examples, which are taken from IRS Publication 15, Employer's Tax Guide, illustrate the IRS's views on classifying these types of workers:

EXAMPLE: Paul is a barber. He signed a lease agreement with Larry, the owner of a barber shop, to use a chair in Larry's shop. Larry bears all the shop expenses, including rent, utilities, advertising, linens and other supplies. Paul keeps 70% of the receipts from his chair, and Larry keeps 30%. Paul puts all receipts in Larry's cash register. At the end of the week, Larry pays Paul the agreed percentage of the receipts. Paul must comply with the shop hours that Larry has posted on the shop door. Paul must take customers in turn, maintain clean premises, use clean towels and sterile equipment and keep a clean personal appearance. Larry's income depends on a percentage of Paul's receipts. Larry retains the right to direct and control Paul to protect his investment and to be assured sufficient profit from the shop. Paul has no investment in the shop, assumes no liability for its operation and furnishes nothing except his personal services. Is Paul Larry's employee?

Yes. Virtually every factor in this example weighs against Paul being an IC and in favor of Paul being an employee. Paul has no risk of loss because he has no investment in the shop and because Larry pays all the expenses. The fact that Larry keeps all the receipts in his cash register and pays Larry a percentage at the end of the week also shows that Paul is an employee—having control over all the money gives Larry the right to control Paul. Larry's control over Paul is also made evident by the fact that Paul must work set hours. All these factors that demonstrate Larry's control over Paul are consistent only with a finding of employee status by the IRS.

EXAMPLE: Charlie, the owner of a barber shop, and Sally, a professional manicurist, have an agreement under which Sally provides manicuring services to shop patrons during business hours. According to the agreement, Sally regulates her own hours, furnishes her own equipment and keeps the proceeds from her work. She does not use the shop cash register nor does she report her earnings to Charlie. She sometimes hires a substitute to fill in for her when she doesn't want to work. Charlie cannot direct the way she performs her services. Either of them can end the agreement at any time. Although Charlie has the right to dismiss Sally by ending the agreement, and although he furnishes her a place to work, he does not have the right to direct and control her work. Is Sally an employee of Charlie's?

No. Sally is self-employed. The fact that Sally pays a fixed monthly fee for the booth, sets her own hours and is free to select her own customers are important factors pointing to her IC status. These all show that Charlie does not control how Sally performs her services. Sally also has a risk of loss.

d. Limousine drivers

The IRS uses a three-prong test to determine whether limousine drivers are employees or ICs. (The word limousine includes sedans, vans and stretch limousines used in a livery service. It does not include taxis.) Each prong must be satisfied for a limousine driver to be classified as an IC under the IRS guidelines:

- Has the driver made an investment in the limousine, either by owning it or leasing it? Drivers who do not make such investments are employees.
- Does the driver have a financial stake in the limousine's profit or loss potential? Drivers without such a risk of loss are employees.
- Does the limousine company have the right to control the driver on the job? If so, the driver is an employee.

Each of these prongs requires a rather detailed analysis. You can find a complete copy of the IRS guidelines on how to classify limousine drivers on the CD-ROM that is included with the book. You can also obtain a copy directly from the IRS by calling 800-TAX-FORM (800-829-3676) or by downloading a copy from the IRS website at www.irs.gov.

e. Van operators

A van operator is the driver of a vehicle that transports household goods such as furniture and other belongings. The IRS guidelines discussed here cover only those van operators who work under a written agreement with a carrier or agent and who own their own trucks or truck tractors.

To determine if a van operator is an IC or employee, the IRS examines several different areas of the relationship between the van company and the operator. Those areas include:

- the operator's financial investment in his or her equipment, either through ownership or lease (this is the most important factor)
- evidence of the operator's potential for profit and loss, including expenses, compensation and the financial burden of hiring his or her own assistants
- who determines the operator's work schedule and manner of performance, and
- other factors that distinguish an IC from an employee, such as training, independent decision-making and termination issues.

You can find a complete copy of the IRS guidelines on how to classify van operators on the CD-ROM that is included with the book. You can also obtain a copy directly from the IRS by calling 800-TAX-FORM (800-829-3676) or by downloading a copy from the IRS website at www.irs.gov.

f. Taxi drivers

Some taxi drivers rent company-owned vehicles while others own their own and contract with a taxi company only to use the company's dispatch services. The IRS takes the position that regardless of whether the driver owns or leases the taxi, he or she is an employee of the company if the driver must pay the company a percentage of the fares he or she earns. The rationale for this view is that in order to determine how much money it's owed, the taxi company must conduct an accounting of all the fares collected by the driver during the shift. The IRS asserts that this right to an accounting means that the taxi company has the right to con-trol the driver and that the driver is therefore the company's employee.

On the other hand, taxi drivers who pay a taxi company a fixed amount—rather than a percentage of their earnings—can be ICs. This is because there is no accounting by the taxi company of the fares the driver receives when the driver pays the company a fixed fee. This is so both for drivers who own their taxis and those who lease them from the taxi company.

However, the IRS will classify as employees even those drivers who pay a fixed fee if other factors indicate that the company controls the driver—for example, the company requires the driver to accept all company dispatch orders.

In addition, the IRS will classify as employees taxi drivers who work for companies that use a voucher system to bill their customers.

HOLLYWOOD FARES

You might get your big break in show biz before you spot a taxi in Los Angeles. Nonetheless, Uncle Sam still wants to know who's really calling the shots between the drivers and dispatchers in LA. An IRS audit of more than 650 taxi drivers concluded that most were employees, even where they paid the taxi company a fixed fee. The rationale was that the taxi companies required their drivers to follow various rules and regulations—all of which showed that the companies controlled the drivers. For instance, drivers could not refuse dispatch orders from the company without suffering adverse consequences. Also, the company had the right to discharge the drivers at any time. And the cars all had to be painted in the company colors. Finally, all of the drivers were included in the company's property damage insurance policy. Whether any of the drivers could play Hamlet was left undecided.

g. Television commercials and professional video production

The IRS has issued extensive guidelines on how to classify workers engaged in creating television commercials and in professional video production. When the IRS uses the term professional video production, it means video productions not intended for television viewing, including corporate video productions typically used for training, employee communications, sales and marketing, public service and public relations.

The IRS has also created a two-step test to determine whether the workers in this field are ICs or employees. In the first step, the IRS looks at whether the production company gives the worker preferential hiring treatment, training or makes payments to the worker's guild or union on his or her behalf. If any one of those elements is present, the worker is classified as an employee and the test is ended. If all three are absent, the IRS goes on to the second step to determine the worker's status. In the second step, the IRS determines where the worker fits into a hierarchy.

 You can find a complete copy of the IRS guidelines on how to classify workers engaged in creating television commercials and in professional video production on the CD-ROM that is included with the book. You can also obtain a copy directly from the IRS by calling 800-TAX-FORM (800-829-3676) or by downloading a copy from the IRS website at www.irs.gov.

h. Truck drivers

Although some trucking companies hire employees to drive company trucks and trailers, most trucking companies use ICs. The trucking industry uses several different types of ICs, including:

- Owner-operators, who are people who own and operate their own trucks, including tractor-trailers or bobtails.
- Subhaulers, who are people or companies that own and operate a single tractor-trailer or a fleet of tractor-trailers that are then leased to prime carriers. Subhaulers are paid a percentage of the freight bill prepared by the prime carrier.
- Pothaulers, who are a subclass of owner-operators. Pothaulers are owner-operators who pick up full sealed containers from the harbor and transport them to the terminal of the prime carrier or break-bulk agent. Pothaulers are usually paid a flat rate for each container hauled.

DIAPERS AND BANANAS AND TAXES, OH MY!

The IRS automatically classifies some truck drivers as employees for employment tax purposes. These include drivers of certain commodities, such as meat and vegetable products, fruit, bakery products, beverages; or laundry or dry cleaning services. (See Section D, below, for a detailed discussion of automatic classification.)

The single most important factor in determining whether a truck driver is an IC or an employee is truck ownership. A trucker who owns or leases his or her own truck may be an IC, but a trucker who uses a company truck will almost always be found to be an employee, even if there are other factors that indicate IC status.

If a truck driver wants to be an IC, it's always best for the driver to buy or lease the truck from someone other than the person or company for whom the driver works. Otherwise, the IRS will analyze the sale or lease very carefully to make sure it isn't a sham designed to help make the driver look like an IC when the driver is really more like an employee. IRS examiners will review the details carefully—especially the title and sale/lease documents. The driver must pay a commercially reasonable purchase or lease price based on the fair market value of the vehicle and must be personally liable for the payments. If the driver financed the purchase, the driver must pay a reasonable interest rate. If the driver leased the vehicle, the lease should usually be for a minimum of one year. A purchase or lease price is reasonable if it is comparable to prices other companies would charge.

In addition to examining the truck ownership, the IRS will also ask whether the driver:

- pays business and traveling expenses
- receives compensation based on a percentage of revenue or miles driven rather than a fixed salary
- hires and pays assistants, drivers and mechanics
- pays his or her own license fees and road taxes
- maintains his or her own truck storage and maintenance facility or business office
- sets his or her own work schedule
- determines the manner of performing the work
- has a choice to accept or reject jobs
- may delegate services to another driver, and
- works for more than one firm at a time.

Doing the above tasks indicates IC status; not doing them indicates employee status. The following example, taken from IRS Publication 15, Employer's Tax Guide (Circular E), illustrates how the IRS classifies truck drivers.

EXAMPLE: A company engages Phil Blue to haul produce to its customers. The company has legal ownership and control of the trucking equipment. The company can require Phil (on an hour's notice) to make deliveries at specific times and specific places. If Phil refuses, he will jeopardize his relationship with the company. He has to operate and maintain the equipment and provide the necessary operators and helpers. He is not allowed to use the company's equipment to haul for others. He is paid on a tonnage basis and is not guaranteed a minimum amount of compensation. He has to pay the operators and helpers out of his tonnage receipts as well as pay for all the in-

surance coverage required by the company. Is Phil an employee of the company?

Yes, but it's a close call. There is a mix of IC and employee factors in this IRS example. The fact that Phil is paid on a tonnage basis and not guaranteed any minimum compensation is on the IC side of the ledger. So is the fact that Phil must personally pay for helpers and all insurance coverage and maintain the vehicles. However, all the other factors indicate employee status. Most importantly, the company owns the truck. The company also exercises substantial control over Phil. He is not allowed to use the company truck to haul for others, and he must accept all assignments offered by the company. The fact that Phil must make deliveries at times and places specified by the company would seem to be a neutral factor—obviously, produce must be delivered according to a certain time schedule.

i. Companion sitters

Companion sitters are people who serve as companions for the sick and elderly. Typically, a companion sitter will find employment through a specialized placement service, rather than hiring the sitter directly.

A special employment tax law provision provides that sitters are not employees of the placement service if the service does not pay them wages—that is, if the companion sitter is paid directly by the person or business whom they are sitting for.

The relationship of the companion sitter to the client is a little more complicated. To sort it out, use the IRS common law test. Under this test, a sitter would be a client's employee if the client has the right to control how the sitter performs the companion sitting services. It seems likely the right of control would be present in most companion sitting situations, except, perhaps, where the client is so ill or elderly he or she doesn't have the physical capacity to exercise any control over the sitter.

Companion sitters who perform their services at the client's home are considered household workers for federal payroll tax purposes. (See Chapter 8 for guidance on dealing with household employees.)

D. Step Three: Check Statutory Employee Rules

This step applies only if you've determined that a worker who is an IC under the common law test discussed in Step Two (see Section C, above) falls into one of the following categories:

- corporate officers (see Section 1, below)
- home workers (see Section 2, below)
- drivers who distribute food products, beverages or laundry (see Section 3, below)
- full-time life insurance salespeople (see Section 4, below), and
- traveling or city salespeople (see Section 5, below).

If a worker you classify as an IC under the common law test comes within one of these categories, and if the additional requirements discussed below are met, the worker is a statutory employee. Statutory employees must be treated as employees for FICA purposes, so you must pay half of their Social Security and Medicare taxes yourself and withhold the other half from their

paychecks. You must also pay federal unemployment taxes for statutory employees. You don't have to withhold federal income tax from the workers' paychecks, regardless of their status as a statutory employee (except for corporate officers). The following chart summarizes what you must pay for statutory employees:

EMPLOYER TREATMENT OF STATUTORY EMPLOYEES

Type of Worker	Income Tax Withholding	Social Security Taxes	Federal Unemployment Taxes
Corporate officer	Withhold	Pay and withhold	Pay
Agent or commission driver	No withholding	Pay and withhold	Pay
Life insurance salesperson	No withholding	Pay and withhold	None due
Traveling or city salesperson	No withholding	Pay and withhold	Pay
Home worker	No withholding	Pay and withhold if total pay is more than $100 in cash during the year	None due

You must give every statutory employee a Form W-2, Wage and Tax Statement, and check the Statutory Employee designation in box 15. The W-2 must show the Social Security and Medicare tax withheld, as well as the Social Security and Medicare income. You must also file a copy with the Social Security Administration. You can obtain Form W-2 and instructions for completing it by calling the IRS at: 800-TAX-FORM (829-3676) or by calling your local IRS office. You may also download those documents from the agency's website at www.irs.gov.

Don't Forget to Check the Safe Harbor

If a worker is a statutory employee, you'll still be able to avoid having to pay employment taxes if you qualify for Safe Harbor protection as discussed in Section E, below. However, it's not likely that many firms that use statutory employees would qualify for the Safe Harbor.

For all statutory employees other than corporate officers, there are three threshold requirements that the worker must meet. (If you are dealing with a corporate officer, you can skip ahead to Section 1, below.) The worker must:

- **Do the work personally.** The worker cannot subcontract the work out to others. A written agreement stating this will satisfy the requirement, but it is not required. If you explicitly tell a worker that he or she must perform the services personally, and the worker agrees, the requirement is satisfied. In addition, this requirement can be implied from the circumstances. For example, telling a person: "I want you to clean my house," implies that you want him or her to perform services for you personally.
- **Make no substantial investment in the equipment or facilities used to perform the services.** This includes things such as office space and furniture and office equipment and machinery. It does not include tools, instruments and clothing commonly provided by employees in the trade—for example, uniforms that employees typically provide for themselves or inexpensive hand tools that carpenters typically have. Nor does it include education, experience or training. Statutory employees can also use vehicles for their transportation or for transporting goods.
- **Have a continuing relationship with the hiring firm.** This includes regular part-time work and regular seasonal employment. But a single project is not enough to constitute a continuing relationship, even if the job takes a long time to complete.

THINGS TO DO IF YOU DON'T WANT STATUTORY EMPLOYEES

You can avoid having a worker classified as a statutory employee by setting up the work relationship so that it does not satisfy one or more of the three threshold requirements described above. For example:

- Sign a written agreement with the worker stating that he or she has the right to subcontract or delegate the work out to others. But note that the agreement must reflect reality—that is, you must really intend to give the worker the right to delegate.
- Avoid having a continuing relationship with the worker. Use the worker for a single project, not ongoing work. Spread your hiring around by using lots of different workers instead of a few favorite ones. Also, avoid giving workers lengthy projects. Break down complex projects into separate tasks and hire different workers to complete them.
- Hire workers with a substantial investment in outside facilities.

Now that you know the threshold requirements, let's look more closely at the categories of workers eligible to be statutory employees.

1. Corporate Officers

If a corporation's president, treasurer, vice president or secretary (1) performs services for the company and (2) receives (or is entitled to receive) compensation, the officer is a statutory employee. (Note that both requirements must be met.) Compensation doesn't just refer to wages. If the officer earns stock options, then this requirement is met.

EXAMPLE: Murray, his sister Rose and his brother-in-law Artie start a catering business, which they set up as a corporation. Murray serves as the president, Rose as the secretary-treasurer and Artie as vice president. Murray and Rose actually run the company. Artie contributed start-up funds, but does not work for the corporation and receives no pay from it. Murray and Rose are statutory employees of the corporation; Artie is not.

2. Home Workers

People who work in a home (theirs or someone else's) or a workshop are statutory employees if they meet the threshold requirements described above and if all of the following criteria apply:

- they do the work away from the hiring firm's place of business—usually in their own home or workshop, or in another person's home
- they do the work on goods or materials furnished by the hiring firm
- they perform the work in accordance with the hiring firm's specifications; generally, such specifications are simple and consist of patterns or samples, and
- the hiring firm requires the worker to return the processed material to the hiring firm or to some person designated by the hiring firm.

This group usually includes people who make or sew buttons, quilts, gloves, bedspreads, clothing, needlecraft products and similar products.

If all these requirements are met, you must pay the employer's share of FICA. However, you do not have to pay FICA tax if you pay the home worker less than $100 for a calendar year.

If the worker does not qualify as an employee under the IRS common law test, you do not have to withhold payroll taxes or pay federal unemployment taxes (FUTA).

EXAMPLE: Rosa sews buttons on shirts and dresses. She works at home. She does work for various companies, including Upscale Fash-

ions, Inc. Upscale provides Rosa with all the clothing and the buttons she must sew. The only equipment Rosa provides is a needle. Upscale gives Rosa a sample of each outfit showing where the buttons are supposed to go. When Rosa finishes each batch of clothing, she returns it to Upscale. Rosa is a statutory employee. Upscale must pay employer FICA (and withhold Rosa's share of FICA). But it need not pay FUTA or withhold federal income tax unless Rosa is an employee under the common law test.

3. Food, Beverage and Laundry Distributors

If they meet the threshold requirements discussed above, drivers who distribute meat or meat products, vegetables or vegetable products, fruits or fruit products, bakery products, beverages other than milk or laundry or dry cleaning are statutory employees.

The products these workers distribute may be sold at retail or wholesale. The drivers may either be paid a salary or by commission. They may operate from their own trucks or trucks belonging to the hiring firm. Ordinarily, they service customers designated by the hiring firm as well as those they solicit.

EXAMPLE: Alder Laundry and Dry Cleaning enters into an agreement with Sharon to pick up and deliver clothing for its customers. Sharon has similar arrangements with several other laundries and arranges her route to serve all the laundries. None of the companies has any control over how she performs her services. She owns her own truck and is paid by commission. Sharon qualifies as an IC under the common law test.

However, she is a statutory employee because all three threshold requirements are met: Her agreement with Alder acknowledges that she will do the work personally, she has no substantial investment in facilities (her truck doesn't count since it's used to deliver the product) and she has a continuing relationship with Alder. Alder must pay employment taxes for Sharon—that is, pay half of her FICA and withhold the other half from her pay, and pay all of the applicable FUTA. However, Alder need not withhold federal income tax since Sharon is an IC under the common law test.

Delivery people who buy and sell merchandise on their own account or deliver to the general public as part of an independent business do not fall within this category. It's easy to tell if drivers have independent businesses. Instead of merely delivering products owned and sold by others, they buy the products themselves and resell them.

4. Life Insurance Salespeople

This group of statutory employees includes salespeople whose full-time occupation is soliciting life insurance applications or annuity contracts, primarily for one life insurance company. The company usually provides work necessities such as office space, secretarial help, forms, rate books and advertising material.

If a life insurance salesperson is a statutory employee, the hiring firm must pay FICA taxes. However, it need not pay FUTA taxes or withhold federal income taxes unless the salesperson is an employee under the common law test.

> **EXAMPLE:** Walter Neff sells life insurance full time for the Old Reliable Life Insurance Company. He works out of Old Reliable's Omaha office, and the company provides him with a desk, clerical help, rate books and insurance applications. Walter is a statutory employee of Old Reliable. The company must pay employer FICA and withhold employee FICA from Walter's pay. It need not pay FUTA or withhold federal income tax unless Walter is an employee under the common law test.

5. Business-to-Business Salespeople

Salespeople are statutory employees if they meet the threshold requirements described above and if they:

- work at least 80% of the time for one person or company, except, possibly, for sideline sales on behalf of someone else
- sell on behalf of, or turn their orders over to, the hiring firm
- sell merchandise for resale or supplies for use in the buyer's business operations (as opposed to goods purchased for personal consumption at home), and
- sell only to wholesalers, retailers, contractors or those who operate hotels, restaurants or similar establishments; this does not include manufacturers, schools, hospitals, churches, municipalities or state and federal governments.

This group does not include drivers who distribute food, beverages or laundry. (For that group of people, see Section 3, above.)

Generally, this category includes traveling salespeople who might otherwise be considered ICs. Such salespeople are ordinarily paid on a commission basis. The details of their work and the means by which they cover their territories are not typically dictated to them by others. However, they are expected to work their territories with some regularity, take purchase orders and send them to the hiring firm for delivery to the purchaser.

> **EXAMPLE:** Linda sells books to retail bookstores for the Simply Sons Publishing Company. Her territory covers the entire Midwest. She works only for Simply and is paid a commission based on the amount of each sale. She turns her orders over to Simply, which ships the books to each bookstore customer. Linda is Simply's statutory employee. The company must pay FICA and FUTA taxes for her. However, Simply need not withhold federal income taxes from her pay unless she qualifies as an employee under the common law test.

E. Step Four: Check the Safe Harbor Rules

The employer's Safe Harbor is a set of legal protections found in a footnote to the Internal Revenue Code. It is called Safe Harbor protection because it provides employers with a refuge from the cold winds and turbulent waters of an IRS audit. If you meet the three requirements for Safe Harbor protection discussed below, the IRS can't impose assessments or penalties against you for worker misclassification, and you can safely and confidently treat the workers involved as ICs.

The Safe Harbor was intended to help employers, who often have a difficult time determining how to classify their workers under the IRS common law test. If the Safe Harbor requirements are met, an employer may treat a worker as an IC for payroll tax purposes even if the worker should have been classified as an employee under the common law test discussed in Step Two.

Unfortunately, experience has shown that few employers are able to take advantage of the Safe Harbor. Most can't satisfy the three requirements discussed in this section. However, this doesn't mean *you* can't satisfy them. If you think a worker should be classified as an employee under the common law test, or you're not sure how to classify a worker under the test, look at the Safe Harbor rules carefully. If you can meet them all, you can treat the worker as an IC for payroll tax purposes.

To receive Safe Harbor protection for a worker, you must do all of the following three things:

- file all required 1099-MISC forms for the worker (see Section 1, below, for more about this form)
- consistently treat the worker—and others doing substantially similar work to that worker—as an IC (see Section 2, below, for more this consistent treatment prong of the Safe Harbor rules), and
- have a reasonable basis for treating the worker as an IC (see Section 3, below, for more about the reasonable basis prong of the Safe Harbor rules).

Safe Harbor Applies Only to Federal Payroll Taxes

If a worker receives Safe Harbor protection, you can safely treat that worker as an IC for the purposes of federal payroll taxes. However, that same worker might still be considered an employee under other rules, such as federal pension plan rules and state rules.

1. First Prong: Filing IRS Form 1099-MISC When Appropriate

The first requirement you have to meet to obtain Safe Harbor protection is to timely file IRS Form 1099-MISC for any unincorporated IC to whom you paid $600 or more in any year after 1977. You must file this form with the IRS by February 28 of the year after the year in which the individual performed work for you.

This simple requirement knocks a great many hiring firms out of the box right from the start, since many fail to file 1099s for workers they treat as ICs. This may be because they are unaware of the requirement, they fear that filing 1099s may get them audited or the worker doesn't provide the information needed for a 1099.

However, you need not file Form 1099-MISC for the following types of ICs:

- ICs to whom you paid less than $600 during the year
- incorporated ICs (except for incorporated doctors and lawyers), and
- ICs who performed services not related to your business (for example, household workers).

If a Form 1099-MISC is not required, you can obtain Safe Harbor protection without filing it.

It's up to you to prove that the 1099s were filed, so be sure to keep copies. If you lack proof, the IRS can check its records to see if the forms were filed, but this require a time-consuming computer run.

2. Second Prong: Consistent Treatment

This prong requires that you treat all workers who hold substantially similar positions the same way, that is, as independent contractors, for federal tax purposes. (See subsection a, below, for an explanation of what substantially similar means.) If you treat even one of the workers as an employee for federal tax purposes, then you cannot use the Safe Harbor rules for any workers who hold substantially similar positions, even if you've always treated those workers as ICs.

How do you treat a worker as an employee for federal tax purposes under this prong? You do any one of the following:

- withhold federal income, Social Security or Medicare taxes from the worker's wages, whether or not you actually pay the withheld money to the IRS
- file a federal employment tax return for the worker (IRS Forms 940 through 943), or
- file a W-2 Wage and Tax Statement for the worker, whether or not you do, in fact, withhold the tax.

An IRS auditor can easily discover whether you've consistently treated workers performing similar services as ICs by examining your payroll tax returns and similar records.

> **EXAMPLE:** A roofing company hired 57 people to work as roofing applicators. The company consistently treated 56 of the applicators as ICs. It didn't withhold payroll taxes, file employment tax returns or provide the workers with W-2 statements. However, the company filed IRS Form 941, the Employer's Quarterly Federal Tax Return, for one applicator and paid his Social Security and Medicare taxes. The IRS ruled that the company could not use the Safe Harbor rules for any of the applicators because they were not all treated as ICs for federal tax purposes.

The consistent treatment requirement applies only to how you treat your workers for *federal tax purposes*. You can treat workers as employees for other purposes and still obtain Safe Harbor protection. (See subsection c, below, for more about this issue.)

The consistent treatment requirement applies only to workers who hold substantially similar positions. (See subsection a, below, for more about this issue.) Workers in different positions can be treated differently.

> **EXAMPLE:** The Reliable Building Co. hired ten painters and ten bricklayers in one year. It treated all the painters as employees—that is, it withheld payroll taxes from their pay, issued them W-2 forms and filed employment tax returns for them. It treated all of the bricklayers as ICs, filing 1099-MISC forms for them. Reliable satisfied the consistent treatment prong of the Safe Harbor rules as to the bricklayers. The fact that Reliable treated the painters as employees doesn't matter because the painters didn't hold positions that were substantially similar to the bricklayers—that is, being a bricklayer is not substantially similar to being a painter.

a. The Meaning of substantially similar positions

How do you know if workers are in substantially similar positions? The IRS looks at the day-to-day services the workers perform and the method by which they perform them—for example:

- A beauty parlor owner classified cosmetologists who leased their chairs from the owner as ICs, and those who worked directly under the owner's control as employees. The owner couldn't qualify for the Safe Harbor because the cosmetologists held substantially similar positions. (*Ren-Lyn Corp. v. U.S.*, 968 F.Supp. 363 (N.D. Oh. 1997).)
- A sign company classified salespeople to whom it paid a salary as employees, and those who worked for commissions on an as-needed basis as ICs. The positions were substantially similar, so no Safe Harbor. (*Lowen Corp. v. U.S.*, 785 F.Supp. 913 (D. Kan. 1992).)

- A shuttle company had two sets of drivers: those who worked under the company's contract with Illinois Bell, who were treated as employees; and those who worked under a contact with Alamo, who were treated as ICs. The positions were substantially similar, so no Safe Harbor. (*Leb's Enterprises v. U.S.*, 11385 AFTR2d 2000-886 (N.D. Ill. 2000).)

Thus, to preserve your right to Safe Harbor protection, you must keep the work that employees and ICs do separate—that is, ICs and employees can't perform similar functions. For example, a trucking company can't classify some drivers as ICs and some as employees and qualify the drivers for the Safe Harbor. The company would have to classify all of the drivers as ICs to satisfy the consistency requirement. However, the company could classify a bookkeeper as an employee without jeopardizing the Safe Harbor for the IC drivers.

Before you hire an employee, make sure you haven't used ICs to perform similar services. Before you hire an IC, make sure you haven't used employees to perform similar services.

b. Timing concerns

The moment you treat any worker as an employee, you lose Safe Harbor protection for all workers performing substantially similar services. But you are not prevented from obtaining Safe Harbor protection for prior years—that is you can still qualify for the Safe Harbor for the years before you treated any worker in a substantially similar position as an employee.

EXAMPLE: Quickie Roofing treats all its applicators as ICs in 2000 and 2001—that is, it does not withhold federal taxes, file employment tax returns or give the workers W-2 forms. In 2002, however, Quickie begins treating some applicators as employees—that is, it does withhold federal tax from their paychecks and files employment tax returns for the workers. Quickie may still obtain Safe Harbor protection for the applicators for 2000 and 2001, but not 2002 or after.

However, if you've purchased your company from somebody else, the prior owner's classification practices apply to you as well as the prior owner. Thus, you can't qualify for the Safe Harbor if a prior owner treated as employees workers performing substantially similar services as workers you wish to classify as ICs.

EXAMPLE: Joe started Acme Trucking in 1988, treating all of his truckers as employees. In 2003, Joe sold the company to Eve. She treats all the truckers as ICs. If the IRS audits Acme for the years after the sale, Eve cannot obtain Safe Harbor protection for the truckers because Joe did not treat them as ICs.

This rule also prevents hiring firms from evading the consistency requirement by reincorporating their businesses.

EXAMPLE: Ace Trucking Inc. treats all its drivers as employees. Ace's owners want to convert all the drivers to IC status. The owners dissolve the corporation and transfer all the assets to a new corporation, Joker Trucking Inc. Joker hires all of Ace's old drivers and classifies them as ICs. Joker Trucking's drivers do not qualify for the Safe Harbor.

c. Inconsistent treatment for other purposes

As we stated above, the consistent treatment requirement means you must treat your workers consistently for *federal tax purposes*. You can treat workers inconsistently for other purposes and still obtain Safe Harbor protection. For example, you could provide a worker with workers' compensation coverage or pay state unemployment compensation taxes for him or her—both of which mean that you are treating the worker as an employee for state tax purposes—and still obtain Safe Harbor protection if you meet the other prongs.

You may wish to do this where your state has particularly strict rules about which workers qualify as ICs for unemployment insurance or workers' compensation purposes. (See Chapter 6 for information about state taxes, including unemployment insurance. See Chapter 7 for information about workers' compensation.)

DON'T FILE FEDERAL TAX FORMS FOR INDEPENDENT CONTRACTORS

If you classify a worker as an employee for state law purposes, don't use any federal tax forms to report your state tax payments or withholding for the worker. If you file such a form, the IRS will think that you are treating the worker as an employee for federal tax purposes—and you'll lose your Safe Harbor protection for that worker and for all workers who hold substantially similar positions.

For example, if you pay state unemployment taxes for a worker you classify as an IC for federal tax purposes, don't include the payments in IRS Form 940, Annual Unemployment Tax Return. List on Form 940 only the state unemployment compensation taxes you've paid for workers you classify as ICs for IRS purposes as well as state purposes.

---

d.   Workers With dual status

It's possible for the same worker to be both an IC and employee—and not violate the consistent treatment prong. This can occur where a worker performs very different services for the same company. For example, an employee bookkeeper for a business might be hired as an IC to design and print an advertising brochure. The fact that the bookkeeper is treated as an employee for the bookkeeping services does not prevent the hiring firm from obtaining Safe Harbor protection for the worker for the design and printing services.

3.   Third Prong: Having a Reasonable Basis for IC Classification

The final and usually most difficult requirement you must satisfy to obtain Safe Harbor protection is showing that you had a reasonable basis for treating the workers involved as ICs. Reasonable basis is just a fancy way of saying that you had a good reason for the IC classification.

There are several ways you can show a reasonable basis for treating a worker as an IC; some are easy and simple, some are more difficult and complex. These include showing that:

- it is a longstanding practice in your trade or industry to treat similar workers as ICs (see subsection a, below, for more about this)
- you relied on advice from an attorney or an accountant that the worker was an IC (see subsection b, below, for more about this)
- you relied on past court decisions or IRS rulings (see subsection c, below, for more about this)
- you relied on a past IRS audit (see subsection d, below, for more about this), or
- that you had some other good reason for classifying the worker as an IC, such as following a favorable ruling from a state agency (see subsection e, below, for more about this).

Ideally, you should take whatever steps are necessary to establish a reasonable basis before you start treating a worker as an IC. If you have already hired ICs, don't wait until an audit occurs to find a reasonable basis. Find one right now and keep your documentation on file in case of an audit. If you're already undergoing an audit, you can still establish a reasonable basis, but your task may be harder.

Let's look in more detail at each of the ways in which you can establish reasonable basis.

a.   Relying on industry practice

One way to establish a reasonable basis for treating a worker as an IC is showing that similar hiring firms in your geographic area treat similar workers as ICs. In other words, if everybody else does it, you can do it, too. However, in practice, it can be difficult to prove this to the IRS or a court.

To satisfy this requirement, you must prove four things: (1) that you relied on the fact that (2) a significant number of firms (3) in your geographic area use the same classification as a (4) longstanding practice.

Let's look at each of these in more detail.

Reliance. If audited, it's acceptable for you to say that you "just knew" that everyone else used same classification. But it's better if you can point to some hard evidence, like a survey of your industry or sworn statements from other business owners. In addition, it's good if you have a paper trail showing that you classified the workers as ICs because it was industry practice—for example, corporate minutes stating that the workers involved are being classified as ICs because this is a longstanding practice in your industry. If you don't have anything in writing to show your reliance on the longstanding practice, all is not lost. If you are ever audited, the auditor will interview you and other key people in your business and ask you why you classified the workers involved as ICs. This will give you the opportunity to explain that you relied upon the longstanding industry practice. The auditor will also interview the workers themselves to determine what reasons you gave them for classifying them as ICs. So be sure you explain to the workers that their IC classification was due to the industry practice. Indeed, it's a good idea to state this in your written IC agreements with the workers. (See Chapter 13 for a discussion of independent contractor agreements.)

Significant number. How much is enough? If you can reach 25%, you don't have to go any farther, But even if you can't reach it, a smaller number may satisfy the IRS depending on the circumstances.

Geographic area. You ordinarily don't have to prove that everybody in the world in the same business as you treats workers similar to yours as ICs. You only need to look at the geographic area in which you do business. If the market in which you compete is limited to your city, then you need only show that firms in your city do the same thing. If, however, you compete in regional or national markets, the geographic area may include that whole region or even the entire United States.

Longstanding practice. No fixed length of time is required for something to be considered longstanding, but the IRS will presume that any practice that has existed for ten years or more is longstanding. If you're in a new business or industry—for example, biotechnology—a much shorter time period should be acceptable.

b. Relying on professional advice

For many hiring firms, the easiest way to establish a reasonable basis is to ask an attorney or accountant whether the workers involved qualify as ICs for IRS purposes. If the answer is yes, your reliance on this advice constitutes a reasonable basis. However, this will work only if you obtain the advice before you begin treating the workers involved as ICs.

EXAMPLE: In 1983, the president of a Tennessee company that hired numerous telemarketers to sell gourmet foods contacted his longtime CPA and asked him whether the workers qualified as ICs. The CPA, who was thoroughly familiar with the company's business, advised the owner that the telemarketers qualified as ICs under the IRS common law test. The company classified all of the telemarketers as ICs for federal tax purposes, and it filed all required Form 1099s for them. The IRS audited the company in 1991 and claimed that the telemarketers should have been classified as employees during 1989-90. The company appealed and won. The court held that it was reasonable for the company to rely on advice from its CPA that the workers were ICs. This reliance satisfied the reasonable basis requirement for Safe Harbor protection. Since the company consistently treated all the telemarketers as ICs, filed all required Form 1099s and satisfied the reasonable basis requirement, it qualified for Safe Harbor protection. As a result, the company didn't have to pay a $3,888,918 IRS assessment.

Get advice about worker status in writing: a letter from the attorney or accountant will do. The letter should explain why the workers qualify as ICs. Keep the letter in your IC file. Once you obtain such a letter, you have the assurance of knowing you'll qualify for Safe Harbor protection so long as you satisfy the other two requirements explained above—filing all Form 1099s and consistently treating the workers as ICs. If you're audited, you won't have to go through the grueling and uncertain process of proving that the workers involved really are ICs under the common law test.

The IRS says you can't rely on advice from just any attorney or accountant; you must go to one who is familiar with business tax issues. You are not required to go to a high-priced tax specialist, nor do you have to independently investigate the attorney or accountant's credentials. However, you must make sure the person advises businesses. For example, the IRS says you couldn't reasonably rely on the advice of a patent attorney since such attorneys ordinarily don't advise businesses on tax matters.

c.   Relying on court decisions and IRS rulings

If any federal court—that is, federal tax court, federal district court, federal court of appeals or the U.S. Supreme Court—holds that workers in similar situations were not employees for federal tax purposes, you can use that holding as a reasonable basis for the Safe Harbor rules.

Published IRS rulings may also be used to show a reasonable basis. These include IRS Letter Rulings and Revenue Rulings. You may also rely on technical advice given to you by the IRS. This includes a specific Letter Ruling or determination letter from the IRS. You may not, however, rely on IRS technical advice given to other taxpayers. If you've purchased your business from someone else, you may not rely on a Letter Ruling issued to your predecessor.

All you need is one supportive opinion or ruling. The ruling need not be from a federal court in your state or judicial district, and it doesn't matter if other opinions or rulings go against you, and it doesn't matter if your business is outside of the court's jurisdiction.

The facts involved in such court decisions or IRS rulings do not have to be absolutely identical to your situation. Nor do they necessarily have to involve the particular industry or business in which you're engaged. They just have to be similar enough for you to rely upon them in good faith. You should provide the IRS auditor with a copy of the court decision or ruling you relied upon and explain why it was reasonable for you to do so.

The IRS requires that the decision or IRS ruling must have been in existence at the time you first began treating the workers involved as ICs. You can't use a decision decided after this time.

Most of the time, you probably won't be able to find a prior court decision or IRS ruling upon which to rely. There are thousands of published IRS rulings, but the vast majority hold that the workers involved were employees. There are not as many federal court rulings on this issue, and the chances of finding a favorable one that may be reasonably relied upon are fairly slim in most cases. However, there are favorable court rulings for some industries—for example, cases involving drywall installers, construction workers and truckers who own their own trucks.

If no other reasonable basis is available, before you classify a worker as an IC, do some legal research to try to find a favorable court decision or IRS ruling. You can do the research yourself, or hire an attorney or CPA to do it for you. (See Chapter 14 for information on doing your own research.)

d.   Relying on past IRS audits

If your business was audited by the IRS any time after 1977, you could be in luck: The audit could establish a reasonable basis for treating your workers as ICs. If, after the audit, you were not assessed back employment taxes for workers you classified as ICs, the IRS cannot later claim that any of your workers holding substantially similar positions are employees.

The audit must have been for your business. An audit of your own personal tax returns doesn't count, nor do audits of your workers' taxes. And you can't rely upon audits by state and local tax authorities.

AN AUDIT BY ANY OTHER NAME IS NOT AN AUDIT

Not all IRS contacts are considered audits. An audit occurs only when the IRS inspects your business's books and records. Mere inquiries or correspondence from an IRS Service Center do not count.

For example, a letter you receive from an IRS Service Center to verify a discrepancy in a Form 1099 you filed for a worker is not an audit. The IRS calls such contacts adjustments. If, however, IRS correspondence includes an examination or inspection of your records to determine the accuracy of deductions claimed on your tax returns, the contact does constitute an audit.

The IRS says that compliance checks in which the IRS asks if a business has filed all required returns, including employment tax returns, do not constitute audits. You'll receive a letter from the IRS saying as much if it conducts a compliance check of your business. However, a compliance check would qualify as an audit if the IRS asks about the reason for your worker classification practices or examines books and records other than those IRS forms the IRS requires you to maintain such as your business's income and employment tax returns.

Be sure to keep all copies of your correspondence and other documentation from the IRS as well as the auditor's business card. Show the auditor copies of this documentation to establish you had a prior audit. The auditor will then verify this by checking IRS records.

If an IRS audit occurred before January 1, 1997, it need not have focused on worker classification or employment taxes or even brought up the subject to enable you to use it for the Safe Harbor rules. Things aren't so simple for audits that occurred after that date, however. A post-1996 audit qualifies as a reasonable basis for purposes of the Safe Harbor rules only if it included an examination of whether the individual workers involved in the current audit or others holding substantially similar positions were properly classified as ICs for employment tax purposes.

EXAMPLE: The IRS examined Acme Corporation's 1996 income tax return in 1997. The auditor did not ask or consider whether ICs hired by Acme qualified as such for employment tax purposes. The IRS audits Acme again in 20XX, and this time the auditor questions the workers' IC classification. Acme may not use the 1997 audit as a reasonable basis because the audit did not include an examination of the worker classification issue.

The prior audit is only useful to you if the workers from that audit (that is, the workers whose IC status was not questioned by the IRS) hold substantially similar positions to the workers who are currently at issue.

EXAMPLE: A nursery and landscaping company hired landscapers and treated them as ICs. The IRS audited the business and determined that the landscapers were ICs. The corporation later hired janitorial workers and also treated them as ICs. The IRS audited the company again and claimed the janitorial workers were employees. The corporation claimed that the prior audit was a Safe Harbor. The IRS refused to grant Safe Harbor protection because the janitors and landscapers did not hold substantially similar positions.

The Safe Harbor rules do not define "substantially similar." The IRS takes the narrow view that it means that the workers must do the same work. However, some courts take a much more liberal approach. They compare the structure of the relationship between the workers and hiring firm, not the type of work involved. This means that workers in different industries could be considered substantially similar for Safe Harbor purposes.

EXAMPLE: The landscaping company in the above example appealed its case to federal court and won. The court held that the landscape workers and janitors held substantially similar positions for Safe Harbor purposes. Even though they did different kinds of work, their relationship with the company was very similar. Both groups of workers were paid on a per job basis and were treated similarly in terms of control, supervision and work demands. Because the prior audit did not challenge the IC status of the landscape workers, the court ruled that the hiring firm qualified for Safe Harbor protection for its subsequently hired janitors.

e. Catchall Provision

If you can't find a reasonable basis in any of the ways we discussed above, you might still be able to squeak through using the catchall provision. If you can demonstrate in any other way a reasonable basis for treating the workers as ICs, you still have a chance at that Safe Harbor. There are many possible ways to show such a reasonable basis, for example:

- Determinations by government agencies: A determination by a state agency or federal agency other than the IRS that the workers involved qualify as ICs may constitute a reasonable basis if the state or federal agency uses the same common law test as the IRS and interprets it similarly. Many states use the common law test for unemployment compensation purposes (see Chapter 6 for a list of these states), and most states use the common law test for workers' compensation

purposes (see Chapter 7 for a list of these states). Decisions by federal agencies such as the U.S. Labor Department could also provide a reasonable basis.

- Good faith application of common law test: Even more significantly, courts have held that a reasonable basis can include a hiring firm's reasonable, good faith—though possibly mistaken—belief that the workers qualified as ICs under the IRS common law test. (See Section C, above, for a discussion of the common law test.)

EXAMPLE: A firm that provided specialized temporary registered nurses to hospitals classified the nurses as ICs. The firm thought the classification was correct under the common law test. The IRS disagreed and claimed that the firm should have classified the nurses as employees. The firm appealed to federal court and the court held that it could use the Safe Harbor because it had reasonably concluded that the nurses qualified as ICs under the IRS common law test. This was enough to provide a reasonable basis for the classification.

REASON IN THE EYE OF THE BEHOLDER — AND THE IRS

You don't have to use one of the reasons we have discussed in this chapter to establish reasonable basis. You are only limited by your imagination—and by the IRS.

Firms have successfully argued reasonable basis in the following situations:

- a firm relied upon information from an industry or trade association or similar group that the workers may be classified as ICs
- a firm relied upon a favorable court decision or IRS ruling issued after it began treating the workers involved as ICs, and
- a firm relied upon an IRS private letter ruling or determination letter issued to one of its competitors stating that similar workers qualified as ICs.

The IRS has stated that the following reasons do not serve as a reasonable basis for classifying workers as ICs:

- the fact that the workers didn't have Social Security numbers
- the fact that it's cheaper for a hiring firm to treat the workers as ICs because it doesn't have to pay half their Social Security taxes or provide them with benefits
- the fact that the workers asked to be treated as ICs so they wouldn't have to have taxes withheld from their pay.

4. Limitations on Safe Harbor Protection

Even if you meet the three-prong test that we describe above, you will not be allowed to use Safe Harbor protection if you are a broker that deals with technical service workers (see subsection a, below) or if you want the protection to shield you during an audit of your pension plan (see subsection b, below).

a. Technical service firms

If you are a broker who contracts to provide certain technical service workers to hiring firms, you may not claim the workers are ICs using the Safe Harbor rules (though the hiring firm may).

Such brokers—also called technical services firms or consulting firms—may not use the Safe Harbor if they contract to provide third-party clients with:

- engineers
- designers
- drafters
- computer programmers
- systems analysts, or
- other similarly skilled workers.

EXAMPLE: Acme Technical Services is a broker that provides computer programmers to others. Acme contracts with Burt, a freelance programmer, to perform programming services for the Old Reliable Insurance Company. Reliable pays Acme who in turn pays Burt after deducting a broker's fee. Acme is a broker, and Burt is a hiring firm. Acme cannot claim the computer programmers are ICs.

b. Retirement plan audits

The IRS has a special group of auditors called the Employment Plans and Exempt Organizations Divisions, or EP/EO, who audit retirement plans. The IRS uses the common law test to determine whether workers are employees or ICs for retirement plan purposes. Safe Harbor protection is unavailable in such audits. If the IRS determines that workers you've classified as ICs are really employees for purposes of your retirement plan, the plan could lose its tax qualified status, resulting in substantial tax liability.

 If You Have a Retirement Plan, Don't Rely Solely on the Safe Harbor

If you are audited by the IRS and win your audit through the Safe Harbor rules, the IRS can still refer your case to the EP/EO for audit. For this reason, if your company has a tax qualified retirement plan, it is wise to make sure workers you've classified as IC qualify as such under the IRS common law test in addition to the Safe Harbor. ∎

IRS Audits

This chapter provides an overview of IRS audits and explains the considerable assessments and penalties that may be imposed on companies that misclassify workers. It also describes an IRS initiative called the Classification Settlement Program, or CSP, that allows many hiring firms to pay reduced assessments if they agree to reclassify the workers involved as employees.

Dealing with IRS audits is a complex subject. This chapter does not cover the entire audit process in detail. For detailed information on handling IRS audits, see *Tax Savvy for Small Business*, by attorney Frederick W. Daily (Nolo).

A. Why Audits Occur

Whenever you classify a worker as an IC, you become a potential IRS target. The IRS would prefer all workers to be classified as employees, not ICs. That way, it could collect workers' income and Social Security taxes directly from their employers through payroll withholding.

If you stay in business long enough, and if you have ICs, it's likely you'll be audited at least once by the IRS. Some businesses are audited far more often. Repeat audits are especially likely if past audits turned up serious problems. You should always be prepared to defend your worker classification practices to the IRS. At the very least, you want to put yourself in a position where the IRS can impose only the minimum assessments and penalties allowed by law if it determines you have misclassified employees as ICs.

B. Audit Basics

An audit is an examination by the IRS of your business, its tax returns and the records used to create the returns.

The IRS can audit your business for many reasons—for example, to determine whether:

- your business has paid the correct employment taxes for employees and filed the proper forms
- you've withheld the proper income taxes from employees' pay, or
- your employee pension plan meets the federal requirements for tax qualified status. (See Section H.)

1. Who Gets Audited

There are a number of ways you can be chosen by the IRS for an employment tax audit.

- You may be chosen for a general tax audit by the IRS computer; a small business has about one chance in 75 of being chosen in any year.
- The IRS may receive complaints from disgruntled workers or even business competitors that you are misclassifying workers.
- You may be in an industry that has worker classification practices the IRS is targeting. In past years, the IRS has targeted hair salons, trucking firms, couriers, securities dealers, high technology firms, roofers, temporary employment agencies, nurses' registries, building contractors and manufacturers' representatives. If you're in a business or industry where classifying workers as ICs is common, the IRS is sure to target it sooner or later.
- The IRS may be notified by a state agency that you have misclassified workers under state law. This most commonly occurs when terminated ICs apply for unemployment compensation and agency officials determine that the ICs should have been classified as employees under state law.
- The IRS may decide to inspect your payroll tax records as part of its general enforcement program—similar to the random checks now

conducted of passengers at airports. You'll be given seven days notice and an auditor will come to your office to conduct the inspection.

- You may come to the IRS's attention through an audit of an IC who hasn't been paying income or self-employment taxes.
- You may file more 1099 forms than average for companies in your industry, leading the IRS to conclude that you may be misclassifying your workers.

2. Audit Time Limits

As a general rule, the IRS has up to 36 months to audit a tax return after it's filed. Employee payroll taxes are reported on employment tax returns, IRS Form 941. The date of filing these returns determines when the time limit for audits concerning your worker classification practices can begin. Employment tax returns must be filed every three months, but for the purposes of this time limit, such returns are all deemed filed on April 15 of the following year.

> **EXAMPLE:** Acme Sandblasting Corporation files quarterly employment tax returns for its employees in 2003. Acme also has workers it classifies as ICs who were not included in the employment tax returns. Acme's four 2003 employment tax returns are all deemed filed on April 15, 2004. This is the day the 36-month audit time limit starts to run. The IRS will lose the right to audit Acme's employment tax returns for 2003 on April 16, 2007. After that date, the IRS may not question Acme's worker classification practices for 2003.

If you have some workers you classify as employees and you file employment tax returns, the IRS will only be able to conduct audits for the previous three years. These are also known as open years. The IRS usually audits only one or two of these open years.

Longer Time Limits If You Fail to File

The audit time limit period—called a statute of limitations—starts to run only if you actually file an employment tax return. In other words, years in which you don't file an employment tax return are theoretically open to IRS scrutiny forever. If you've never hired employees, but have hired ICs, there is no time limit on a worker classification audit because you have never filed an employment tax return.

In addition, there is no time limit on IRS audits where you filed a false or fraudulent return with the intent of evading taxes. This won't apply where a worker misclassification was due to an innocent or negligent mistake. But the IRS might invoke the fraud rule if it believes you knew the workers involved were employees and deliberately classified them as ICs to evade payroll taxes. In this event, the IRS may impose extremely harsh penalties. (See Section D2.)

Fortunately, the IRS has a general policy of not going back more than six years in conducting audits, even in cases of fraud or failure to file.

3. What the Auditor Does

As a first step, the IRS auditor will interview you. If your business is very small—a sole proprietorship grossing less than $100,000 per year—the auditor will probably request that you come to the local IRS office.

But if your business is a corporation, partnership or sole proprietorship grossing more than $100,000 per year, the IRS will usually seek to conduct the audit at your place of business. This is also known as a field audit. You're entitled to request that the audit be conducted elsewhere—for example, the IRS office or the office of your attorney or accountant. Explain that your business will be disrupted if the auditor comes there. It is usually a good idea to ward off on-site audits because you don't want an IRS auditor snooping around your business premises.

The auditor will also try to talk to any workers he or she thinks might be misclassified. You can't prevent the auditor from doing this.

The auditor will seek detailed information about any workers you've classified as ICs, including their names and addresses, the services they performed, when they worked for you, how they were paid, whether you've filed 1099s reporting your payments and whether you have signed independent contractor agreements.

IRS auditors have broad powers to inspect your records. To identify workers who may have been misclassified as ICs, IRS auditors often ask to see the following documents for the years being audited:

- copies of all IRS Form 1099s you've issued reporting payments of $600 or more to a worker in a year
- your payroll records and cash disbursement journals
- accounts payable records, and
- copies of all written contracts requiring outside workers to perform services on your behalf.

Among other things, IRS auditors will look for large payments to workers classified as ICs and try to trace whether payments have been made regularly over a number of years. Both may indicate employee status.

4. What You Need to Prove in an Audit

Unless the worker involved is a statutory IC (which is only possible for licensed real estate agents and direct sellers) the auditor will first attempt to determine whether you qualify for Safe Harbor protection. To qualify for the Safe Harbor, you must have:

- filed all required 1099 forms reporting to the IRS payments made to the workers
- consistently treated all workers holding substantially similar positions as ICs for federal tax purposes, and
- had a good reason for treating the workers as ICs.

Most hiring firms are unable to meet these requirements. (See Chapter 4 for more information about statutory ICs and the Safe Harbor protection.)

If you don't qualify for Safe Harbor protection, the auditor will then determine whether the workers involved qualify as ICs or employees under the common law test. You'll need to convince the auditor that the workers are in business for themselves.

Examples of the information and documentation you should provide the auditor include:

- your signed IC agreements with the workers (see Chapter 13 for information on drafting independent contractor agreements)
- documentation provided by the workers showing that they're in business for themselves, such as proof of insurance, business cards and stationery, copies of advertisements, professional licenses and copies of articles of incorporation
- a list of any employees of the workers
- a list of the equipment and facilities owned by the workers
- the invoices the workers submitted for billing purposes
- the names and addresses of other firms the workers have worked for, preferably at the same time they worked for you, and
- copies of the 1099 forms you filed reporting the payments made to unincorporated workers to the IRS.

You should already have all this documentation and information in your IC files. (See Chapter 12 for information on IC files.) If you don't have it at hand, obtain it as quickly as possible.

If the workers do qualify as ICs under the common law test, the auditor's last task is to determine whether they are statutory employees—this status may apply only to corporate officers, home workers, life insurance salespeople, business-to-business salespeople and drivers who distribute laundry, food or beverages. (See Chapter 4 for more information about statutory employees.)

For detailed guidance on dealing with IRS auditors, see *Tax Savvy for Small Business*, by attorney Frederick W. Daily (Nolo).

5. Audit Results

After the audit ends, the IRS will mail to you an examination report. This signals that the IRS considers the audit to be completed. Read the report carefully. If you're fortunate, you'll receive a "No Change Letter" stating that the auditor could not find sufficient basis for demanding any changes in your workers' status. On the other hand, if the auditor decides that you don't qualify for Safe Harbor protection and that you have misclassified workers under the common law test, the letter will demand that you change their status and it will impose assessments and penalties. However, if you qualify, the auditor may offer you a special settlement under the IRS Classification Settlement Program. In return for paying a reduced assessment, you must agree to treat the workers involved as employees in the future. (See Section C of this chapter for more information on the settlement program.)

If assessments and penalties have been imposed, check to see that they've been calculated correctly. (See Section D of this chapter for more about IRS penalties.)

6. Appealing the Audit

Examination reports are not set in stone. You can fight back by negotiating with the auditor or, if that fails, by appealing to the IRS Appeals Office, the tax court or the federal district court for your district.

a. Informal negotiations

Before entering the world of appeals, you should informally negotiate with the IRS. Start with the person who audited you. It's not helpful to simply ask—or beg—the auditor to lower the amount of the assessments. Instead, you need to show the auditor that he or she was mistaken on the legal issues involved. You must show either that:

- you're entitled to Safe Harbor protection, or
- even if you're not entitled to Safe Harbor protection, the auditor was mistaken in finding that the workers failed to qualify as ICs under the common law test.

If you can't get satisfaction from the auditor, you may have more success speaking with the auditor's manager. IRS managers are often more reasonable than field auditors.

b. Administrative appeals

If informal negotiations don't work, you can appeal the examination report. One way to do this is to file an appeal with the IRS appeals office, a department of the IRS that is separate from the audit division. An IRS appeals officer will handle your administrative appeal. You may be given an opportunity to have a face-to-face meeting, or the entire matter may be handled by mail. Although the appeals office is a branch of the IRS, many taxpayers have been successful in appealing IRS audits there.

To begin the process of appealing, file a written protest with the local IRS district director who will forward it to the appeals office. You must do this within 30 days of the date of the examination report or no later than 30 days of the date of an IRS 30-Day Letter. A 30-Day Letter will be sent to you if you fail to respond to the examination report within 30 days. It is your formal notice that your case is in dispute and you have 30 days to appeal. If you miss the deadline, you can still file an appeal in tax court or federal district court.

The IRS has a special program that allows hiring firms to appeal employment tax issues on an expedited basis—before the IRS audit ends and you receive the auditor's final examination report. To do this, you must submit a written request to the case manager. There is no additional fee for an early appeal.

c. Tax court appeals

Whether or not you pursue an appeal to the IRS appeals office, you may appeal to the tax court. The tax court is a special federal court that just handles tax cases. Its procedures are less formal than those of the federal district courts. But what is most advantageous about tax court is that you may file an appeal without first paying the tax and penalties the IRS claims are due. This is not the case if you appeal in regular federal district court. (See subsection d, below.)

To obtain tax court review of your case, you must file a petition with the court no later than 90 days after receiving an employment tax determination from the IRS. While your case is pending in tax court, you may start treating the workers whose employment status is involved—or those in similar positions—as employees rather than ICs. The tax court is not allowed to take this change into account in determining whether you properly classified the workers involved in your appeal as ICs.

d. Federal district court appeals

You also have the right to appeal in federal court. You can do this if you are dissatisfied with the outcome in the IRS administrative appeal, or you can forgo the administrative appeal and go straight to district court. But before you can appeal in court, you must pay the tax and penalties due and file a claim for refund with the IRS. After the IRS rejects the claim, you can sue for a refund in federal district court or federal claims court.

 For detailed guidance on IRS appeals, see *Stand Up to the IRS*, by attorney Frederick W. Daily (Nolo).

 You have the right to be represented by a lawyer or CPA in an audit and during the administrative and court appeals process. If you are facing the possibility of having to pay substantial assessments and penalties—over $5,000—it's probably sensible to hire professional help. An accountant, general business attorney or other small business people in your community may be able to refer you to a good local tax professional.

C. The Classification Settlement Program

When the IRS determines that hiring firms have misclassified employees as ICs, the Classification Settlement Program (or CSP) gives the firms the chance to pay reduced assessments in return for agreeing to classify the workers involved as employees in the future. The program is intended to encourage hiring firms to resolve worker classification cases as quickly as possible, saving themselves and the IRS time and money.

1. When the CSP Is Used

The CSP comes into play only if the IRS determines that you don't qualify for Safe Harbor protection and that the workers involved don't qualify as ICs under the common law test. In this event, the examiner will determine if you qualify for a CSP offer and make one if you do.

To qualify, you must have filed the required 1099 forms for the workers involved. However, your failure to file a small number of 1099 forms will not disqualify you from the CSP.

> **EXAMPLE:** The Acme Factory Outlet Store treated 150 workers as ICs. Acme filed all required 1099 forms for the workers except for three who were missed by the processing department. Acme's failure to file such a small number of 1099 forms does not disqualify it from the CSP.

2. CSP Offers

There are two different types of CSP offers. Which one you receive depends on whether the examiner believes you may have satisfied the requirements for Safe Harbor protection.

CSP Settlement Offers

1099s Timely Filed?	Hiring Firm Entitled to Safe Harbor Protection?	Type of CSP Offer
No	No	None
Yes	No	1 year's tax + employee treatment
Yes	Maybe	25% of 1 year's tax + employee treatment

a. One full year of assessments

If the examiner concludes that you clearly don't qualify for Safe Harbor protection because you didn't consistently treat the workers involved as ICs or you clearly lacked a reasonable basis for the IC classification, your CSP offer will require you to pay the full IRS employment tax assessment for the workers involved for the year under audit. However, no IRS penalties will be imposed. You must also agree to begin treating the workers involved as employees.

EXAMPLE: The Acme Masonry Company hired two bricklayers in 2000. The two workers performed identical duties, but Acme treated one as an IC and the other as an employee—that is, it filed a 1099 for one and a W-2 for the other. The IRS audited the company. Acme is entitled to a CSP offer because it filed a 1099 for the worker it treated as an IC. However, it is absolutely clear that Acme is not entitled to Safe Harbor protection because it did not treat the similarly situated workers consistently. As a result, the CSP offer will be for one year's full employment tax assessments.

b. 25% of one year's assessments

The CSP offer will require you to pay only 25% of one year's employment tax assessments if you've filed the required 1099 forms and if the IRS auditor concludes you might have a good argument that you're entitled to Safe Harbor protection. These will be cases where you have a problem establish-

ing that you treated all your workers holding substantially similar positions as ICs, where it's not completely clear that you had a reasonable basis for classifying them that way, or both.

EXAMPLE: The IRS audits the owner of the Larkspur Dock and questions the status of several IC workers. The owner filed all required 1099 forms for the workers and consistently treated them all as ICs. The owner claims he had a reasonable basis for treating the workers as ICs because an accountant told him they qualified as such. The IRS auditor questions the accountant. It turns out the accountant gave the advice orally and can no longer remember what facts were provided. The owner has a potential reasonable basis, but has not clearly established such a basis because the advice was not in writing and the accountant can't remember why he gave it. Under these circumstances, the auditor proposes a CSP offer with a 25% assessment.

3. CSP Procedures

If you accept the CSP offer, the auditor will provide you with a standard closing agreement to sign. You will be required to begin treating the workers involved as employees on the first day of the calendar quarter following the date you sign the agreement. For example, if you sign the agreement on February 1, you'd have to begin employee treatment on April 1. Such treatment must extend not only to those workers who worked for you during the year under audit, but to all workers you hire subsequently to perform equivalent duties, regardless of their job titles.

You are free to reject a CSP offer if you wish. If you reject the offer initially, you can change your mind and accept it during the entire examination process.

Rejecting a CSP offer is not supposed to affect the outcome of the audit. However, the audit will be expanded to include all your open tax years instead of just one year.

TO ACCEPT OR NOT ACCEPT A CSP OFFER

Hiring firms that are given CSP offers by the IRS often accept them. But this doesn't mean you should. If you conclude that you erred in classifying the workers involved as ICs, then the CSP offer may be a good deal. However, if you believe that you have a strong case for Safe Harbor protection or that the workers involved are ICs under the common law test, you may be better off rejecting the CSP offer and fighting the IRS. This may be particularly true if you provide generous pension or stock ownership benefits to your employees. An admission to the IRS that the workers involved are really employees may lead the workers to sue you for employee benefits.

Accepting a CSP offer could cost you in another way as well. Once you accept the offer, you will have to treat the workers as employees for all future years. Even if the workers don't sue you for back benefits, you will feel the pinch in the increased employment tax, workers' compensation premiums and unemployment insurance expenses. Indeed, these added expenses could cost you more than an appeal would have.

So, if you've got a leg to stand on, stand on it. Despite the cost of the appeal, you may end up saving money in the long run.

D. IRS Assessments for Worker Misclassification

The assessments the IRS can impose for worker misclassification vary enormously, depending upon whether the IRS views your misclassification as intentional or unintentional. The most strict penalties, of course, are imposed for intentional misclassification—where you knew the workers were your employees but classified them as ICs anyway to avoid payroll taxes. The IRS will likely conclude your misclassification was intentional if you admit you knew the workers were employees or if it should have been clear to any reasonable person that the workers were employees under the common law test.

> **EXAMPLE:** Bolo Press, a publisher of sports books, has a six-person production department. Bolo reclassifies its production employees as ICs so it can stop paying payroll taxes for them. After the reclassification, Bolo's owners treat the production workers just the same as when they were classified as employees—they tell the workers what time to come in and leave, closely supervise their work and give them fringe benefits such as health insurance and pension benefits. The production workers work solely for Bolo and make no attempt to market their services elsewhere.
>
> In an audit, the IRS concludes that the workers are employees. IRS auditors would likely conclude that the misclassification was intentional. Bolo clearly knew the production workers were really employees and reclassified them as ICs in disregard of the law simply to avoid paying payroll taxes.

On the other hand, worker misclassification is unintentional if you believed in good faith, though mistakenly in the view of the IRS, that the workers were ICs. This can involve tricky semantics. The common law test for worker classification used by the IRS is complex and difficult to apply and often does not provide a conclusive answer about how to classify a worker.

Many workers fall into a gray area where it is unclear how to classify them. If you can show that some of the common law factors indicate IC status, your misclassification should be regarded as unintentional. You should be able to do this in all but the most blatant misclassification cases.

1. Penalties for Unintentional Misclassification

When you hire an unincorporated IC, you are normally required to report the payments made to the worker on IRS Form 1099-MISC. There are two ranges of assessments the IRS may impose for unintentional worker misclassification: One is imposed where you filed all required 1099 forms for the workers the IRS claims you misclassified, and the other is imposed where you did not file the 1099 forms.

a. 1099 forms filed

If 1099 forms were filed, you will be required to pay a sum equal to:

- 20% of the FICA taxes (Social Security and Medicare) the employees should have had withheld from their pay—that is, 1.24% of the misclassified workers' wages up to the FICA Social Security tax ceiling plus 0.29% of all the workers' wages, plus
- 100% of the FICA taxes you should have paid on the workers' behalf as their employer—that is, 6.2% of the employees' wages up to the Social Security tax ceiling plus 1.45% of all the employees' wages, plus
- 1.5% of all the wages that were paid to the misclassified workers—a penalty for your failure to withhold federal income taxes from the workers' paychecks, plus
- all FUTA taxes (federal unemployment taxes) that should have been paid—the FUTA tax rate is 6.2% of the first $7,000 in employee wages, or .08% of the first $7,000 if the applicable state unemployment tax was timely paid; if a worker was paid $7,000 or more for a year, this amounts to either $434 or $56.

FICA SOCIAL SECURITY TAX CEILING

FICA taxes actually consist of two separate taxes: a 6.2% Social Security tax and a 1.45% Medicare tax on both the employer and employee. There is a ceiling on the Social Security tax—that is, a salary level beyond which the tax need not be paid. The ceiling increases every year. In 2003, the ceiling was $87,000. However, the Medicare tax must be paid on all the compensation paid to an employee.

You must pay the assessments for your failure to withhold employee FICA and income taxes from misclassified workers' compensation even if the workers paid all these taxes themselves. And these assessments will not be reduced where you can prove the workers paid the taxes. This means that the IRS could end up collecting more tax than would have been due had you classified the workers as employees and paid payroll taxes.

Together, these assessments amount to 16.88% of the compensation you paid each misclassified worker up to the $7,000 FUTA tax ceiling and then 10.68% of compensation up to the FICA Social Security tax ceiling. Any payments to a worker in excess of the Social Security tax ceiling are assessed at a 3.24% rate.

EXAMPLE: The IRS decides that Acme Sandblasting Corporation unintentionally misclassified five workers as ICs during 2003. Acme paid each worker $20,000 during that year and reported the payments on Form 1099. Based on this $100,000 in payments, the IRS assessment would be $12,620. This is calculated as follows:

20% of employee FICA tax	= $1,300
100% of employer FICA tax	= $7,650
1.5% of all employee wages	= $1,500
6.2% FUTA tax for five workers each paid $20,000	= $2,170

b.   1099 forms not filed

If you failed to file the 1099 forms, the employee FICA and income tax assessments are doubled. You must pay a sum equal to:

- 40% of the FICA (Social Security and Medicare) taxes the employee should have had withheld—that is, 2.48% of the misclassified workers' wages up to the FICA Social Security tax ceiling plus 0.58% of all the workers' wages, plus
- 100% of the FICA taxes you should have paid on the misclassified workers' behalf as their employer—that is, 6.2% of the employees' wages up to the Social Security tax ceiling plus 1.45% of all the employees' wages, plus
- 3% of all the wages that were paid to each misclassified worker as a penalty for your failure to withhold federal income taxes from the workers' paychecks, plus
- all FUTA taxes that should have been paid— 6.2% or .08% of the first $7,000 in compensation.

EXAMPLE: Recall the example above, in which $12,620 was assessed on $100,000 in payments to five misclassified workers. If, however, you did not file Form 1099 for those workers, you'd have to pay $15,880. This would break down as follows:

40% of employee FICA tax	=	$3,060
100% of employer FICA tax	=	$7,650
3% of all employee wages	=	$3,000
6.2% FUTA tax for five workers each paid $20,000	=	$2,170

2.   Penalties for Intentional Misclassification

IRS assessments are far higher if the IRS concludes that you intentionally misclassified as ICs workers you knew to be employees. You will be required to pay out of your own pocket all the FICA tax that you should have withheld from the employees' paychecks. You must pay:

- 100% of the FICA (Social Security and Medicare) taxes the misclassified workers should have had withheld—that is, 7.65% of the employee's wages subject to FICA, plus
- 100% of the FICA taxes you should have paid on the workers' behalf as their employer—that is, 7.65% of the employee's wages subject to FICA, plus
- 20% of all the wages that were paid to the workers to make up for your failure to withhold federal income taxes from their paychecks, plus
- all FUTA taxes that should have been paid— 6.2% of the first $7,000 in worker compensation or .08% if state unemployment taxes were paid.

Together, these assessments amount to a whopping 41.50% of worker compensation up to the $7,000 FUTA tax ceiling and then 35.3% of payments up to the Social Security tax ceiling.

Comparing these assessments with those that can be imposed for unintentional misclassification is a sobering exercise. As illustrated above, if you paid $100,000 to five workers the IRS claimed you unintentionally misclassified as employees during 2002, the assessments would total $12,620 if you filed 1099 forms, or $15,880 if you failed to file 1099 forms. But if the IRS claims you intentionally misclassified the workers, the assessments would total $37,470. This breaks down as follows:

100% of employee FICA tax	=	$7,650
100% of employer FICA tax	=	$7,650
20% of all employee wages	=	$20,000
6.2% FUTA tax for five workers who were each paid $20,000	=	$2,170

a.   Offsets for worker income tax payments

The only good thing about the intentional misclassification assessment is that the income tax portion can be reduced if you can prove that the misclassified worker paid his or her income taxes for the years in question. Such a reduction is called an offset or abatement.

The IRS will not help you prove income taxes were paid. IRS examiners will not request that workers provide copies of their income tax returns nor will the IRS give these returns to you. Instead, you need to file IRS Form 4669, Employee Wage Statement. This form states how much tax the worker paid on the wages. The worker must sign the form under penalty of perjury. You must file a Form 4669 for each worker involved along with Form 4670, Request for Relief From Payment of Income Tax Withholding, which is used to summarize and transmit the Form 4669.

The IRS examiner has the discretion to accept Forms 4669 and 4670 before the examination is closed and reduce the assessment. Otherwise, you must file them with your IRS service center.

EXAMPLE: The IRS determines that Acme Sand-blasting Corporation intentionally misclassified a computer consultant as an IC in 2002. Acme paid the worker $100,000. The IRS assessment is $30,848.40. However, the consultant paid all income taxes due on her compensation. Acme has the consultant sign IRS Form 4669 and submits it to the examiner along with Form 4670 before the IRS examination is closed. The examiner wipes out the entire 20% income tax penalty. The assessment is reduced by $20,000.

b. Offsets for worker FICA tax payments

Theoretically, if the misclassified workers paid their FICA taxes, you may also be entitled to an offset of the employee FICA portion of the assessment. However, in practice, this offset is difficult or impossible to obtain because a misclassified worker has a right to claim a refund for all the self-employment taxes he or she paid for the years covered by the audit. If the worker claims the refund, you can't get the offset. Because of this right, the IRS will not give you an employee FICA offset unless the misclassified worker fails to file a claim for a refund of these taxes within the statutory time limit, either two or three years.

INTENTIONAL MISCLASSIFICATION ASSESSMENTS MAY BE LOWER

Oddly, if you are able to get an offset for the income tax portion of an intentional misclassification assessment, the final assessment may be less than that which could be imposed for an unintentional misclassification. However, you are not allowed to choose which assessment rules will be used. If your misclassification was unintentional, the assessment rules will apply and you will not be entitled to any offsets. Some hiring firms have actually attempted to convince the IRS that a misclassification was intentional so that they could obtain assessment offsets.

E. Penalties for Worker Misclassification

In addition to the assessments discussed above, the IRS has the option of imposing an array of other penalties on hiring firms that misclassify workers.

1. Trust Fund Recovery Penalty

As far as the IRS is concerned, an employer's most important duty is to withhold FICA and income taxes from its employees' paychecks and pay the money to the IRS. Employee FICA and federal income taxes are also known as trust fund taxes because the employer is deemed to hold the withheld funds in trust for the U.S. government. The IRS considers failure to pay trust fund taxes to be a very serious transgression.

The IRS may impose a penalty known as the trust fund recovery penalty, formerly the 100% penalty, against individual employers or other people associated with the business. These are people the IRS deems responsible for failing to withhold employee FICA and federal income taxes and pay the withheld sums to the IRS. Failure to pay payroll taxes is willful if you knew the taxes were due and didn't pay them. The IRS will conclude you have acted willfully if you should have known the workers involved were employees, not ICs.

The trust fund recovery penalty is also known as the 100% penalty because the amount of the penalty is equal to 100% of the total amount of employee FICA and federal income taxes the employer failed to withhold and pay to the IRS. This can be a staggering sum.

EXAMPLE: The IRS determines that Acme Sandblasting Corporation intentionally misclassified a computer consultant as an IC in 2002. Acme paid the consultant $100,000. The IRS decides to impose the trust fund recovery penalty against Acme. Acme should have withheld and paid to the IRS $7,650 in employee FICA taxes and withheld $25,000 in federal income taxes, for a total of $32,650 in trust fund taxes. The 100% penalty is $32,650.

a.   Liability for 100% penalty

If you're a business owner, you'll be personally liable for the 100% penalty—in other words, you will have to pay it out of your own pocket. Business owners include sole proprietors, general partners and corporate officers such as the president, vice president, secretary and treasurer, whether or not they own any stock.

However, the scariest thing about the trust fund recovery penalty is that nonowner employees such as office managers, accountants, bookkeepers and even some clerks may also be held personally liable for it. They may be on the hook if the IRS concludes they willfully prevented the IRS from collecting the unpaid payroll taxes—in other words, they knew the taxes were due and didn't do anything about it. Most vulnerable are those who:

- made the business's financial decisions
- had authority to sign checks
- had the power to decide which bills to pay, or
- signed the business's payroll tax returns, such as the quarterly IRS Form 941.

b.   Appealing a penalty

If an IRS revenue officer decides you are responsible, you will be sent a notice and tax bill. You are entitled to appeal the penalty and have a hearing before an IRS appeals officer. You must file an appeal within 30 days.

 For a detailed discussion of IRS appeals, see *Stand Up to the IRS*, by attorney Frederick W. Daily (Nolo).

2.   Other Penalties

The IRS has the option of imposing many other penalties on hiring firms that misclassify workers. These include:

- A $50 penalty for each W-2 that you failed to file for misclassified workers. The penalty is larger if the failure to file was intentional. (IRC 6721.)
- A $50 penalty for each W-2 you failed to send a misclassified employee. The penalty is $100 if the failure to file was intentional. (IRC 6722.)
- A $50 penalty for each 1099 form you failed to file. (IRC 6721.)
- If the IRS determines you intentionally disregarded the rules requiring 1099 forms to be filed, a penalty equal to the greater of $100 or 10% of the compensation paid the worker can be imposed. (IRC 6721(e)(1).)
- If employment tax returns were not filed, a delinquency penalty of up to 25% of the tax determined to be due. (IRC 6651(a)(1).)
- A penalty for failure to pay taxes of ½ % per month on the unpaid taxes for up to 50 months. (IRC 6651(a)(2).)
- For failing to deposit the taxes found to be due, a penalty of up to 15% of the additional tax. (IRC 6656.)
- For negligently or intentionally disregarding IRS rules and regulations, a penalty of up to 20% of the underpayment that is due to the negligence. (IRC 6662.)

• A fraud penalty of 75% of the underpayment if the IRS determines that the underpayment is due to fraud; no negligence penalty is imposed in this event. (IRC 6663.)

Generally, the more severe penalties are imposed only where you intentionally misclassified workers.

F. Interest Assessments

The IRS can impose interest on employment tax assessments and penalties. The interest rate is adjusted every three months and compounded daily. It is currently around 9%.

THE BOTTOM LINE: ALL YOU COULD OWE

Factoring in all these assessments, penalties and interest, you can make a rough estimate of what you'll have to pay.

If the IRS determines you unintentionally misclassified a worker for whom you filed all required 1099 forms, you'll have to pay about 20 cents for every dollar you paid the worker, and 25 cents for every dollar if you didn't file 1099 forms. But if the IRS finds your misclassification intentional, you'll have to pay about 50 cents for each dollar you paid the worker.

G. Criminal Sanctions

In rare cases where a hiring firm has intentionally misclassified workers, the IRS may conduct a criminal investigation and have the U.S. Justice Department prosecute. Criminal fines and even jail time can be imposed if you're convicted of tax fraud.

H. Retirement Plan Audits

If your company has a retirement plan, you should be concerned about IRS retirement plan audits. Retirement plans are not audited as part of an ordinary business or employment tax audit. Instead, the IRS has specially trained revenue agents in every district just for retirement plan audits. This type of audit may derive from a prior business audit or from a review of annual IRS tax reporting Form 5500, which is required for most retirement plans.

Hiring firms with tax qualified retirement plans may have special problems with retirement plan audits where they classify workers as ICs.

1. Tax Qualified Retirement Plans

A tax qualified retirement plan is a retirement plan that covers business owners and employees and that satisfies the requirements of the federal Employee Retirement Income Security Act, or ERISA. That law is enforced by the U.S. Department of Labor, the IRS and the Pension Benefit Guarantee Corporation.

Contributions to a tax qualified retirement plan are tax deductible by the business, as are contributions by participating employees. In addition, income from retirement plan investments is tax free until it is withdrawn by the plan participants.

2. Anti-Discrimination Rules

You must satisfy complex ERISA rules to obtain these tax benefits. The most important are anti-discrimination requirements providing that the principal owners of a business cannot provide benefits only to themselves, corporate officers or highly paid employees. If there are other employees, many, but not all, must be included in the plan as well. In general, employees don't have to be covered the moment they're hired—but if they're employed long enough and are old enough, you have to bring them into the plan.

ERISA has even more complex rules concerning which workers must be counted under the anti-discrimination rules and how many need to be covered. The anti-discrimination rules are satisfied, for example, if 70% of employees are covered. There are other ways to satisfy the rules that may require that fewer employees be included in the plan.

3. Losing Tax Qualified Status

If the IRS determines that workers you classify as ICs are really employees for ERISA purposes, it's possible that not enough employees will be covered to satisfy the anti-discrimination rules. This can mean that your pension plan will lose its tax qualified status. In this event, all previous tax deductions for benefits or contributions to the plan can be thrown out. Your business can lose the deductions, and the benefit recipients will have to pay taxes on the benefits.

> **EXAMPLE:** Acme Sandblasting Corporation has a tax-qualified retirement plan. Acme has 100 employees and another 100 workers classified as ICs. Seventy of the 100 employees are covered by the pension plan, apparently satisfying the anti-discrimination rules because 70% of workers Acme classifies as employees are covered. However, the IRS determines that the 100 ICs should be classified as employees for ERISA purposes. Acme really has 200 employees and 140 had to be covered. As a result, Acme's retirement plan loses its tax qualified status.

The IRS uses the common law right of control test to determine if workers are employees or ICs for ERISA purposes. If a worker qualifies as an employee for federal payroll tax purposes, he or she is an employee for ERISA purposes as well.

Get Help
This is an extraordinarily complex area of the law, beyond the competence of most attorneys, let alone lay people. You should discuss this issue with your retirement plan administrator or seek advice from a retirement plan consultant or an attorney or CPA specializing in this field.

I. Worker Lawsuits for Pensions and Other Benefits

A company that provides its employees with pensions, stock options and other benefits faces the possibility that workers it has incorrectly classified as ICs will file expensive lawsuits asserting that they are really employees and therefore entitled to the benefits. This happened in a highly publicized case involving the Microsoft Corporation in which the company was sued by several workers it had improperly classified as ICs for federal payroll tax purposes. After lengthy litigation, the court held that the workers were entitled to full employee benefits for the entire time they had worked for Microsoft, including coverage under Microsoft's discount stock purchase plan and 401(k) plan. (*Vizcaino v. Microsoft,* 173 F.3d 713 (9th Cir. 1999).)

Companies that offer generous employee retirement or stock options plans like Microsoft's can avoid the problems Microsoft encountered by making sure that their plan eligibility provisions explicitly exclude workers whom the company has classified as ICs or as contract employees. Coverage should not depend on how the IRS or any other agency classifies the workers. The workers should sign IC agreements in which they waive any claims to such benefits. Companies should talk with their benefit plan administrators to make sure their plans contain such language. If the plans do not have such language, then the plans should be amended to add the language. ■

State Payroll Taxes

Employers in all states must pay and withhold state payroll taxes for employees. These taxes include:

- state unemployment taxes (in all states) (see Section A, below)
- state income tax withholding (in most states) (see Section E, below), and
- state disability taxes (in a few states) (see Section D, below).

In contrast, you do not have to withhold state payroll taxes for ICs. Thus, whenever you hire a worker, you must decide whether the worker is an employee or IC under your state's payroll tax laws. This is not a decision to be taken lightly, because state payroll tax audits are the most common type of audits you have to fear.

Don't Forget Workers' Compensation

In addition to state payroll taxes, you must purchase workers' compensation insurance for employees (but not for independent contractors). Often, this involves analyzing workers under yet another test. We discuss this issue in detail in Chapter 7.

A. State Unemployment Compensation

Federal law requires that all states provide most types of employees with unemployment compensation insurance. Employers are required to contribute to a state unemployment insurance fund. Employees make no contributions, except in Alaska, New Jersey, Pennsylvania and Rhode Island where

small employee contributions are withheld from employees' paychecks by their employers.

Unemployment compensation (UC) is only for employees; ICs cannot collect it. Firms that hire ICs don't have to pay unemployment compensation taxes for them. This is one of the significant benefits of classifying workers as ICs, since unemployment compensation taxes typically amount to hundreds of dollars per year for each employee.

THE COST OF UNEMPLOYMENT COMPENSATION INSURANCE

The unemployment tax rate varies from state to state and depends partly on the age of the hiring firm, the type of industry and how many claims have been filed by a firm's employees. Employers who maintain a stable payroll and file and pay their unemployment taxes on time will generally have a lower unemployment tax rate than employers with high turnovers or large fluctuations in their payroll and those who do not file or pay their taxes on time.

As a general rule, however, the unemployment tax rate is usually somewhere between 2% to 5% of wages—up to the maximum amount of wages that are taxable under the state's unemployment compensation law. The taxable limit in a majority of states ranges from $7,000 to $10,000, but in some states is much higher.

1. Unemployment Compensation Audits

You're more likely to be audited by a state UC auditor than by any other type of government auditor, including the IRS. There are two main reasons for this. First, most states have become very aggressive in auditing hiring firms for UC purposes. The more workers that are classified as ICs for UC purposes, the less money there is for the state's UC fund—and states are increasingly more aggressive about guarding these funds. In addition, state unemployment auditors are often the first to become aware of a firm's worker classification practices because ICs often apply for unemployment compensation when their work for a hiring firm ends.

When a worker classified as an IC files an unemployment compensation application, state unemployment auditors will investigate the hiring firm to determine if the worker was in fact an employee under the state's unemployment compensation law. If the state auditors determine the worker should have been classified as an employee, they will require the hiring firm to pay all the unemployment taxes it should have paid for the worker going back several years—three years is common—plus interest.

In addition, auditors will usually impose penalties for the misclassification. Penalties vary from state to state. A 10% penalty is common, but penalties are much higher in some states. For example, if a California employer willfully misclassifies a worker as an IC—that is, classifies the worker as an IC even though the firm knows he or she is an employee—a penalty equal to about 50% of the total compensation paid the worker for the prior three years may be imposed.

Unfortunately for hiring firms, unemployment compensation agencies in a great many states share information with other state agencies and the IRS. For example, they inform other agencies that a worker was misclassified for UC purposes. The IRS and other agencies will likely assume that the worker has been misclassified for their purposes as well and conduct an audit. An unemployment compensation audit may only be the first of many audits: workers' compensation, state income tax and IRS audits may well follow. Clearly, deciding how to classify a worker for unemployment compensation purposes is a very important decision for any hiring firm.

2. Threshold Requirements for UC Taxes

Before going to the time and trouble of trying to decide whether workers are employees or ICs un-der your state UC law, first see whether you're required to pay for UC coverage for your employees. In most states, if your payroll is very small, you won't have to pay UC taxes. It will make no difference to you whether a worker is an IC or employee; either way, no UC taxes will be due.

In most states, you must pay state UC taxes for employees if you're paying federal UC taxes, also called FUTA taxes. This means you must pay state UC taxes if:

- you pay $1,500 or more to employees during any calendar quarter—that is, any three-month period, or
- you have at least one employee during any day of a week during 20 weeks in a calendar year (the 20 weeks need not be consecutive).

But a large number of states have more strict requirements.

Nine states provide the broadest possible UC coverage by requiring employers to pay UC taxes for any employee whose earnings or hours worked surpass a threshold level. These states are Alaska, Colorado, Hawaii, Maryland, Minnesota, Pennsylvania, Rhode Island, Washington and Wyoming.

Ten states have payroll or service requirements that are less than the FUTA requirements. For example, a California employer must pay UC taxes if it pays one or more employees $100 or more per quarter. Other states in this category include Massachusetts, Montana, Nevada, New Jersey, New Mexico, New York, Oregon, Utah and Wyoming.

Contact your state unemployment agency for the exact service and payroll amounts. (See Section C for contact details.)

B. State UC Classification Tests

Each state has its own unemployment compensation law administered by a state agency, often called the department of labor. Each state's law defines who is and who is not an employee for unemployment compensation purposes. Almost all states fall into one of three categories:

- the common law test
- a three-part ABC test, and
- a modified ABC test.

Find the category for your state on the list below and then read the appropriate discussion in Section 1, 2 or 3. This should give you a general idea of whether a particular worker is an employee or IC for UC purposes. For more detailed information, contact the unemployment compensation agency in your state. Most of these agencies have websites and free information pamphlets. (See Section C for contact details.) Michigan, Oregon, Wisconsin and Wyoming do not fit into any of the three standard categories. We discuss the tests for these states in Section 4, below.

1. The Common Law Test

Many of the most populous states—including California, Florida, New York and Texas—use the common law test to determine whether a worker is an employee for UC purposes. Under this test, a worker is an employee if the person for whom he or she works has the right to direct and control how the work is performed, both as to the final results, and as to the details of when, where and how the work is to be done.

This is the same test that the IRS uses to determine if a worker is an employee or IC for federal unemployment tax (FUTA) purposes, although not all states use the test in exactly the same way as does the IRS. See Chapter 4 for a discussion of the common law test as applied by the IRS.

Generally, any worker who qualifies as an IC under the IRS's version of the common law test would also be an IC under a state unemployment agency's common law test. However, there are no guarantees. Classifying a worker under the common law test is far from an exact science and, particularly in borderline cases, opinions may differ. State unemployment agencies are not bound by a determination by the IRS that a worker is an IC, so it is possible that worker could be deemed an IC by the IRS and an employee by the hiring firm's

unemployment compensation agency. It's a good idea to obtain detailed information about how your state unemployment agency applies the common law test. All state unemployment agencies have websites or you can call or visit your agency. See the end of this chapter for contact information for all state unemployment compensation agencies.

2. The ABC Test

About half the states use a statutory test written by their legislatures to determine if a worker is an employee for unemployment compensation purposes. This test is called the ABC test because it contains three parts.

THE STRICTEST TEST AROUND

The full-blown ABC test is the most strict worker classification test. It is possible for a worker to qualify as an IC for IRS and other purposes under the less strict common law test and still be an employee under the ABC test for state unemployment compensation purposes. This means that you could classify a worker as an IC for IRS purposes and as an employee for state UC purposes. You wouldn't withhold or pay federal payroll taxes, but would pay state UC taxes.

But this poses practical problems. Paying UC taxes for a worker makes the worker look like your employee. You could attempt to explain to an IRS auditor that your state has an extremely strict ABC test, but the auditor will still likely view payment of state IC taxes for a worker as a strong indicator of employee status. The safest course is to classify a worker who fails the ABC test as an employee for all purposes.

STATE TESTS FOR UNEMPLOYMENT COMPENSATION

State	Test
Alabama	Common Law
Alaska	ABC
Arizona	Common Law
Arkansas	ABC
California	Common Law
Colorado	Modified ABC (AC)
Connecticut	ABC
Delaware	ABC
District of Columbia	Common Law
Florida	Common Law
Georgia	ABC
Hawaii	ABC
Idaho	Modified ABC (AC)
Illinois	ABC
Indiana	ABC
Iowa	Common Law
Kansas	Modified ABC (AB)
Kentucky	Common Law
Louisiana	ABC
Maine	ABC
Maryland	ABC
Massachusetts	ABC
Michigan	Other (Economic Reality)
Minnesota	Common Law
Mississippi	Common Law
Missouri	Common Law

State	Test
Montana	Modified ABC (AC)
Nebraska	ABC
Nevada	ABC
New Hampshire	ABC
New Jersey	ABC
New Mexico	ABC
New York	Common Law
North Carolina	Common Law
North Dakota	Common Law
Ohio	Common Law
Oklahoma	Modified ABC (AB or AC)
Oregon	Other (8 factors)
Pennsylvania	Modified ABC (AC)
Rhode Island	ABC
South Carolina	Common Law
South Dakota	Modified ABC (AC)
Tennessee	ABC
Texas	Common Law
Utah	ABC
Vermont	ABC
Virginia	Modified ABC (AB or AC)
Washington	ABC
West Virginia	ABC
Wisconsin	Other
Wyoming	Other

To qualify as an IC for state unemployment compensation purposes, a worker must satisfy all three prongs of the ABC test. You must show that:

- The worker is free from your control or direction in performing the services, both in any oral or written contract of service and in reality. (See subsection a, below.)
- The worker's services are either outside your firm's usual course of business, or performed outside of all of your places of business. (See subsection b, below.)
- The worker is carrying on an independently established trade, occupation, profession or business. (See subsection c, below.)

If any one of the three prongs of the ABC test is not satisfied, the worker will be classified as an employee for unemployment compensation purposes—and you must pay state unemployment compensation taxes for that individual.

a.   Prong A: Control or direction of the work

The first part of the ABC test, Prong A, requires that you not have the right to exercise control or direction over the worker's services. Your control must be limited to accepting or rejecting the results the worker achieves, not how he or she achieves them. This is simply a restatement of the common law right of control test—the test used to determine worker status for IRS and many other purposes. (See Chapter 3 for a discussion of the IRS test.)

The factors state UC auditors examine to determine if you have the right to control a worker differ somewhat from state to state and are determined by state UC laws, regulations and court rulings. For example, Maryland regulations provide that a worker is considered to be free from a hiring firm's direction or control if the firm does not:

- require the worker to comply with detailed instructions about when, where and how the person is to work
- train the worker
- establish set hours of work
- establish a schedule or routine for the worker, or

- have the power to fire the worker for failing to obey specific instructions. (Md. Regs. Code title 24, § 24.02.01.18(B)(3)(a).)

In Oklahoma, unemployment compensation auditors focus on a slightly different set of factors, including whether the hiring firm:

- provides the worker with tools and equipment
- pays the worker's business expenses
- assumes all financial risks involved with the work
- hires the worker's assistants, and
- obtains and maintains all business, tax and occupational licenses.

To find out the details of your state's test, you will have to contact the agency in your state that enforces unemployment compensation laws. (See Section C, below, for contact details.)

b.   Prong B: Outside service

The second part of the ABC test focuses on whether the worker's services are outside your normal business. Prong B is satisfied if either:

- the worker's service is outside the usual course of your business operations, or
- the work is performed completely outside your usual places of business.

Usual course of business operations. State auditors seek to determine whether the worker's services are an integral part of—that is, closely related to—your normal daily business operations. You're likely to exercise control over such workers because they are so important to your business's success or continuation.

EXAMPLE 1: Jeremy works part time on the assembly line at the General Widget Corp. Jeremy helps assemble widgets, which is what General Widget is in the business of producing. Jeremy's services are essential to the nature of General Widget's business because it can't produce widgets without people working on the assembly line. Jeremy therefore can't satisfy Prong B because he does not work outside the hiring firm's normal course of business.

EXAMPLE 2: General Widget Corp. hires Jessica, an attorney with her own practice, to defend it in a products liability lawsuit. General Widget is in the business of producing widgets, not defending lawsuits, so Jessica's services are outside General's normal business, satisfying Prong B.

Work performed outside the business. Even if a worker's services are an integral part of your business operations, you can still satisfy Prong B if the worker's services are performed outside your place of business. In other words, the worker must not work on any of your firm's business premises.

EXAMPLE: General Widget Corp. contracts with Arnie to provide important component parts for its widgets. Arnie builds the components in his own workshop and delivers them to General. Arnie's services are an integral part of General's business operations, but Prong B is still satisfied because Arnie performs the services at his own business premises.

Some states that use the ABC test take the position that if a hiring firm has no fixed place of business—for example, a sales firm—a worker cannot satisfy the off-premises test if the services are performed at a temporary work site or where customers or prospective customers are located. This can make it impossible for workers for many types of hiring firms to qualify as ICs for unemployment compensation purposes.

EXAMPLE: Sam is a home widget installer. He works for a number of different widget sales companies, including Best Buy Widgets. When Best Buy obtains an order, it tells Sam and he goes to the customer's house to install the widget. He does no widget installing at Best Buy's sales office. Sam cannot meet the off-premises test in most states that use the ABC test be-

cause he works at temporary work sites where Best Buy's customers are located—their homes. He would be deemed an employee of Best Buy for unemployment compensation purposes.

c. Prong C: Independent business or trade

The final part of the ABC test requires that the worker be engaged in an independently established trade, occupation, profession or business. This means that the worker's business activity must exist independently of, and apart from, the service relationship with the hiring firm. It must be a stable, lasting enterprise that will survive termination of the relationship with the hiring firm.

Some of the ways you can show that a worker is in an independent business or trade include proof that the worker:

- has a separate office or business location
- maintains a business listing in the telephone directory
- owns the equipment needed to perform the services
- employs assistants
- has a financial investment in the business and the ability to incur a loss
- has his or her own liability or workers' compensation insurance
- performs services for more than one unrelated hiring firm at the same time
- is paid by the job rather than by the hour
- possesses all applicable business licenses, and
- files business (Schedule C) federal income tax returns.

3. Modified ABC Tests

Eight states use a modified version of the ABC test. These states do not require that all three prongs of the standard ABC test discussed above be satisfied; they drop one of the three requirements. The following list shows which prongs of the ABC test these states use.

STATES USING A MODIFIED ABC TEST

State	Prongs Used
Colorado	AC
Idaho	AC
Kansas	AB
Montana	AC
Oklahoma	AB or AC
Pennsylvania	AC
South Dakota	AC
Virginia	AB or AC

Colorado, Idaho, Montana, Pennsylvania and South Dakota drop the B outside-service prong. In these states, a worker will be considered an IC for unemployment compensation purposes if he or she is not under the direction and control of the hiring firm and is engaged in an independent business and trade.

Kansas drops the C independent-business prong. In Kansas, a worker will be an IC for unemployment purposes if he or she is not under the hiring firm's direction and control and the work is either outside the hiring firm's usual business or is performed outside the firm's business premises.

In Oklahoma and Virginia, a worker qualifies as an IC if either the AB or AC prongs are satisfied—that is, lack of control plus outside service; or lack of control plus independent business.

Obviously, it is somewhat easier to establish that a worker is an IC in these states than in those that require that all three prongs of the ABC test be met.

4. Other Tests—Michigan, Oregon, Wisconsin and Wyoming

Four states—Michigan, Oregon, Wisconsin and Wyoming—do not use either the ABC test or a modified ABC test.

a. Michigan

Michigan uses an economic reality test to determine if a worker is an employee. This test focuses on the economic reality of the relationship between worker and hiring firm, rather than looking exclusively at the right to control the worker. A worker who is economically dependent upon the hiring firm is the firm's employee. The factors are:

- who controls the worker's duties (control by the hiring firm indicates employee status)
- how the worker is paid (hourly payment indicates employee status, payment by the project indicates IC status)
- whether the hiring firm has the right to fire and discipline the worker (if so, employee status is strongly indicated), and
- whether the performance of the worker's duties are an integral part of the hiring firm's business toward the accomplishment of a common goal.

(*Williams v. Cleveland Cliffs Iron Co.,* 476 N.W.2d 414 (1991).)

b. Oregon

Oregon has a single test that is used to determine the employment status of workers for unemployment compensation, workers' compensation and state income tax purposes. Under this test, a worker is an IC only if all the following eight factors are met:

- the worker is free from the hiring firm's direction and control in performing the services, although the firm can specify the desired results
- the worker is responsible for obtaining all applicable business licenses and registrations
- the worker furnishes the tools and equipment needed to perform the services
- the worker has the authority to hire and fire assistants
- payment is made on completion of specific portions of the project or is made on the ba-

sis of an annual or periodic retainer and not hourly

- the worker is registered with the state if required by Oregon law
- federal and state income tax returns in the name of the worker or the worker's business (Schedule C) were filed for the previous year if the person worked as an IC the previous year, and
- the worker is engaged in an independently established trade or business.

(Oregon Revised Statutes 670.600.)

c.   Wisconsin

In Wisconsin, a worker is an IC for UC purposes if he or she (1) holds or has applied for an employer identification number from the IRS or has filed business or self-employment income tax returns with the IRS for the previous year, and (2) meets six or more of the following conditions:

- the individual maintains a separate business with his or her own office, equipment, materials and other facilities
- the individual operates under contracts to perform specific services for specific amounts of money under which the worker controls the means and method of performing the services
- the individual incurs the main expenses for the services performed
- the individual is responsible for the satisfactory completion of the services and is liable for failure to satisfactorily complete them
- the individual is paid solely on a commission or per-job or competitive-bid basis
- the individual may realize a profit or suffer a loss
- the individual has recurring business liabilities or obligations, or
- the success or failure of the individual's business depends on the relationship of business receipts to expenditures.

(Wisconsin Statutes 108.02(12)(b).)

d.   Wyoming

Wyoming looks at three factors to determine if a worker is an employee for UC purposes. A worker is an IC if he or she:

- is free from control or direction over the details of the performance of services by contract and in fact
- represents his or her services to the public as a self-employed individual or an independent contractor, and
- may substitute another individual to perform the services.

(27 Wyoming Statutes Section 27-3-104(b).)

5.   Statutory Employees

Federal law requires that certain types of workers must be covered by unemployment insurance, even if they qualify as ICs:

- corporate officers
- drivers who distribute food products, beverages or laundry, and
- traveling or city salespeople.

These workers are called statutory employees. (See Chapter 4 for a detailed discussion of statutory employees.)

Most states also require that state unemployment compensation be paid for statutory employees. The only exceptions are Georgia, Maryland, Massachusetts, Montana and New Hampshire. If you hire a statutory employee in one of these states, you must pay the full 6.2% FUTA tax, since you won't receive a credit for paying state unemployment taxes.

However, the following 14 states exclude some or all corporate officers from receiving state unemployment insurance: Alaska, California, Delaware, Hawaii, Iowa, Michigan, Minnesota, New Jersey, North Dakota, Oklahoma, Oregon, Texas, Washington and Wisconsin. If you live in one of these states, check with your state unemployment agency for more information.

CALIFORNIA RULES FOR CONSTRUCTION CONTRACTORS AND AUTHORS

California contractors must pay careful attention to some especially strict unemployment compensation rules. If you hire an unlicensed worker or unlicensed subcontractor to perform work requiring a contractor's license, you're automatically deemed the worker's or subcontractor's employer for all state payroll tax purposes, including unemployment compensation and state income tax. (Cal. Unemployment Ins. Code § 621.5, Cal. Labor Code § 2750.5.)

EXAMPLE: Tom, a licensed contractor, agrees to do a room addition. Lacking the time to do the job himself, he subcontracts the work out to Bill, who does not have a construction contractor license. Although Bill would easily qualify as an IC under the normal rules, he is considered Tom's employee because he is unlicensed. Tom must pay all applicable California payroll taxes for Bill.

Neither the IRS nor virtually any other state has a rule similar to California's. Bill, in the example above, would be an IC for IRS purposes and would be an IC in most other states as well.

In addition, California law provides that the author of a work commissioned by another is deemed the employee of the commissioning party for state payroll tax purposes if the work is done under a written agreement specifying that the work is made for hire.

6. Exemptions From Coverage

Most states exempt certain services from unemployment compensation coverage. This includes services performed by:

- your spouse, minor children or parents (but services by a parent are not exempt in New York)
- licensed real estate brokers who work on commission, and
- real estate salespeople who work on commission.

But the most important exemption from unemployment compensation coverage is for casual labor. Casual labor is a term used by hiring firms to describe temporary or part-time workers. Under the laws of most states, workers performing casual labor are not covered by unemployment compensation if the services are not performed within the hiring firm's course of trade or business.

EXAMPLE: The Leopold and Loeb law firm hires John to paint one of its offices. Painting does not fall within the law firm's trade or business, so John may qualify for the casual labor exemption.

FIGHTING UNEMPLOYMENT COMPENSATION CLAIMS

If a worker you classified as an IC files a claim for unemployment compensation, you don't have to simply accept the worker's assertion that he or she should have been classified as an employee. You have the right to fight the worker's claim, both in administrative proceedings before the state unemployment agency and, if this fails, in state court.

Procedures differ from state to state, but are generally handled in the following way.

First, the worker will file a claim with the state UC agency. You'll be notified in writing of the claim and can file a written objection, usually within seven to ten days. Be sure to review your state's worker classification test and timely file an objection explaining why the worker is an IC. Include copies of documentation showing that the worker is in business for himself or herself. You should already have this material in your files. (See Chapter 12.)

Next, the UC agency will determine if the worker is eligible to receive UC benefits. There's usually no hearing at this stage.

If either you or the worker doesn't like the UC agency's ruling, you can demand a hearing. This is usually held at the UC agency's office before a hearing officer on the agency's staff, called a referee in many states. You should present your written documentation showing that the worker was an IC, not your employee. You can testify yourself and also present oral testimony from witnesses—for example, supervisors or other people who dealt with the worker. The more relevant persuasive evidence you have, the better off you'll be.

Before the hearing, ask to see the UC agency's complete file on the claim, since it may contain inaccurate statements you'll need to refute.

You're entitled to have an attorney represent you at the hearing. If you can afford it, this is not a bad idea, because an adverse ruling may result in audits of other workers you've classified as ICs by the UC agency and other government agencies, including the IRS.

Either side can then appeal the UC hearing officer's ruling to a state administrative agency such as a board of review. You should usually hire a lawyer to do this. Such appeals are usually not successful.

Finally, you can appeal to your state courts. Again, you will probably need the help of a lawyer to do this. Your appeal will likely fail unless you can show the prior rulings were contrary to law or not supported by substantial evidence.

However, the casual labor exemption is lost if the worker performs services for more than 24 days during a calendar quarter—that is, any three-month period—or during the previous calendar quarter.

EXAMPLE: John, the painter, works for Leopold and Loeb for 25 days in March and 15 days in April. He doesn't qualify for the casual labor exemption for either the first or second calendar quarter. He worked more than 24 days during the January-February-March calendar quarter, so the exemption is lost for that quarter. In addition, the exemption is lost for the April-May-June calendar quarter because he worked more than 24 days during the previous quarter.

The following states do not have a casual labor exemption: Delaware, Idaho, Illinois, Iowa, Kansas, Maine, Michigan, Missouri, Nevada, New Jersey, New Mexico, New York, Oklahoma, South Dakota, Tennessee, Texas, West Virginia, Wisconsin and Wyoming.

C. State Unemployment Tax Agencies

Below is a list of state unemployment tax agencies. If the telephone number listed for your state is a long distance call from your area, check your telephone book under the name of your state's agency to find a local number.

STATE UNEMPLOYMENT TAX AGENCIES

Alabama
Department of Industrial Relations
Montgomery, AL
334-242-8025
http://dir.state.al.us

Alaska
Employment Security Division
Juneau, AK 99802-5509
907-465-2712
www.labor.state.ak/esd

Arizona
Department of Economic Security
Phoenix, AZ
602-952-1815
www.de.state.az.us

Arkansas
Employment Security Department
Little Rock, AR
501-682-3200
www.state.ar.us/esd/index.htm

California
Employment Development
Department
Sacramento, CA
800-300-5616
www.edd.cahwnet.gov

Colorado
Department of Labor and
Employment
Unemployment Insurance Tax Branch
Denver, CO
800-480-8299 or 303-318-9100
www.coworkforce.com/UIT

Connecticut
Unemployment Tax Division
Labor Department Administrative
Offices
Wethersfield, CT
860-566-1018 or 203-248-4270
www.ctdol.state.ct.us

Delaware
Department of Labor
Division of Unemployment Insurance
Newark, DE
302-761-8058
www.delawareworks.com/divisions/
unemployment/welcome.htm

District of Columbia
Department of Employment Services
Tax Division
Washington, DC
202-724-7273
http://does.dc.gov/services/
tax_liability.shtm

Florida
Department of Revenue
Tallahassee, FL
850-488-9719 or 800-482-8293
www.floridajobs.org

Georgia
Department of Labor
Unemployment Insurance Division
Atlanta, GA
404-656-3129
www.dol.state.ga.us/employers.html

Hawaii
Department of Labor and Industrial
Relations
Unemployment Insurance Division
Honolulu, HI
808-586-9077
http://dlir.state.hi.us

Idaho
Department of Labor
Unemployment Insurance Division
Boise, ID
208-332-3576 or 800-448-2977
www.labor.state.id.us

Illinois
Department of Employment Security
Chicago, IL
312-793-4880 or 800-247-4984
www.ides.state.il.us

Indiana
Division of Workforce Development
Indianapolis, IN
1-888-WORKONE
www.dwd.state.in.us

Iowa
Workforce Development
Des Moines, IA
515-281-5387 or 800-JOB-IOWA
www.iowaworkforce.org

Kansas
Department of Human Resources
Division of Employment Security
Topeka, KS
785-296-5026
www.hr.state.ks.us

Kentucky
Department of Employment Services
Unemployment Insurance
Frankfort, KY
502-564-2900
www.desky.org/ui

Louisiana
Department of Labor
Baton Rouge, LA
225-922-0182
www.laworks.net

Maine
Department of Labor
Bureau of Unemployment
Compensation
Augusta, ME
207-287-2338
www.state.me.us/labor

Maryland
Office of Unemployment Insurance
Baltimore, MD
410-767-3246
www.dllr.state.md.us

Massachusetts
Department of Employment and
Training
Boston, MA
617-727-6560
www.detma.org

State Unemployment Tax Agencies (continued)

Michigan
Bureau of Workers' and
Unemployment Compensation
Detroit, MI
313-456-2010 or 800-638-3994
www.michigan.gov/bwuc

Minnesota
Department of Economic Security
St. Paul, MN
612-296-6141
www.mnworkforcecenter.org

Mississippi
Employment Security Commission
Jackson, MS
601-961-7755
www.mesc.state.ms.us

Missouri
Division of Employment Security
Jefferson City, MO
573-751-3215
www.dolir.state.mo.us

Montana
Department of Labor and Industry
Helena, MT
406-444-6900
http://uid.dli.state.mt.us

Nebraska
Division of Unemployment Insurance
Lincoln, NE
402-471-9835
www.dol.state.ne.us

Nevada
Department of Employment, Training
and Rehabilitation
Employment Security Division
Carson City, NV
775-687-4545
http://detr.state.nv.us/es/
esd_employers.htm

New Hampshire
Department of Employment Security
Concord, NH
603-228-4100
www.nhes.state.nh.us

New Jersey
Department of Labor
Division of Unemployment Insurance
Trenton, NJ
609-292-7163
www.state.nj.us/labor

New Mexico
Department of Labor
Unemployment Compensation Bureau
Albuquerque, NM
505-841-2000
www3.state.nm.us/dol/dol_esd.html

New York
Department of Labor
Albany, NY
888-899-8810 or 518-485-8589
www.labor.state.ny.us

North Carolina
Employment Security Commission
Raleigh, NC
919-733-7506
www.ncesc.com

North Dakota
Job Service
Bismarck, ND
800-732-9787 or 701-328-2868
www.state.nd.us/jsnd/
jobinsurance.htm

Ohio
Office of Unemployment
Compensation
Columbus, OH
614-466-6282
www.state.oh.us/odjfs/ouc/index.stm

Oklahoma
Employment Security Commission
Oklahoma City, OK
405-557-0200
www.oesc.state.ok.us

Oregon
Employment Department
Salem, OR
503-378-4824
http://findit.emp.state.or.us/uiinfo.cfm

Pennsylvania
Department of Labor and Industry
Harrisburg, PA
717-787-5279
www.dli.state.pa.us

Rhode Island
Department of Labor and Training
Providence, RI
401-243-9100
www.dlt.state.ri.us/ui

South Carolina
Employment Security Commission
Columbia, SC
803-737-3071
www.sces.org

South Dakota
Unemployment Insurance Division
Aberdeen, SD
605-626-2452
www.state.sd.us/dol/dol.htm

Tennessee
Division of Employment Security
Bureau of Unemployment Insurance
Nashville, TN
615-741-2486
www.state.tn.us/labor-wfd

Texas
Workforce Commission
Austin, TX
800-832-9394
www.twc.state.tx.us

Utah
Department of Workforce Services
Salt Lake City, UT
801-526-9400 or 800-222-2857
http://jobs.utah.gov/ui

Vermont
Department of Employment and
Training
Montpelier, VT
802-828-4000
www.det.state.vt.us

State Unemployment Tax Agencies (continued)

Virginia
Employment Commission
Richmond, VA
804-786-5085
www.vec.state.va.us/index.htm

Washington
Employment Security Department
Olympia, WA
360-902-9303
www.wa.gov/esd/ui.htm

West Virginia
Bureau of Unemployment Programs
Charleston, WV
304-558-0291
www.state.wv.us/bep/default.shtm

Wisconsin
Department of Workforce
Development
Madison, WI
608-266-3131
www.dwd.state.wi.us/ui

Wyoming
Department of Employment
Unemployment Insurance Division
Casper, WY
307-235-3253
http://wydoe.state.wy.us

D. State Disability Insurance

Five states have disability insurance that provides employees with coverage for injuries or illnesses that are not related to work. These states are: California, Hawaii, New Jersey, New York and Rhode Island. Puerto Rico also has a disability insurance program.

In these states, employees make disability insurance contributions, which are withheld from their paychecks by their employers. Employers must also make contributions in Hawaii, New Jersey and New York.

Except in New York, the disability insurance coverage requirements are the same as for UC insurance. (New York uses the common law right of control test, the same test it uses for workers' compensation coverage.) If you pay UC for a worker, you must withhold and pay disability insurance premiums as well.

In California, New Jersey and Rhode Island, disability insurance is handled by the state unemployment compensation agency. The same employee records are used for UC and disability—and employers submit contribution reports for both taxes at the same time. New York's disability program is administered by the Workers' Compensation Board. In Hawaii, the Temporary Disability Insurance Division of the Department of Labor and Industrial Relations handles disability insurance.

E. State Income Taxes

All states except Alaska, Florida, Nevada, South Dakota, Texas, Washington and Wyoming have income taxation. If you do business in a state that imposes state income taxes, you must withhold the applicable tax from your employees' paychecks and pay it over to the state taxing authority. No state income tax withholding is required for workers who qualify as ICs.

It's very easy to determine whether you need to withhold state income taxes for a worker: If you are withholding federal income taxes, then you must withhold state income taxes as well. Contact your state tax department for the appropriate forms.

But if a worker qualifies as an IC for IRS purposes and no federal income taxes need be withheld, you won't need to withhold state income taxes, either.

A list of state income tax offices follows.

STATE TAX OFFICES

Alabama
Department of Revenue
Montgomery, AL
334-242-2677
www.ador.state.al.us

Alaska
Department of Revenue
Juneau, AK 99802-5509
907-465-2300
www.revenue.state.ak.us

Arizona
Department of Revenue
Phoenix, AZ
602-542-8173
www.revenue.state.az.us

Arkansas
Department of Finance and
Administration
Division of Revenue
Little Rock, AR
501-682-4663
www.accessarkansas.org/dfa/
index.html

California
Franchise Tax Board
Taxpayer Services Center
Sacramento, CA
800-852-5711 or 916-845-6500
www.ftb.ca.gov

Colorado
Department of Revenue
Denver, CO
303-866-3091
www.revenue.state.co.us

Connecticut
Department of Revenue Services
Hartford, CT
860-297-5962 or 800-382-9463
www.drs.state.ct.us

Delaware
Division of Revenue
Wilmington, DE
302-577-8205 or 800-292-7826
www.state.de.us/revenue

District of Columbia
Office of Tax and Revenue
Customer Service Center
Washington, DC
202-747-4829
http://cfo.dc.gov/etsc/main.shtm

Florida
Department of Revenue
Tallahassee, FL
850-488-6800 or 800-352-3671
www.myflorida.com/dor

Georgia
Department of Revenue
Atlanta, GA
404-417-4477 or 877-602-8477
www.gatax.org

Hawaii
Department of Taxation
Honolulu, HI
800-222-3229 or 808-587-4242
www.state.hi.us/tax

Idaho
State Tax Commission
Boise, ID
208-334-7660 or 800-972-7660
www2.state.id.us/tax

Illinois
Department of Revenue
Springfield, IL
800-732-8866
www.revenue.state.il.us

Indiana
Department of Revenue
Indianapolis, IN
317-232-2240
www.state.in.us/dor

Iowa
Department of Revenue and Finance
Taxpayer Services
Des Moines, IA
515-281-3114 or 800-367-3388
www.state.ia.us/tax/index.htm

Kansas
Department of Revenue
Topeka, KS
785-296-3909
www.ksrevenue.org

Kentucky
Revenue Cabinet
Frankfort, KY
502-564-4581
www.revenue.state.ky.us/index.htm

Louisiana
Department of Revenue
Baton Rouge, LA
225-219-2448
www.rev.state.la.us

Maine
Revenue Services
Augusta, ME
207-287-2076
www.state.me.us/revenue

Maryland
State Comptroller
Revenue Administration Center
Annapolis, MD
410-260-7980 or 800-MD-TAXES
www.comp.state.md.us

Massachusetts
Department of Revenue
Taxpayer Service Division
Chelsea, MA
617-887-6367 or 800-392-6089
www.dor.state.ma.us

Michigan
Department of Treasury
Lansing, MI
517-373-3200
www.michigan.com/treasury

Minnesota
Department of Economic Security
St. Paul, MN
612-296-6141
www.mnworkforcecenter.org

STATE TAX OFFICES (CONTINUED)

Mississippi
State Tax Commission
Jackson, MS
601-923-7000
www.mstc.state.ms.us

Missouri
Department of Revenue
Jefferson City, MO
573-751-7191 or 800-877-6881
www.dor.state.mo.us

Montana
Department of Revenue
Helena, MT
406-444-6900
www.discoveringmontana.com/
revenue/css/default.asp

Nebraska
Department of Revenue
Lincoln, NE
402-471-5729
www.revenue.state.ne.us

Nevada
Department of Taxation
Carson City, NV
775-687-4820
www.tax.state.nv.us

New Hampshire
Department of Revenue
Administration
Concord, NH
603-271-2191
www.state.nh.us/revenue

New Jersey
Department of Revenue
Trenton, NJ
609-292-1720
www.state.nj.us/treasury/index.html

New Mexico
Department of Taxation and Revenue
Santa Fe, NM
505-827-0700
www.state.nm.us/tax

New York
Department of Taxation and Finance
Albany, NY
800-225-5829
www.tax.state.ny.us

North Carolina
Department of Revenue
Raleigh, NC
919-733-3991
www.dor.state.nc.us/index.html

North Dakota
Tax Department
Bismarck, ND
701-328-2770
www.state.nd.us/taxdpt

Ohio
Department of Taxation
Taxpayer Services Division
Columbus, OH
888-405-4039 or 614-466-6401
www.state.oh.us/tax

Oklahoma
State Treasury
Oklahoma City, OK
405-521-3191
www.treasurer.state.ok.us

Oregon
Department of Revenue
Salem, OR
503-378-4988 or 800-356-4222
www.dor.state.or.us

Pennsylvania
Department of Revenue
Harrisburg, PA
717-787-1064
www.revenue.state.pa.us

Rhode Island
Division of Taxation
Providence, RI
401-222-1040
www.tax.state.ri.us/ui

South Carolina
Department of Revenue
Taxpayer Service Center
Columbia, SC
803-898-5000
www.sctax.org/dor/default.htm

South Dakota
Department of Treasury
Pierre, SD
605-773-3311
www.state.sd.us/revenue/
revenue.html

Tennessee
Department of Revenue
Taxpayer Services
Nashville, TN
615-253-6000 or 800-342-1003
www.state.tn.us/revenue

Texas
Comptroller of Public Accounts
Austin, TX
512-463-3961 or 800-832-9394
www.cpa.state.tx.us

Utah
State Tax Commission
Salt Lake City, UT
801-297-2200 or 800-662-4335
www.tax.utah.gov

Vermont
Department of Taxes
Montpelier, VT
802-828-2865
www.state.vt.us/tax

Virginia
Department of Taxation
Richmond, VA
804-367-8037
www.tax.state.va.us

Washington
Department of Revenue
Olympia, WA
800-647-7706
http://dor.wa.gov

West Virginia
Department of Tax and Revenue
Charleston, WV
304-558-3333
www.state.wv.us/taxdiv

Wisconsin
Department of Revenue
Madison, WI
608-266-2772
www.dor.state.wi.us

Wyoming
Department of Revenue
Cheyenne, WY
307-235-3253
http://revenue.state.wy.us

Workers' Compensation

This chapter provides an overview of the workers' compensation system. It also explains when you need to provide workers' compensation insurance for workers and what happens if you don't.

A. Basics of the Workers' Compensation System

Each state has its own workers' compensation system that is designed to provide replacement income and medical expenses for employees who suffer work-related injuries or illnesses. Benefits may also extend to the survivors of workers who are killed on the job. To pay for this, employers in all but two states—New Jersey and Texas, where workers' compensation is optional—are required to pay for workers' compensation insurance for their employees, either though a state fund or a private insurance company. Employees do not pay for workers' compensation insurance.

Before the first workers' compensation laws were adopted about 80 years ago, an employee injured on the job had only one recourse: sue the employer in court for negligence—a difficult, time-consuming and expensive process. The workers' compensation laws changed this by establishing a no-fault system. Although employees can't sue in court, they are entitled to receive compensation without having to prove that the employer caused the injury. In exchange for paying for workers' compensation insurance, employers are spared from having to defend lawsuits by injured employees and paying out damages.

An employee who is injured on the job can file a workers' compensation claim and collect benefits from your workers' compensation insurer, but cannot sue you in court except in rare cases where you intended to cause the injury—for example, where you beat up an employee. Workers' compensation benefits are set by state law and are usually modest. Employees can obtain reimbursement for medical and rehabilitation expenses and lost income, but can't collect benefits for pain and suffering or mental anguish caused by an injury.

EXAMPLE: Sam, a construction worker for the Acme Building Company, accidentally severs a muscle in his arm while using a power saw on an Acme construction site. Since Sam is an Acme employee, he is covered by Acme's workers' compensation insurance policy.

Sam may file a workers' compensation claim and receive benefits from Acme's workers' compensation insurer. Under the law of Sam's state, Sam is entitled to receive a maximum of $2,520 to make up for lost income plus medical and rehabilitation expenses. All of this is paid by Acme's workers' compensation insurer, not by Acme itself. This is all Sam is entitled to collect. He cannot sue Acme in court for damages arising from his injuries.

Your workers' compensation premiums will likely go up if many employees file workers' compensation claims, but the premiums will almost certainly be cheaper than defending employee lawsuits.

1. ICs Are Excluded

You generally need not provide workers' compensation for a worker who qualifies as an IC under your state workers' compensation law. (See Section C.) This can result in substantial savings. However, unlike employees who are covered by workers' compensation, ICs can sue you for work-related injuries. (See Section B.)

2. Cost of Coverage

The cost of workers' compensation varies from state to state and depends upon a number of factors including:
- the size of the employer's payroll
- the nature of the industry involved, and
- how many claims have been filed in the past by the employer's employees.

As you might expect, it costs far more to insure employees in hazardous occupations such as construction than it does to provide coverage for those in relatively safe jobs such as clerical work. It might cost $200 to $300 a year to insure a clerical worker and perhaps ten times as much to insure a roofer or lumberjack.

Depending on the state in which you live, you can obtain workers' compensation insurance from a state fund, a private insurer or both. (See Section I.)

B. Injured ICs' Rights to Sue You

An IC who is not covered by workers' compensation can sue you for damages for personal injuries if your negligence—that is, carelessness or failure to take proper safety precautions—caused or contributed to the injury. You will also be held responsible for the negligence of your employees.

EXAMPLE: Trish, a self-employed trucker, contracts to haul produce for the Acme Produce Company. Trish is an IC, and Acme does not provide her with workers' compensation insur-

ance. Trish loses her little finger when an Acme employee negligently drops a load of asparagus on her hand. Since Trish is an IC, she can't collect workers' compensation benefits from Acme's insurer, but she can sue Acme in court for negligence. If she can prove Acme was negligent, Trish can collect damages not only for her lost wages and medical expenses, but for her pain and suffering as well.

These damages could far exceed the modest sums that workers' compensation benefits would have provided. Had Trish been Acme's employee, it might have cost Acme several hundred dollars a year to provide workers' compensation coverage for her. But since she was an IC, it could cost Acme tens of thousands of dollars to defend her lawsuit and pay out damages.

Of course, an IC must actually prove that your negligence or that of your employees caused or contributed to the work-related accident to recover any damages at all. So if you were not negligent, the IC may end up losing a lawsuit or decide not to file one in the first place.

C. The Need for Liability Insurance

No matter how small your business, if you hire ICs, it is vital that you obtain general liability insurance to protect yourself against personal injury claims by people who are not your employees. A general liability insurer will defend you in court if an IC, customer or any other nonemployee claims you caused or helped cause an injury. The insurer will also pay out damages or settlements up to the policy limits. Such insurance can be cheaper and easier to obtain than workers' compensation coverage for employees, so you can still save on insurance premiums by hiring ICs rather than employees.

If you don't have general liability insurance already, contact an insurance broker or agent to obtain a policy.

D. Requiring ICs to Obtain Their Own Coverage

Many hiring firms require workers classified as ICs to obtain workers' compensation coverage for themselves. Such coverage is available in most states, even if an IC is running a one-person business.

If you don't do this, your own workers' compensation insurer might require you to cover the IC and pay additional premiums. Insurance companies do this because there is a risk that an injured IC might later claim to be an employee just to get workers' compensation benefits. Your workers' compensation insurer will audit your payroll and other employment records at least once a year to make sure you're paying the proper premiums.

If you require an IC to be insured, obtain a certificate of insurance from the worker. A certificate of insurance is issued by the workers' compensation insurer and is written proof that the IC has a workers' compensation policy. Keep it in your files and make it available to your workers' compensation insurer when you're audited.

For detailed guidance on workers' compensation insurance audits, see *Comp Control: The Secrets of Reducing Workers' Compensation Costs*, by Edward J. Priz (Oasis Press), and *Slash Your Workers' Comp Costs: How to Cut Premiums Up to 35%—And Maintain a Productive and Safe Workplace*, by Thomas Lundberg (Amacom).

Even if an IC has his or her own workers' compensation insurance, you'll still need to have liability insurance because the IC can sue you in court if he or she is injured due to your negligence. As we explained above, the workers' compensation provisions barring lawsuits by injured employees won't apply to you because you are not the IC's employer. Injured ICs or their workers' compensation insurers may file these lawsuits.

E. Providing Coverage for IC Employees

In all states except Alabama, California, Delaware, Iowa, Maine, Rhode Island and West Virginia, you might have to provide workers' compensation benefits for the employees of ICs—depending on the circumstances. Under state laws that define statutory employees, an IC's uninsured employees are considered to be your employees for workers' compensation purposes if:

- the IC fails to obtain workers' compensation insurance for them, and
- the IC's employees perform work that is part of your regular business—that is, work customarily carried out in your business and other similar businesses.

The purpose of these laws is to prevent employers from avoiding paying for workers' compensation insurance by subcontracting work out to uninsured ICs.

EXAMPLE: The Diamond Development Company, a residential real estate developer, is building a housing subdivision. It hires Tom, a painting subcontractor, to paint the houses. Tom is an IC who has sole control over the painting work. Tom hires 40 painters to do the work for him. They are all Tom's employees. Tom fails to provide his employee-painters with workers' compensation coverage.

Andy, one of Tom's employees, is injured on the job. Since Tom has no workers' compensation insurance, Andy can file a workers' compensation claim against Diamond Development, even though he was not Diamond's employee. This is because Andy is Diamond's statutory employee under the state law and house painting is clearly a part of Diamond's regular business of constructing new housing.

Because of these statutory employee rules, it's very important for you to require any IC who uses employees to perform services for you to provide them with workers' compensation insurance. Ask to see an insurance certificate establishing that an IC's employees are covered by workers' compensation insurance. In many states you can also call the state workers' compensation agency to determine if an IC has coverage for his or her employees. (See Section J for contact details.)

If your own workers' compensation insurer audits your company and discovers that you have hired an IC whose employees do not have workers' compensation coverage, it will likely classify that worker as your own employee for workers' compensation purposes and require you to pay an additional workers' compensation premium.

If you are required to provide workers' compensation benefits to an IC's employees, you are entitled to seek reimbursement for the cost from the IC. But if the IC has no money or can't be located, this legal right will be useless.

 California Rule for Unlicensed Construction Workers

Under California law, a construction contractor who hires unlicensed subcontractors or construction workers is automatically considered to be their employer for workers' compensation purposes. (Calif. Labor Code § 2750.5.) This is so even if the workers are ICs under the usual common law rules. This means the contractor has to provide the workers with workers' compensation coverage. The California State License Board determines who must be licensed to perform services in the construction industry in California. If you're not sure whether the work involved requires a license, contact the Board. If a contractor's license is required, ask to see one before hiring a construction subcontractor or worker. Otherwise, you'll have to provide workers' compensation coverage.

F. Determining Who Must Be Covered

You must use a two-step analysis to determine whether you must provide a worker with workers' compensation insurance.

First, determine if workers' compensation coverage is necessary if the worker is qualified as an employee under your state workers' compensation law. Most states exclude certain types of workers from workers' compensation coverage. (See Section G.) You won't have to provide coverage for workers who fall within these exclusions. Some states also don't require coverage unless you have a minimum number of employees.

Second, if there is no exclusion for the workers involved, you must determine whether the workers should be classified as employees or ICs under your state's workers' compensation law. If they're employees, you'll have to provide coverage; if they're ICs, you won't. States use different tests to classify workers for workers' compensation purposes. (See Section H.)

G. Exclusions From Coverage

Most states exclude certain types of workers from workers' compensation coverage. The nature and scope of these exclusions vary somewhat from state to state. Check the workers' compensation law of your state—or ask your workers' compensation carrier to do so—to see how these exclusions operate in your state.

1. States With Employee Minimums

The workers' compensation laws of several states exclude employers having fewer than a designated number of employees. In other words, if you have fewer than this minimum number of employees, you don't need to obtain workers' compensation insurance for anyone—employees or ICs.

STATE REQUIREMENTS FOR WORKERS' COMPENSATION COVERAGE

State	Employees Required
Alabama	five or more
Arkansas	three or more
Florida	four or more (one or more for construction trades)
Georgia	three or more
Michigan	three or more
Mississippi	five or more
Missouri	five or more
New Mexico	three or more
Rhode Island	four or more
South Carolina	four or more
Tennessee	five or more
Virginia	three or more
Wisconsin	three or more

2. Casual Labor

Most states exempt casual workers from workers' compensation coverage. Who qualifies as a casual worker varies from state to state. In most states, casual labor is for a brief time period and is outside the hiring firm's usual course of business. These states include Alabama, Arizona, Colorado, Connecticut, Delaware, Florida, Georgia, Idaho, Indiana, Iowa, Minnesota, Montana, Nevada, New Jersey, New Mexico, North Carolina, North Dakota, Ohio, Oregon, South Carolina, Tennessee, Utah, Vermont, Virginia, Wisconsin and Wyoming.

EXAMPLE: The Acme Widget Company hires Sue, a caterer, to cater a retirement dinner for Acme's president. Catering is outside Acme's usual course of business—manufacturing widgets. And Sue is hired for a temporary period—to plan a single event. Sue would qualify as a casual laborer under most state laws and would not have to be covered by workers' compensation.

This exception is narrow. For example, people hired to do temporary maintenance or repair work would generally not be casual laborers because such work is usually considered part of a firm's normal course of business.

EXAMPLE: A partition broke at a soft drink distributor's place of business, smashing hundreds of bottles. The firm hired two workers for a single day to clean up the bottles. The workers were not casual laborers because such clean-up work was a regular part of a soft drink distributor's business; such breakage was an inherent risk of the business. (*Graham v. Green*, 156 A.2d 241 (1959).)

Some states have more liberal rules. For example, New Jersey excludes from workers' compensation coverage all types of work that are not in the hiring firm's usual course of business, whether they're casual or not—that is, temporary or transitory.

To find out about your state's law, contact your state workers' compensation office. (See Section J for contact details.)

3. Domestic Workers

The states listed in the chart below require that domestic workers who work in private homes be covered by workers' compensation if their salary and/or time worked exceed a threshold amount. States not listed in the chart exclude from workers' compensation coverage these domestic employees. Domestic or household workers include housekeepers, gardeners, babysitters and chauffeurs. (See Chapter 8 for more information about dealing with these types of workers.)

WORKERS' COMPENSATION REQUIREMENTS FOR DOMESTIC WORKERS

State	Domestic Workers Who Must Be Covered
Alaska	All, except part-time babysitters, cleaners and similar part-time help
California	All who, during 90-day period preceding injury, work 52 or more hours or earn more than $100
Colorado	All who work more than 40 hours per week for five or more days per week for one employer
Connecticut	All who work more than 24 hours per week for one employer
Delaware	All paid $750 or more in any three-month period by single private home
Hawaii	All whose wages are $225 or less during the current calendar quarter and during each completed calendar quarter of the preceding 12-month period
Illinois	All who work 40 or more hours per week for 13 or more weeks during a calendar year for any household or residence
Iowa	All who earn $1,500 or more during the 12 months before an injury
Kansas	All, if employer had a $20,000 or more gross payroll for all employees (domestic and non-domestic) during the preceding year
Kentucky	All if two or more work in a private home 40 or more hours per week
Maryland	All paid $750 or more in any calendar quarter by single private home
Massachusetts	All who work 16 or more hours per week for one employer

State	Domestic Workers Who Must Be Covered
Michigan	All employed more than 35 hours per week for 13 weeks or more during the previous 52 weeks
Minnesota	All who earn $1,000 or more in any three-month period or $1,000 or more in any three-month period during the previous year from the same single, private household
New Hampshire	All
New York	All employed by the same employer for 40 or more hours per week
North Carolina	All, if employer employs 10 or more full-time non-seasonal workers
Ohio	All who earn $160 or more in any calendar quarter from one employer
Oklahoma	All, if employer had a $10,000 or more gross payroll for all domestic employees during the preceding year
South Carolina	All if four or more domestic workers are employed, except employers whose total annual payroll the previous calendar year was less than $3,000
South Dakota	All employed 20 or more hours in any calendar week and for more than six weeks in any 13-week period
Utah	All regularly employed for 40 or more hours per week by the same employer
Washington	All if two or more domestic workers are regularly employed in a private home 40 or more hours per week

H. Classifying Workers for Workers' Compensation Purposes

If none of the exclusions discussed above applies, you must determine whether a worker is an employee or IC under your state's workers' compensation law. If the worker qualifies as an employee, you must provide workers' compensation coverage. (Remember: Even if you know what a worker's classification is under the IRS rules and under your state's unemployment laws, you must still check your state's workers' compensation rules, because a worker may be an IC under some rules but an employee under others.) Each state has its own workers' compensation law with its own definition of who is an employee. However, these state laws follow one of three patterns.

- Most states classify workers for workers' compensation purposes using the common law right of control test. (See Section 1.)
- Other states use a relative nature of the work test, either alone or in conjunction with the common law test. (See Section 2.)
- A few states use different classification schemes. (See Section 3.)

Find your state in the chart below and read the applicable discussion. For more detailed information on your state's workers' compensation laws, contact the state workers' compensation agency. (See Section J for contact information.)

When reading about your state's law, keep in mind that most state workers' compensation agencies and state courts interpret their workers' compensation laws to require coverage. This is because the workers' compensation laws are designed to help injured workers, and it's considered beneficial for society as a whole to have as many workers as possible covered. Generally, if there is any uncertainty as to how a worker should be classified for workers' compensation purposes, state workers' compensation agencies and courts find that the worker is an employee who should be covered.

1. Common Law States

A majority of state workers' compensation statutes define an employee as one who works for, and under the control of, another person for hire. The right to control the details of the work is the primary test used to determine whether an employment relationship exists. (See Chapter 3 for a detailed discussion of the common law test.)

The list of factors used to measure control varies somewhat from state to state. But the goal of the test is the same: to determine whether the hiring firm has the right to direct and control the worker in the way he or she works, both as to the final results, and as to the details of when, where and how the work is to be done.

The following states use a four-factor test to determine if a hiring firm has the right of control: Alabama, Idaho, Kansas, Mississippi, Montana, New Jersey, North Dakota, Oregon, South Carolina and West Virginia. These states ask whether

- there is direct evidence that the hiring firm has the right to control the performance of the work itself, including how, when and where it is performed
- the hiring firm has the right to discharge the worker and the worker has the right to quit at any time
- the worker is paid by the job or on a time basis—hourly, weekly, monthly, and
- the hiring firm supplies the worker with valuable equipment.

In Chapter 3, we discuss all of these factors in detail.

It is far harder to prove that a person is an IC than an employee for workers' compensation purposes. Because the states want as many workers as possible to qualify as employees, it is not necessary for all four factors to indicate that there is an employment relationship for a worker to be deemed an employee for workers' compensation purposes. Rather, one or two factors are usually sufficient. For example, a worker's compensation auditor who discovers that you have the right to fire a worker at any time for any reason, or for no reason at all, will likely stop the audit right there

STATE TESTS USED TO CLASSIFY WORKERS

State	Test
Alabama	Common law
Alaska	Relative nature of work
Arizona	Common law
Arkansas	Common law
California	Common law and other (economic reality)
Colorado	Common law
Connecticut	Common law
District of Columbia	Common law
Delaware	Common law
Florida	Common law
Georgia	Common law
Hawaii	Common law and relative nature of work
Idaho	Common law
Illinois	Common law
Indiana	Common law
Iowa	Common law
Kansas	Common law
Kentucky	Common law
Louisiana	Common law
Maine	Common law
Maryland	Common law
Massachusetts	Common law
Michigan	Other (economic reality)
Minnesota	Common law and other
Mississippi	Common law and relative nature of work

State	Test
Missouri	Common law
Montana	Common law
Nebraska	Common law
Nevada	Common law
New Hampshire	Common law
New Jersey	Common law and relative nature of work
New Mexico	Common law
New York	Common law
North Carolina	Common law
North Dakota	Common law and relative nature of work
Ohio	Common law
Oklahoma	Common law
Oregon	Other (8 factors)
Pennsylvania	Common law
Rhode Island	Common law
South Carolina	Common law
South Dakota	Common law
Tennessee	Common law
Texas	Common law
Utah	Common law
Vermont	Common law
Virginia	Common law
Washington	Other (6 factors)
West Virginia	Common law
Wisconsin	Other (9 factors)
Wyoming	Common law

are conclude that the worker is your employee. But even workers who cannot be discharged without cause may be employees.

EXAMPLE: Joanna, a driver who delivers dry cleaning for Ace Cleaners, designates her own delivery schedules and routes and is otherwise not controlled by Ace. She has a one-year contract with Ace that provides that she cannot be terminated or quit unless there is a material breach of the contract.

However, Ace provides her with a delivery truck and pays her by the hour. These two factors alone are enough to show an employment relationship for workers' compensation purposes. The combination of a hiring firm providing a driver with a vehicle and paying by the hour is almost always enough to show employment for workers' compensation purposes.

To establish IC status, you will usually have to satisfy all the factors discussed above, with the possible exception of the method of payment.

EXAMPLE: An Oregon country club hired Marcum, an unemployed logger, to prune dead wood from some trees on the golf course. He was injured after a few days on the job and filed a workers' compensation claim alleging that he was the club's employee. The court concluded that Marcum was an IC. The court examined all four factors and found that three indicated IC status, the fourth was neutral.

- *Control:* There was no direct evidence of control over Marcum by the club. A club member testified that he simply told Marcum what trees to prune. He did not tell him how to do the work or what hours to work. Marcum hired an assistant and paid him himself. Marcum had no continuing relationship with the club—he had never worked for it before.
- *Right to fire:* The club member who hired Marcum stated that he felt he could

terminate Marcum's contract only if he was not properly doing the job.
- *Equipment:* Marcum furnished all his own equipment, including saws and a pickup truck.
- *Method of payment:* Marcum was paid $25 per tree. Such piecework payment indicated neither IC nor employee status.

(*Marcum v. State Accident Ins. Fund,* 565 P.2d 399 (1977).)

2. Relative Nature of the Work Test

Despite the fact that most states now use the common law test discussed above, there is a growing trend to use a test that makes it more difficult to establish that a worker is an IC: the relative nature of the work test. This test is based on the simple notion that the cost of industrial accidents should be borne by consumers as a part of the cost of a product or service. If a worker's services are a regular part of the cost of producing your product or service, and the worker is not conducting an independent business, this test dictates that you should provide workers' compensation insurance for the worker.

On the other hand, you don't need to provide workers' compensation if a worker is running an independent business and the worker's services are not a normal everyday part of your business operations—the cost of which you regularly pass along to your customers or clients.

To determine whether a worker is an employee or IC under the relative nature of the work test, ask two questions:
- Is the worker running an independent business?
- Are the workers' services a regular part of the cost of your product or service?

If the answer to both questions is yes, the worker is an employee for workers' compensation purposes.

Many states use the relative nature of the work test in conjunction with the common law control test. If a worker's status is unclear under the common law test, these states use the second test. Other states use only the relative nature of the work test. Check the chart, above, to find out what your state does.

a. Independent business

If a worker is running an independent business and has the resources to provide his or her own insurance coverage for work-related accidents, it's reasonable not to require the worker's clients or customers (meaning you) to provide such coverage.

It's much easier for highly skilled and well paid workers to qualify as ICs under the test than low-skill low-pay workers. Highly skilled workers are most likely to have their own independent businesses and to earn enough to be financially responsible for their own accidents.

Workers' compensation agencies and courts might also examine many of the factors from the common law test. (See Chapter 4 for a complete discussion of the IRS common law test.) A worker is more likely to be viewed as operating an independent business if he or she:

- makes his or her services available to the public—for example, by advertising
- does not work full time for you
- has multiple clients and income sources, and
- has the right to reject jobs you offer.

b. Part of the cost of your product or service

A worker's services will likely be viewed as a regular part of the cost of your product or service if:

- the worker's services are a regular part of your company's daily business operations
- the work is continuous rather than intermittent, and
- the duration of the work indicates continuous services as opposed to contracting for a particular job.

c. Examples

EXAMPLE 1: Ceradsky was killed while operating a milk truck owned by Purcell. Purcell had contracted with a cheese manufacturer to pick up milk from farmers along a specific route and deliver it to the cheese factory. Although Purcell and Ceradsky had been classified as ICs by the cheese company, Ceradsky's survivors applied for workers' compensation benefits from the company. The court held that they were entitled to benefits because both Ceradsky and Purcell were employees of the cheese company under the relative nature of the work test.

The milk hauling was not an independent business, but only an aid to the cheese company's production process. Purcell and Ceradsky hauled milk exclusively for the cheese company six days a week for years. They did not earn enough money from the work to be expected to purchase their own insurance. In addition, the milk hauling work was a regular and essential part of the company's cheese production process, the costs of which were passed on to cheese consumers. (*Ceradsky v. Mid-America Dairymen, Inc.*, 583 S.W.2d 193 (Mo. App. 1979).)

EXAMPLE 2: Ostrem suffered an eye injury while installing a diesel engine in a piece of heavy equipment owned by a construction company. He applied for workers' compensation benefits from the company and was denied them because he was an IC under the relative nature of the work test. First, the court found that he operated an independent business: he was highly skilled, established his own rate of pay and hours, took out a business license, was generally unsupervised, had multiple clients and made his services available to the public. Second, Ostrem's work was not part of the construction company's regular business. He had been hired to install one engine only and had never worked for the company before. The job should have taken only a few days. He had been hired to complete a single job, not to do regular work of the construction company. (*Ostrem v. Alaska Workmen's Compensation*, 511 P.2d 1061 (Alaska 1973).)

3. Other Tests

A few states have somewhat different tests for determining who qualifies as an employee for workers' compensation purposes. The tests used in Michigan, Minnesota, Oregon, Washington and Wisconsin define who is an employee much more clearly than the common law or relative nature of the work tests. If you're doing business in one of these states, consider yourself fortunate. California is another story, however.

a.   California

California uses at least two tests—the common law test and a second economic reality test. If a worker is an IC under the common law test, the California Workers' Compensation Appeal Board and courts will use the second broader economic reality test to try to find employee status for the workers involved.

Under the California version of the common law control test, a worker is more likely to be viewed as an IC if he or she:

- has the right to control the manner and performance of his or her own work
- has a monetary investment in the work
- controls when the work begins and ends
- supplies tools and instruments needed for the work
- has a license to perform the work
- is paid by the project rather than by unit of time (such as hourly payment)
- is engaged in a distinct occupation or business
- is highly skilled
- can't quit at any time
- was hired for a temporary and fixed, rather than indefinite, time, and

- believes, along with the hiring firm, that the relationship is an IC relationship.

California uses the same economic reality test that applies to federal labor laws. (See Chapter 9 for a discussion of how to determine if someone is an IC under federal labor laws.) This test emphasizes whether the worker functions as an independent business or is economically dependent upon the hiring firm. Under this test, a worker is more likely to be viewed as an IC if:

- the worker has the right to control the manner and performance of his or her own work
- the worker's opportunity for profit or loss depends on his or her managerial skill
- the worker supplies his or her own tools and instruments
- the services rendered require a special skill
- the working relationship is temporary rather than permanent, and
- the services rendered are not an integral part of the hiring firm's business.

(*S.G. Borello & Sons, Inc. v. Dept. of Indus. Relations*, 48 Cal.3d 341 (1989).)

b.   Michigan

Michigan uses an economic reality test to determine a worker's status for both workers' compensation and unemployment compensation purposes. (See Chapter 6, Section B4, for more information on this test.)

c.   Minnesota

Minnesota uses the four-factor common law test described above, but has designed special rules for 34 specific occupations that are intended to serve as a safe harbor—that is, workers who come within the rules are deemed ICs. These occupations include: artisans, barbers, bookkeepers and accountants, bulk oil plant operators, collectors, consultants, domestic workers, babysitters, industrial home workers, laborers, orchestra musicians, several types of salespeople or manufacturer's representatives, agent drivers, photographers, models, some professional workers, medical doctors providing part-time services to industrial firms, real estate and securities salespeople, registered and practical nurses, unlicensed nurses, taxicab drivers, timber fellers, buckers, skidders and processors, sawmill operators, truck owner-drivers, waste materials haulers, messengers and couriers, variety entertainers, sports officials, jockeys and trainers. (See Minn. R. § 5224 and following.)

d. Oregon

Oregon uses an eight-factor statutory test to determine a worker's status for both workers' compensation and unemployment compensation purposes. (See Chapter 6, Section B4, for more information on this test.) However, one Oregon court has used the four-factor common law test discussed in Section 1, above. (*Oregon-Drywall-Sys., Inc. v. National Council on Comp. Ins.*, 153 Or. App. 662, 958 P.2d 195 (1998).)

e. Washington

In Washington, a worker is an IC for workers' compensation purposes if all the following six conditions are met:
- the worker is free from control while performing the services
- the worker's services are either:
  - ▴ outside the hiring firm's usual course of business, or
  - ▴ performed outside the firm's places of business, or
  - ▴ performed at a workplace for which the worker pays
- the worker is engaged in an independent business, or has a principal place of business that is eligible for a federal income tax business deduction
- the worker is responsible for filing a Schedule C or similar form with the IRS listing the worker's business expenses

- the worker pays all applicable state business taxes, obtains any necessary state registrations and opens an account with the State Department of Revenue, and
- the worker maintains a separate set of books or records showing all income and expenses of the worker's business.

(Wash. Rev. Code § 18.27.)

f. Wisconsin

Under Wisconsin's test, a worker is an IC for workers' compensation purposes if the worker satisfies nine conditions. He or she must:
- maintain a separate business with his or her own office, equipment, materials and other facilities
- hold or have applied for a federal employer identification number
- operate or contract to perform specific services or work for specific amounts of money, with the worker controlling the means of performing the services or work
- incur the main expenses related to the service or work that he or she performs under contract
- be responsible for completing the work or services and be liable for failing to complete it
- receive compensation for work or services performed under a contract on a commission, per job or competitive bid basis and not on any other basis—for example, hourly payment
- be able to realize a profit or suffer a loss under the contracts
- have continuing or recurring business liabilities or obligations, and
- have a business set-up in which success or failure depends on the relationship of business receipts to expenditures.

(Wis. Stat. § 102.07(8).)

4. Consequences of Misclassifying Workers

You will suffer harsh penalties if you misclassify an employee as an IC for workers' compensation purposes and have no workers' compensation insurance.

Most state workers' compensation agencies maintain a special fund to pay benefits to injured employees whose employers failed to insure them. You will be required to reimburse this fund or pay penalties to replenish it.

In addition, in most states, the injured worker can sue you in court for personal injuries. Most states try to make it as easy as possible for injured employees to win such lawsuits by not allowing you to raise legal defenses you might otherwise have, such as that the injury was caused by the employee's own carelessness.

You will also have to pay fines imposed by your state workers' compensation agency for your failure to insure. These fines vary widely, ranging from $250 to $5,000 per employee or may be based on the amount of workers' compensation premiums that should have been paid. The workers' compensation agency may also obtain an injunction—a legal order—preventing you from doing business in the state until you obtain workers' compensation insurance.

If you are doing business as a sole proprietor or partnership, you will be personally liable for these damages and fines. And the fact that your business may be a corporation won't necessarily shield you from personal liability. In some states, shareholders of an uninsured corporation may be personally liable for the injuries sustained by the corporation's employees. For example, in California, any shareholder of an illegally uninsured corporation who holds 15% or more of the corporate stock, or at least a 15% interest in the corporation, may be held personally liable for the resulting damages and fines.

Finally, in almost all states, failure to provide employees with workers' compensation insurance is a crime—a misdemeanor or even a felony. An uninsured employer may face criminal prosecution, fines and, in rare cases, prison.

I. Obtaining Coverage

Some states allow an employer to self-insure—a process that typically requires the business to maintain a hefty cash reserve earmarked for workers' compensation claims. Usually, this isn't practical for small businesses. Most small businesses buy insurance through a state fund or from a private insurance carrier.

If private insurance is an option in your state, discuss it with an insurance agent or broker who handles the basic insurance for your business. Often you save money on premiums by coordinating workers' compensation coverage with property damage and public liability insurance. A good agent or broker may be able to explain the mechanics of a state fund where that's an option or is required.

 For detailed guidance on workers' compensation insurance audits, see *Comp Control: The Secrets of Reducing Workers' Compensation Costs,* by Edward J. Priz (Oasis Press), and *Slash Your Workers' Comp Costs: How to Cut Premiums Up to 35%—And Maintain a Productive and Safe Workplace,* by Thomas Lundberg (Amacom).

J. State Workers' Compensation Offices

A list of state Workers' Compensation Offices follows.

YOU OWE DOUGH!

PENALTY

State Workers' Compensation Offices

Alabama
Workers' Compensation Division
Department of Industrial Relations
Montgomery, AL
334-242-2868
http://dir.state.al.us/wc

Alaska
Workers' Compensation Division
Department of Labor
Juneau, AK
907-465-2970
www.labor.state.ak.us/wc/wc.htm

Arizona
Industrial Commission
Phoenix, AZ
602-542-4661
www.ica.state.az.us

Arkansas
Workers' Compensation Commission
Little Rock, AR
501-682-3930
www.awcc.state.ar.us

California
Division of Workers' Compensation
Sacramento, CA
800-736-7401
www.dir.ca.gov/dwc/dwc_home_page.htm

Colorado
Division of Workers' Compensation
Denver, CO
800-390-7936 or 303-318-8700
www.coworkforce.com/DWC

Connecticut
Workers' Compensation Commission
Hartford, CT
860-493-1500
www.ctdol.state.ct.us

Delaware
Division of Industrial Affairs
Office of Workers' Compensation
Wilmington, DE
302-761-8200
www.delawareworks.com/divisions/industaffairs/
workers.comp.htm

District of Columbia
Department of Employment Services
Labor Standards Bureau
Office of Workers' Compensation
Washington, DC
202-671-1000
http://does.dc.gov/services/wkr_comp.shtm

Florida
Department of Financial Services
Division of Workers' Compensation
Tallahassee, FL
800-342-1741
http://www.fldfs.com/wc

Georgia
Board of Workers' Compensation
Atlanta, GA
404-656-3875
www.state.ga.us/sbwc

Hawaii
Disability Compensation Division
Department of Labor and Industrial Relations
Honolulu, HI
808-586-9174
http://dlir.state.hi.us

Idaho
Industrial Commission
Boise, ID
208-334-6000 or 800-950-2110
www2.state.id.us/iic

Illinois
Industrial Commission
Chicago, IL
312-814-6611
www.state.il.us/agency/iic

Indiana
Workers' Compensation Board
Indianapolis, IN
800-824-COMP or 317-232-3809
www.in.gov/workcomp

Iowa
Division of Workers' Compensation
Des Moines, IA
515-281-5387 or 800-562-4692
www.iowaworkforce.org/wc

State Workers' Compensation Offices (continued)

Kansas
Division of Workers' Compensation
Department of Human Resources
Topeka, KS
785-296-3441
www.hr.state.ks.us/wc/html/wc.html

Kentucky
Department of Workers' Claims
Frankfort, KY
502-564-5550
http://labor.ky.gov/dwc

Louisiana
Office of Workers' Compensation Administration
Baton Rouge, LA
800-201-2499 or 225-342-7555
www.laworks.net

Maine
Workers' Compensation Board
Augusta, ME
207-287-3751 or 888-801-9087
www.state.me.us/wcb

Maryland
Workers' Compensation Commission
Baltimore, MD
800-492-0479 or 410-864-5100
www.wcc.state.md.us

Massachusetts
Department of Industrial Accidents
Boston, MA
800-323-3249 or 617-727-4900
www.state.ma.us/dia

Michigan
Bureau of Workers' and Unemployment Compensation
Lansing, MI
517-322-1296 or 888-396-5041
www.michigan.gov/bwuc

Minnesota
Workers' Compensation Division
Department of Labor and Industry
St. Paul, MN
800-342-5354 or 651-284-5032
www.doli.state.mn.us/workcomp.html

Mississippi
Workers' Compensation Commission
Jackson, MS
601-987-4200
www.mwcc.state.ms.us

Missouri
Division of Workers' Compensation
Department of Labor and Industrial Relations
Jefferson City, MO
573-751-4231
www.dolir.state.mo.us/wc/index.htm

Montana
Department of Labor and Industry
Helena, MT
406-444-6543
http://dli.state.mt.us

Nebraska
Workers' Compensation Court
Lincoln, NE
402-471-6468 or 800-599-5155
www.state.ne.us/home/WC

Nevada
Division of Industrial Relations
Carson City, NV
775-684-7260
http://dirweb.state.nv.us

New Hampshire
Workers' Compensation Division
Department of Labor
Concord, NH
800-272-4353 or 603-271-3176
www.labor.state.nh.us/workers_compensation.asp

New Jersey
Department of Labor
Division of Workers' Compensation
Trenton, NJ
609-292-2515
www.state.nj.us/labor/wc/wcindex.html

New Mexico
Workers' Compensation Administration
Albuquerque, NM
505-841-6000
www.state.nm.us/wca

New York
Workers' Compensation Board
Albany, NY
518-474-6674
www.wcb.state.ny.us/index.html

North Carolina
Industrial Commission
Raleigh, NC
800-688-8349
www.compstate.nc.us

STATE WORKERS' COMPENSATION OFFICES (CONTINUED)

North Dakota
Workers' Compensation Bureau
Bismarck, ND
800-777-5033 or 701-328-3800
www.ndworkerscomp.com

Ohio
Bureau of Workers' Compensation
Columbus, OH
800-644-6292
www.state.oh.us/odjfs/ouc/index.stm

Oklahoma
Workers' Compensation Court
Oklahoma City, OK
800-522-8210 or 405-522-8600
www.owcc.state.ok.us

Oregon
Workers' Compensation Division
Salem, OR
503-947-7810 or 800-452-0288
www.cbs.state.or.us/external/wcd

Pennsylvania
Bureau of Workers' Compensation
Harrisburg, PA
717-787-5279
www.dli.state.pa.us

Rhode Island
Department of Labor and Training
Division of Workers' Compensation
Cranston, RI
401-462-8100
www.dlt.state.ri.us/webdev/wc/default.htm

South Carolina
Workers' Compensation Commission
Columbia, SC
803-737-5700
www.wcc.state.sc.us

South Dakota
Division of Labor and Management
Department of Labor
Pierre, SD
605-773-3681
www.state.sd.us/dol/dlm/dlm-home.htm

Tennessee
Workers' Compensation Division
Labor and Workforce Development
Nashville, TN
615-532-2731
www.state.tn.us/labor-wfd/wcomp.html

Texas
Workers' Compensation Commission
Austin, TX
513-933-1899
www.twc.state.tx.us

Utah
Industrial Accident Division
Salt Lake City, UT
801-530-6800
www.ind-com.state.ut.us/indacc/indacc.htm

Vermont
Department of Labor and Industry
Workers' Compensation Division
Montpelier, VT
802-828-2286
www.state.vt.us/labind/wcindex.htm

Virginia
Workers' Compensation Commission
Richmond, VA
804-367-8600 or 877-664-2566
www.vwc.state.va.us

Washington
Department of Labor and Industries
Olympia, WA
360-902-5999
www.lni.wa.gov

West Virginia
Workers' Compensation Division
Charleston, WV
304-926-5000
www.state.wv.us/scripts/bep/wc

Wisconsin
Workers' Compensation Division
Madison, WI
608-266-1340
www.dwd.state.wi.us/wc/default.htm

Wyoming
Workers' Safety and Compensation Division
Cheyenne, WY
307-777-6763
http://wydoe.state.wy.us/doe.asp?ID=9

Hiring Household Workers and Family Members

This chapter provides guidance if you have hired, or intend to hire, a person to work in or around your home—or if you hire a parent, spouse or child to work at any location. It explains a host of rules that often make life a little easier for people who hire these types of workers.

A. Household Workers

Household workers include housecleaners, cooks, chauffeurs, housekeepers, nannies, babysitters, gardeners, private nurses, health aides, caretakers and others who work in the home.

1. Federal Payroll Tax Status

Federal payroll taxes include Social Security tax (FICA), federal unemployment taxes (FUTA) and federal income tax withholding (FITW). You don't have to pay or withhold any federal payroll taxes for household workers who are ICs. FICA and FUTA must be paid for employee household workers whose salaries exceed certain amounts. (See Section A2.)

You need to apply the IRS test discussed in Chapter 4 to determine if a household worker is an IC or employee for federal payroll purposes. Under this test, a worker is an employee if you have the right to control how the worker performs the services. It's highly likely that any full-time household worker would be viewed as an employee under this test—you'll have a very hard time convincing the IRS you don't have the right to control someone who works full-time in your home.

However, it is possible for part-time household workers to qualify as ICs under the test. The key is that the worker must be running an independent business.

EXAMPLE: Anne hires David to clean her house every two weeks, a task that takes him about two hours. David has 20 clients in addition to Anne, provides his own cleaning equipment and ordinarily does the cleaning work when Anne is not home. Anne has the right to ac-

cept or reject the results David achieves in cleaning her home, but she does not supervise how he does the work. David is likely an IC under the IRS test.

Part-time housecleaners, cooks, chauffeurs, housekeepers, gardeners, caretakers or maids may qualify as ICs under the common law test, but it seems likely that in-home child care workers would not, even if they only work part time. Even the most callous parent would probably insist on having the right to control how a babysitter, nanny or similar worker cares for his or her children. Undoubtedly, most parents actually exercise this right. The only exception might be where you obtain the worker through an agency (see below). In addition, child care workers who provide care outside your home can be ICs.

a. The IRS Safe Harbor

Even if a household worker is an employee under the common law test, you won't have to pay employment taxes if you qualify for Safe Harbor protection. To qualify, you must satisfy two requirements:

- You must never have treated any worker performing similar services since 1977 as an employee for federal tax purposes; for example, if your household worker is a nanny, you must have never done any of the following for that worker or any other nanny you've hired since 1977: (1) withheld federal income tax or FICA tax from the worker's wages; (2) filed a federal employment tax return for the worker on IRS Form 942; or (3) filed a W-2 Wage and Tax Statement for the worker, whether or not tax was actually withheld.
- You must have had a reasonable basis for treating the worker as an employee. The most likely basis would be that the classification is a recognized practice of a significant segment of the worker's industry. After all, treating household workers as ICs has long been a common practice. However, as a

practical matter, it can be hard to convince the IRS or courts that you have a reasonable basis for your IC classification. Moreover, as a result of the special payroll tax rules for household workers enacted in 1995 (see Section A2), it's likely that many household workers are now being treated as employees, making the common practice argument harder to prove.

(See Chapter 4 for a detailed discussion of the Safe Harbor).

1099s NOT REQUIRED FOR HOUSEHOLD WORKERS

You don't need to file 1099-MISC forms reporting to the IRS your payments in excess of $600 to household workers. This is because 1099s need only be filed when your hire a worker to work in your business. They need not be filed when you hire someone to work in your home for non-business purposes—for example, to clean your home.

b. Workers obtained through agencies

Generally, household workers obtained through an agency are not your employees if the agency is responsible for who does the work and how it is done. A babysitter you hire through a placement agency to come to your home to care for your child is not your employee if the agency sets and collects the fee, pays the sitter and controls the terms of work—for example, provides the sitter with rules of conduct and requires regular performance reports. The agency is the sitter's employer, not you.

c. Independent contractor agreements

It's wise to have IC household workers sign independent contractor agreements before they start

work. The agreement should make clear that the worker is an IC and you have no right to control the means and manner in which the work is performed—only the final results. (See Chapter 13 for guidance on creating your own IC agreements.)

Unfortunately, because many household worker relationships are informal, it may be difficult to get the worker to sign such an agreement. Do the best you can. It may be helpful to point out that such an agreement benefits the worker as well as you because it helps prevent possible disputes by setting forth the worker's duties and your payment obligations.

2. Payroll Tax Rules

Even if a household worker qualifies as an employee, you still may not have to pay federal payroll taxes.

A LITTLE HISTORY

Before 1995, people who hired household employees were supposed to pay Social Security (FICA) taxes for any such employee who was paid more than $50 in any three-month period. FICA taxes were due for all but the most temporary household employees.

However, this requirement went largely ignored—both by employers and the IRS—until Zoe Baird, President Clinton's first Attorney General nominee, admitted she had violated it by failing to pay FICA taxes for a full-time nanny and gardener she employed. In the wake of the Nannygate scandals involving Baird and several other presidential nominees, Congress passed the Social Security Domestic Employment Reform Act in 1994. The Act took effect in 1995 and eased tax reporting requirements for many of the estimated two million Americans who owe Social Security and other taxes on household employees.

Under the Social Security Domestic Employment Reform Act, FICA taxes need to be paid for a household worker who qualifies as an employee under the common law test only if the worker is paid more than a threshold amount. The amount is adjusted annually to account for inflation. For 2003, it was $1,400. To find out the amount for subsequent years, refer to IRS Publication 926, Household Employer's Tax Guide. You can find a copy of that publication on the CD-ROM at the back of this book. You can also obtain it from your local IRS office or from the IRS website at www.irs.gov.

Employers who pay a household worker less than the threshold amount need not file federal tax forms for that worker. But household employees who earn less than $1,000 still must pay their own income, FICA and FUTA taxes unless their overall income is so low that they're not required to file a tax return.

If you do pay a household employee $1,000 or more per year, however, you must comply with a number of federal tax requirements. The following IRS chart summarizes these rules.

FEDERAL TAX REQUIREMENTS FOR HOUSEHOLD WORKERS

Type of Tax	ICs	Employees
FICA	None due	FICA tax is due if you pay cash wages of $1,400 or more during the year. But don't count wages you pay to: • your spouse • your child under age 21 • your parent (but see Section B1c for exception), or • any employee under age 18 (but see Section A2a for exception).
FUTA	None due	FUTA tax is due if you pay cash wages of $1,000 or more in any calendar quarter. But don't count wages you pay to: • your spouse • your child under age 21, or • your parent.
FITW	None due	FITW need not be withheld unless the employee requests it and you agree.

a. FICA taxes

If you pay a household employee who is over 18 years of age $1,400 or more in cash wages in any year, you must withhold FICA taxes from the employee's earnings and make a matching contribution. Currently, the employer and employee must each pay an amount equal to 7.65% of the employee's wages to the IRS.

There is an exemption from FICA taxes for household employees who were under 18 any time during the calendar year and for whom household service is not a primary occupation. But FICA must be paid if domestic service is a teenager's principal employment. In other words, FICA taxes are not due if a teenager works occasionally to earn extra money and not to earn a living. FICA must be paid, however, if a teenager does household work to earn a living. If a teenager is a student, providing household services is not considered to be his or her principal occupation.

EXAMPLE 1: The Bartons hire Eve, a 17-year-old high school student, to babysit their children two or three times a month. The Bartons need not pay FICA for Eve even if they pay her $1,400 or more during the year.

EXAMPLE 2: The Smiths hire Jane to provide childcare services in their home. Jane is a 17-year-old single mother who left school and works as a childcare giver to support her family. This is clearly her principal occupation. The Smiths must pay FICA for Jane if they pay her $1,400 or more during the year.

There is also a special exemption for family members. (See Section B.)

b. FUTA taxes

If you pay a household employee $1,000 or more in cash wages during any calendar quarter—that is, any three-month period—you must also pay FUTA taxes. The rate varies from state to state depending on the amount of state unemployment taxes, but it is usually 0.8% of the first $7,000 of annual wages paid to an employee, or $56 per year.

Beware of Changing State Laws

Most states have already amended—or are expected to amend—their unemployment taxation laws to parallel the federal rule. Check with your state labor department to find out the current requirements in your state. (See Chapter 9, Section F.)

c. FITW taxes

Federal income taxes need not be withheld from a household employee's wages unless the employee requests it and the employer agrees. The employer does not have to agree. The same rule is followed under most state income tax laws.

It's unlikely that a worker would make such a request since most workers prefer not having tax withheld from their paychecks. But if a worker does ask you to withhold income tax, it's probably not in your interest to agree since it will create extra bookkeeping headaches for you.

d. Paying FICA and FUTA taxes

You are responsible for paying your household employee's share of FICA taxes as well as your own. You can withhold the employee's share from his or her wages. Withholding means you deduct the taxes due from the worker's pay and keep it in your bank account. IRS Publication 926, Household Employer's Tax Guide (see below), contains a table showing you how much you should withhold from the wages you pay a household employee. Instead of withholding the employee's share of these taxes, you can pay them from your own funds. Obviously, if you do this, you should reduce the employee's compensation to make up for the tax payments you're making on the employee's behalf.

Federal unemployment or FUTA taxes work differently. You cannot withhold FUTA taxes from an employee's wages. You must pay them from your own funds.

When you file your federal income tax return, you must add to your income all the FICA and FUTA taxes due on the wages you paid your household employee. The amount you owe on this additional "income" is due to the IRS with your tax return by April 15.

If you have several household employees or pay them a lot, you could have substantial extra taxes due when you file your tax return. You can avoid this by paying estimated taxes during the year to the IRS to cover the amount of employment taxes due. Alternatively, if you are employed, you can have your employer increase the amount of federal tax withheld from your paychecks. Note that the estimated tax penalty does not apply to employment taxes for household employees for 1997 or earlier.

If you don't pay estimated tax or have enough tax withheld from your paychecks, you may have to pay the IRS an estimated tax penalty. Basically, you'll have to pay a penalty if the amount you have withheld from your paychecks or pay as estimated tax during the year is less than 90% of your total tax due for the current year. This amount is increased if your income is over $150,000.

 For detailed information, see IRS Publication 505, Withholding and Estimated Tax, which you can find on the CD-ROM at the back of this book.

If you withhold or pay FICA taxes or withhold federal income tax, you must file IRS Form W-2 after the end of the year. To complete Form W-2, you will need both an employer identification number and your employee's Social Security number.

 Household Employers Must Obtain Federal ID Numbers

If you hire a household employee, the IRS requires that you obtain a federal employer identification number or EIN. An EIN is a nine-digit number the IRS assigns to employers for tax filing and reporting purposes. The IRS uses the EIN to identify the employer. EINs are free and easy to obtain. Use your EIN on all your employment tax returns, employment tax checks and other employer-related documents you send the IRS.

You obtain an EIN by filing IRS Form SS-4, Application for Employer Identification Number,

with the IRS. Filling out the form is simple and the SS-4 form has detailed instructions. You can obtain your EIN by mailing the completed SS-4 to the appropriate IRS service center listed in the form's instructions. The IRS will mail the EIN to you in about four weeks. If you need an EIN right away, you can get it over the phone by using the IRS's Tele-TIN program. Review the SS-4 instructions for details.

 You can find a copy of IRS Form SS-4 in Appendix 4 and on the CD-ROM at the back of this book.

 For detailed guidance, refer to IRS Publication 926, Household Employer's Tax Guide, which you can find on the CD-ROM at the back of this book.

3. Insurance for Injuries to Household Workers

Household workers can become injured on the job. For example, a babysitter could slip on a toy carelessly discarded by your child and suffer a back injury. After the sitter finishes yelling at your child, he or she will undoubtedly look to you to pay the medical and other expenses caused by the job-related accident.

You could be liable for such injuries. For example, you'll normally be liable for a work-related injury to a household worker that is caused by your or family members' negligence or unsafe conditions in your home. But, even if you're not liable, you could still be sued by an injured household worker and have to hire an attorney and pay other legal expenses.

Paying for these expenses out of your own pocket could prove ruinous. You should have insurance to cover them. This normally takes the form of a homeowner's insurance policy that also provides workers' compensation coverage for injuries to household employees.

a. Coverage for household ICs

If you own your home, you probably already have a homeowner's insurance policy since all lenders require them. Homeowner's policies contain liability coverage that insures you if a household worker who is an IC sues you for bodily injury or property damage occurring at your home. The homeowner's insurer will pay the costs of defending such a lawsuit and pay any damages up to the policy limits. It will also pay the injured person's medical expenses.

b. Coverage for household employees

Injuries to household employees may not be covered by your homeowner's policy. Such policies typically exclude coverage for injuries to employees. Instead, you have to purchase workers' compensation insurance. This is the type of insurance that employers normally obtain to cover injuries to their employees. (See Chapter 7.)

If you only use ICs and never hire a household employee, you don't need workers' compensation insurance. Unfortunately, it can be difficult to know for sure whether a worker is an employee or IC for workers' compensation purposes. States use different tests to classify workers for this purpose. These rules can be complex and difficult to apply. (See Chapter 7.) Don't gamble that a household worker is an IC. Your homeowner's insurer may disagree with you and claim that the worker is your employee. It will then deny coverage to an injured worker under the bodily injury and medical payment provisions of your policy.

You can usually obtain workers' compensation coverage for household employees from your homeowner's insurer. Your homeowner's policy may already include this coverage. Or you may have to specifically ask for it and pay extra. Check your policy or ask your insurance agent about it. If your policy doesn't already include this coverage, you'll need to purchase a rider or endorsement covering household employees.

c. Renters

If you're a renter, you should obtain a renter's policy with this same coverage. Don't assume you'll be covered by your landlord's insurance.

4. Federal Minimum Wage and Overtime Regulations

The federal Fair Labor Standards Act (FLSA) requires most types of employees to be paid at least the federal minimum wage and time-and-a-half for overtime. The FLSA is enforced by the Department of Labor, which may impose fines against employers who violate the FLSA.

You may be surprised to discover that the FLSA applies to household employees if they:

- receive at least $50 in cash wages in a calendar quarter from their employers, or
- work a total of more than eight hours a week for one or more employers.

These federal wage and overtime regulations apply only to household employees, not ICs. Unfortunately, it can be hard to know for sure whether a household worker is an employee or IC under the FLSA. (See the discussion below.) If you're not sure whether a household worker is an employee or IC, the safest course is to assume he or she is an employee and obey the minimum wage and overtime rules. (See Section 4a, below.) These rules do not place a very great financial burden on you.

CLASSIFYING WORKERS UNDER THE FLSA

The Department of Labor uses an economic reality test to determine a worker's status for FLSA purposes. (See Chapter 6, Section B4, for a discussion of this test.) To qualify as an IC, a household worker will generally have to provide services for several different households simultaneously and be able to show some opportunity for profit or loss. Profit or loss can be shown where a worker earns a set fee instead of an hourly wage, or where a worker has business expenses that could exceed business income—for example, salaries for assistants or equipment costs.

Of course, you cannot closely supervise the work of a household worker and expect him or her to qualify as an IC. Instead, your control must be limited to accepting or rejecting the worker's final results. For example, you can tell a gardener to mow your lawn and rake leaves, but you can't supervise how he or she does the work. This lack of supervision is impractical for many types of household workers, such as most child care providers.

Any worker who works solely for you and makes no attempt to obtain other clients or customers will almost surely be viewed as your employee by the Department of Labor. For example, a live-in housekeeper or child care provider is almost certainly an employee.

a.   Minimum wage laws

The federal minimum wage is $5.15 per hour. However, you may pay a $4.25 per hour training wage to a household worker under 20 years of age for the first three months he or she is on the job.

If your state has established a higher minimum wage, you must pay that amount. In California, for example, the minimum wage is $5.75 per hour. A number of other states also have minimum wage rates higher than the federal minimum. Check with your state labor department to find out what the current minimum wage is in your state. (See Chapter 9, Section F.) In the few states that have a minimum wage lower than the federal rate, the federal rate controls.

You must pay the minimum wage to any non-exempt domestic employee who:

- earns at least $50 in wages from one employer in any calendar quarter, or
- works at least eight hours a week for one or more employers.

If a household employee works less than eight hours a week for you, but works for others as well, you'll have to find out how many hours he or she works for other employers.

Casual babysitters and people who help care for people who can't care for themselves are exempt from federal minimum wage requirements if less than 20% of their hours are spent on general household work. But this exemption does not apply to trained personnel whose vocation is babysitting or caring for others—for example, registered and practical nurses.

The Department of Labor defines a casual babysitter as one who cares for others' children for less than 20 hours per week for all the people he or she works for together. The casual babysitter exemption also applies to a sitter who accompanies your family on vacation, provided that the vacation doesn't exceed six weeks.

You must pay a household employee the minimum wage regardless of whether payment is made by the hour or with a regular salary. You must pay minimum wage for each hour worked, including all hours an employee must be on duty at your home or at any other prescribed workplace, such as a vacation house. However, you are permitted a credit for the value of room and board you provide to a household employee.

HOW ROOM AND BOARD FIGURE INTO MINIMUM WAGE

Under the FLSA, employers may take a credit against minimum wage requirements for the reasonable cost or fair value of food and lodging or other facilities customarily furnished to an employee. But an employer may take this credit only when the employee voluntarily agrees to the arrangement.

Federal and state regulations define appropriate meal and lodging credits. In California, for example, when credit for lodging is used to meet part of the employer's minimum wage obligation, no more than $20 per week may be credited for a room occupied by one person.

b. Compensation for overtime

Most household employees must be paid overtime at the rate of one and one-half times their regular wage rate for all hours worked beyond a 40-hour workweek. In computing overtime pay, you must treat each workweek separately—that is, you can't average hours over two or more weeks.

You do not have to pay overtime to an au pair, housekeeper or other household employee who lives in your home. You must, however, pay the minimum wage for each hour worked.

Overtime is also not required for people who help care for people who can't care for themselves.

5. Immigration Requirements

Many household workers in the United States are immigrants. Some work illegally—that is, they are not U.S. citizens and don't have a green card or other documentation of their legal status. The federal government is cracking down on people who illegally hire undocumented household employees.

All employers, including those who hire most types of household employees, are required to verify that the employee is either a U.S. citizen or national, or a legal alien authorized to work in the United States.

You are not required to verify citizenship when you hire an IC. The government uses the common law right of control test to determine whether a worker is an employee or IC for immigration purposes. (See Chapter 3 for a discussion of the common law test.) A worker who qualifies as an IC for tax purposes will likely be an IC for immigration purposes as well.

Verification is also not required for employees who work in your home on only a sporadic basis—for example, a babysitter you hire now and then who sits for a few hours. Nor is verification necessary for employees of domestic agencies—for example, a housekeeper you hire from an agency where the worker is the agency's employee and you pay the agency, not the worker directly. Finally, the verification requirements don't apply to any employees hired before November 7, 1986.

Although you are not required to verify the immigration status of ICs or others coming within these exceptions, it is still illegal for you to hire any worker whom you know to be an illegal alien.

If you want to help a household worker become legal, see *How to Get a Green Card*, by Loida Nicolas Lewis and Len T. Madlansacay (Nolo). Also, contact the INS about any federal programs or special visas for nannies or au pairs that are available from time to time.

B. Family Members As Workers

Family members work with and for each other all of the time. If a family member is an IC under the tests discussed in this book, then that's great—you don't have to worry about such things as payroll taxes and unemployment compensation (depending on the test, of course). And even if the family member is your employee under these tests, you may still escape payroll taxes under special state rules. In Section 1, below, we discuss federal rules. In Section 2, below, we discuss state rules.

1. Federal Payroll Taxes

To determine if a family member is an IC for IRS purposes, follow the same steps that we describe in Chapter 4. If the family member is an IC, then you can stop there. If the family member is an employee, however, you may still escape federal payroll taxes (FICA and FUTA). Read on.

a. Children employed by parents

A parent need not pay FUTA taxes for services performed by a child who is younger than 21 years old. This is so regardless of the type of work the child does.

FICA taxes need not be paid for a child younger than 18 who works for a parent in a trade or business, or a partnership in which each partner is a parent of the child. If the services are for work other than a trade or business—such as domestic work in the parents' home—the parent does not have to pay FICA taxes until the child reaches 21.

EXAMPLE: Lisa, age 16, works in a bakery owned by her mother and operated as a sole proprietorship. Although Lisa is an employee under the IRS test, her mother need not pay FUTA for Lisa until she reaches 21 and need not pay FICA taxes for her until she reaches 18.

However, these rules do not apply—and FICA and FUTA must be paid—if a child works for:
- a corporation, even if it is controlled by the child's parent
- a partnership, even if the child's parent is a partner, unless each partner is a parent of the child, or
- an estate, even if it is the estate of a deceased parent.

EXAMPLE: Ron works in a bicycle repair shop that is half owned by his mother and half owned by her partner, Ralph, who is no relation to the family. FICA and FUTA taxes must be paid for Ron because he is working for a partnership and not all the partners are his parents.

If a child is paid regular cash wages as an employee in a parent's trade or business, he or she may be subject to federal income tax withholding regardless of age.

b. One spouse employed by another

If one spouse pays another wages to work in a trade or business, the payments are subject to FICA taxes and federal income tax withholding, but not to FUTA taxes.

EXAMPLE: Kay's husband, Simon, is a lawyer with his own practice. Kay works as his secretary and is paid $1,500 per month. Simon must pay the employer's share of FICA taxes for Kay and withhold employee FICA and federal income taxes from her pay.

However, neither FICA nor FUTA need be paid if the spouse performs services in other than a trade or business—for example, domestic service in the home.

EXAMPLE: Jill is a medical doctor with a busy practice. Her husband, Bob, stays home and takes care of the house and children. Jill gives Bob $1,000 a month as walking around money. These payments are not subject to any federal payroll taxes—FICA, FUTA or FITW.

But these rules do not apply—and FICA, FUTA and FITW must all be paid—if a spouse works for:
- a corporation, even if it is controlled by the individual's spouse
- a partnership, even if the individual's spouse is a partner, or
- an estate, even if it is the estate of a deceased spouse.

EXAMPLE: Laura's husband, Rob, works as a draftsperson in Laura's architectural firm. The firm is set up as a corporation solely owned and controlled by Laura. The corporation must pay FICA, FUTA and FITW for Rob.

c. Parent employed by child

The wages of a parent employed by a son or daughter in a trade or business are subject to income tax withholding and FICA taxes.

EXAMPLE: Don owns and operates a restaurant and employs Art, his father, as a part-time waiter. Since the restaurant is a business, Don must pay the employer's share of FICA taxes for Art and withhold employee FICA and federal income taxes from his pay.

FICA taxes do not have to be paid if the parent's services are not for a trade or business—for example, domestic services in the home. However, this rule is subject to one exception. Wages for domestic services by a parent for a child are subject to FICA taxes if:

- the parent cares for a grandchild (that is, the parent's child's child) who is either younger than 18 or requires adult supervision for at least four continuous weeks during a calendar quarter due to a mental or physical condition, and
- the parent's child is a widow or widower, divorced, or married to a person who, because of a physical or mental condition, cannot care for the grandchild.

EXAMPLE: Sally is a divorcee with two small children who live with her. Sally works during the day so she hires Martha, her mother, to care for the children during working hours. Sally pays Martha $250 a week. Sally must pay the employer's share of FICA taxes for Martha and withhold employee FICA and federal income taxes from her pay.

You do not have to pay FUTA taxes when you hire a parent to perform household services.

2. State Payroll Taxes

State payroll taxes consist of unemployment compensation which employers are required to pay directly to a state fund and state income tax that employers must withhold from employees' paychecks.

a. Unemployment compensation

Every state except New York exempts from unemployment compensation coverage services performed by a person employed by his or her child or spouse. In New York, unemployment compensation must be paid where a child employs a parent.

All states except New Hampshire exclude from unemployment compensation coverage minor children employed by their parents. In over half the states, a minor child is one under 21 years old. In most of the other states, a minor is a child under 18. In Wyoming, the age is 19.

b. State income taxation

All states except Alaska, Florida, Nevada, South Dakota, Texas, Washington and Wyoming have income taxation. If a family member is an employee of your business and is paid regular wages, you may have to withhold state income taxes from his or her pay. Check with your state's tax authority.

No income tax withholding is required for family members who qualify as ICs under your state's income tax law.

Labor and Anti-Discrimination Laws

mployees enjoy a wide array of rights under federal labor and anti-discrimination laws. Among other things, these laws:

- impose minimum wage and overtime pay requirements on employers
- make it illegal for employers to discriminate against employees on the basis of race, color, religion, gender or national origin
- protect employees who wish to unionize, and
- make it unlawful for employers to knowingly hire illegal aliens.

Most states have similar laws protecting employees.

In recent years, a growing number of employees have brought lawsuits against employers alleging violations of these laws. Some employers have had to pay hefty damages to their employees. In addition, various watchdog agencies, such as the U.S. Department of Labor and the U.S. Equal Employment Opportunity Commission, have authority to take administrative or court action against employers who violate these laws.

One of the advantages of hiring ICs is that few of these laws apply to them. However, this does not mean you can freely discriminate against ICs.

For more information about labor and anti-discrimination laws as they apply to employees, refer to *Everyday Employment Law: The Basics*. If you want detailed information about these laws, including the text of the laws and government resources, refer to *Federal Employment Laws: A Desk Reference*. Both are by attorneys Amy DelPo and Lisa Guerin, and both are published by Nolo.

A. Federal Wage and Hour Laws

The main federal law affecting workers' pay is the federal Fair Labor Standards Act or FLSA (29 U.S.C. §§ 201 and following), which establishes a national minimum wage and overtime standards for covered employees.

Most businesses are covered by the FLSA, but not all workers are included in its coverage. ICs are not subject to this law. Nor are employees who fall within any of the several exempt categories discussed below.

Don't Forget State Laws

This discussion only pertains to the federal wage and hour law. It does not address state laws, with which you must also comply. Contact your state labor department for more information. (See Section F of this chapter for contact information.)

1.   When the FLSA May Apply

You are required to pay employees working for you either the federal minimum wage ($5.15 per hour) or, if your state has a higher minimum wage, you are required to pay that wage. One possible exception is for household workers. (See Chapter 8 for guidance on hiring household workers.)

The reason you need to be concerned about the FLSA is because of overtime pay requirements. The FLSA requires that all non-exempt employees be paid an additional one-half times their regular rates of pay for all hours of work over 40 hours in a week. If you've classified as ICs workers who are really non-exempt employees under the FLSA, you will likely have to pay each misclassified worker an additional one-half of that worker's regular rate for all hours worked in excess of 40 per week during the previous two or three years. This could be a substantial sum if your workers regularly put in long work weeks. If you refuse to pay, you could face legal action by the Labor Department or by the affected workers and possible fines. You could also be held personally liable for FLSA violations.

The Department of Labor doesn't have the large investigative staff that the IRS does, but it doesn't need it. It relies on complaints by disgruntled workers who believe they're entitled to overtime pay. Since informants' identities are kept confidential, and since they can't be fired for complaining to the Labor Department, workers really have nothing to lose if they think they might qualify as employees and be entitled to the protection of the FLSA.

Before trying to determine how workers will be classified by the Department of Labor (see Section A4), you should first see if either your business or workers are exempt from FLSA coverage. You don't need to worry about this particular worker classification issue or the Department of Labor if your business or workers are exempt.

2. Covered Businesses

Your business is covered by the FLSA if you take in $500,000 or more in total annual sales or if you're engaged in interstate commerce. This covers nearly all workplaces, because the courts have broadly interpreted interstate commerce to include, for example, any business that regularly uses the U.S. mail to send or receive letters to and from other states or makes or accepts telephone calls to and from other states.

If your business is covered by the FLSA, it makes no difference how you compensate workers. If they are employees not exempt from the FLSA, they must be paid time-and-a-half for overtime. This is so whether they are paid by the hour, week or month; paid a commission on sales; paid on a piecework basis; compensated only by tips; or paid a set fee for the work.

⚠ Businesses Exempt From the FLSA
A handful of businesses are exempt from the FLSA—for example, most small farms are not covered. It's not likely your business falls within any of these exemptions, but for details of these exemptions, check with the nearest office of the U.S. Labor Department's Wage and Hour Division. (See Section F.)

3. Workers Exempt From Overtime Requirements

Several categories of workers are exempt from the FLSA, even if their employer is covered by the law and even if they themselves are employees. They can work as much overtime as they want and you won't have to pay time-and-a-half. The most common exemptions are for white collar workers and outside salespeople.

a. White-collar workers

Many white-collar workers are exempt from the FLSA. The FLSA divides such workers into three categories:

- **Executives.** Employees who manage two or more employees within a business or a department, and who can hire, fire and promote employees.
- **Administrators.** Employees who perform specialized or technical work related to management or general business operations.
- **Professionals.** Employees who perform original and creative work or work requiring advanced knowledge normally acquired through specialized study—for example, engineers and accountants.

To be exempt from the FLSA, these employees must be paid a minimum weekly salary or fee of $250 and spend at least 80% of the workday performing duties that require them to use discretion and independent judgment.

 These exemptions are explained in a free booklet titled *Regulations Part 541: Defining the Terms—Executive, Administrative, Professional and Outside Sales*. It's available from the nearest office of the Wage and Hour Division of the U.S. Department of Labor. You can find a list of all the Wage and Hour Division offices throughout the country at www.dol.gov/esa/public/contacts/whd/america2.htm. You can also look in the federal government pages of your phone book.

b. Outside salespeople

An outside salesperson is exempt from FLSA coverage if he or she:

- regularly works away from your place of business while making sales or taking orders, and
- spends no more than 20% of work time doing work other than selling for your business.

Typically, an exempt salesperson will be paid primarily through commissions and will require little or no direct supervision.

c. Computer specialists

Computer system analysts and programmers whose primary duty is systems analysis, systems design or high-level programming are exempt from the FLSA if they receive a salary of at least $170 a week or, if paid by the hour, receive at least $27.63 an hour.

d. Other workers

Several other types of workers are exempt from the overtime pay provisions of the FLSA. The most common include:

- inside salespeople whose regular rate of pay is more than one and one-half times the minimum wage and who receive more than half their pay from commissions
- taxicab drivers
- truck drivers and other trucking company employees whose maximum working hours are set by the Department of Transportation
- employees of seasonal amusement or recreational businesses
- employees of local newspapers having a circulation of less than 4,000
- newspaper delivery workers
- announcers, news editors and chief engineers of certain small radio and TV stations
- employees of motion picture theaters
- switchboard operators employed by phone companies that have no more than 750 stations
- workers on small farms, and
- seafarers on all vessels.

4. Classifying Workers Under the FLSA

If a worker does not fall into any of the exempt categories discussed above, the FLSA will apply only if the worker is an employee. The Department of Labor and courts use an economic reality test to determine the status of workers for FLSA purposes.

The economic reality test is also used to determine employee state for the Family and Medical Leave Act (which entitles workers to unpaid leave under certain circumstances) and the Worker Adjustment and Retraining Act (which requires employers give advance notice of plant closings and mass layoffs). It is also applied frequently by courts in determining employee status in cases involving Title VII of the Civil Rights Act of 1964, the Age Discrimination in Employment Act and the Americans with Disabilities Act.

You can find a lot of free information about these employment laws on Nolo's website at www.nolo.com. Click on the Plain-English Law Centers Tab at the top of the home page. Then click on the Employment Law tab on the left side of the page. Under Employers' Rights and Responsibilities, find the heading for Preventing Discrimination in the Workplace. There, you will find an article called *Federal Anti-Discrimination Laws*.

Under this test, workers are employees if they are economically dependent upon the businesses for which they render services. Economic dependence equals an employment relationship. This can be a rather difficult test to apply. After all, taken to its logical extreme, all workers could be considered employees because all workers, to some extent, are economically dependent on the people they work for.

As a general rule, however, the economic reality test will classify as employees all workers who would be considered employees under the common law test (see Chapter 3 for an in-depth discussion of this test). It will also classify as employees workers whom government agencies and courts feel need and deserve the special protections. These are primarily low-skill, low-paid workers—the type of workers labor and workers' compensation laws were originally intended to help.

This is borne out by the type of factors courts examine to gauge the degree of a worker's dependence on a hiring firm. They include:

- the skill required to do the work
- the amount of the worker's investment in facilities and equipment
- the worker's opportunities for profit or loss
- whether the worker's relationship with the hiring firm is permanent or brief
- the extent to which the services provided by the worker are an integral part of the hiring firm's business
- whether the hiring firm has the right to control how the work is done, and
- the amount of initiative, judgment or foresight required for the success of the worker's independent enterprise in open market competition with others.

Highly skilled, highly paid workers with substantial investments in tools and equipment are likely to be considered ICs under this test so long as they don't work full time for just one firm. In contrast, a worker who doesn't earn much, has low skills, no investment in tools or equipment and doesn't have to use much individual initiative to earn a living will probably be an employee.

A few court decisions help illustrate what a judge may emphasize when applying the economic realities test.

In one case, a natural gas pipeline construction company hired pipe welders and classified them as ICs. Twenty of them sued the company, claiming they were entitled to overtime pay because they were really employees. The court concluded that the workers were ICs under the economic reality test and therefore not entitled to overtime pay. The court noted that:

- The welders' jobs were highly specialized and required great skill.
- The welders moved from company to company and from job to job, usually working no more than six weeks at a time for any one company.
- The company exercised no control over how the welders did their jobs. Instead, the company's customers specified the type of welding procedures to be used and then tested the finished results.

- The welders owned all their own welding equipment and trucks, with an average cost of $15,000.
- The welders' success depended on using their initiative to find consistent work by moving from job to job.
- Although they were paid an hourly rate, the welders' opportunity for profit or loss depended mostly on their abilities to find work and minimize welding costs.

Based upon these facts, the court concluded that the welders were ICs. (*Carrell v. Sunland Constr. Inc.*, 998 F.2d 330 (5th Cir. 1993).)

In another case, the Department of Labor claimed that a nightclub operator had incorrectly classified topless dancers as ICs and was liable for overtime pay and for failing to pay the minimum wage. The court agreed. Even though the dancers' compensation was derived solely from tips they received from customers, the court found they were employees under the economic reality test. The dancers were economically dependent upon the nightclub because it set their work schedules and the minimum amounts they could charge for table dances and couch dances. Moreover, the club played the major role in luring customers through advertising, providing customers food and beverages and other means. The only initiative the dancers provided was deciding what to wear and how provocatively to dance. (*Reich v. Circle C. Investments, Inc.*, 998 F.2d 334 (5th Cir. 1993).)

In some circumstances, it is possible for even skilled workers to be considered employees under the economic reality test. For example, one federal court found that professional nurses were employees protected by the overtime pay provisions of the Fair Labor Standards Act. This was so even though the court admitted the nurses were highly skilled, worked for several different patients or hospitals at a time, were free to decline referrals and exercised independence and initiative in the way they did their work. (*Brock v. Superior Care, Inc.*, 840 F.2d 1054 (2d Cir. 1988).)

5. Avoiding Problems

The easiest way to avoid problems with FLSA overtime pay requirements is to prevent workers from putting in more than 40 hours a week. If a person is clearly an employee, you can simply prohibit him or her from working overtime. But if you classify a worker as an IC, you should not directly specify how many hours he or she should work—either orally or in a written IC agreement. Doing so makes the worker look like an employee, not only for FLSA purposes but for IRS and other purposes as well. It's really none of your business how long an IC works. You can only be concerned with the results an IC achieves, not how the worker achieves them.

Avoid giving workers who are not clearly ICs more work than they can do in a 40-hour week. This may mean you have to plan ahead so you can lengthen deadlines or hire more ICs to do the needed work.

6. Recordkeeping Requirements

The FLSA requires you to keep records of wages and hours for employees. You do not have to keep such records for independent contractors.

B. Federal Labor Relations Laws

The National Labor Relations Act or NLRA (29 U.S.C. §§ 151 and following) gives most employees the right to unionize. This enables them to negotiate collective employment contracts through union representatives rather than having to deal with employers individually.

The National Labor Relations Board (NLRB) administers the law and interprets its provisions. The NLRB conducts union elections and enforces the NLRA's rules of conduct, determining whether employers have engaged in unfair labor practices.

1. Only Employees Covered

The NLRA applies only to employees. ICs have the right to form a union if they wish to do so, but they are not protected by the NLRA. You can decline to use the services of ICs who form a union or simply express support for a union. You can't do this with employees who are covered by the NLRA.

2. Employees Exempt From the NLRA

Not all private sector employees are covered by the NLRA. Exempt employees include:
- managers and supervisors
- confidential employees—such as company accountants
- farm workers
- members of an employer's family
- most domestic workers, and
- workers in certain industries—such as the railroad industry—that are covered by other labor laws.

3. Determining Worker Status

If a worker does not fall within one of the classes of NLRA-exempt employees, you need to decide whether he or she is an employee or IC for NLRA purposes. The common law right of control test is used for this purpose. (See Chapter 4 for a discussion of the IRS common law test.)

C. Anti-Discrimination Laws

The federal government and most states have laws prohibiting discrimination in the workplace. Most of these laws apply only to employees, not ICs.

1. Federal Anti-Discrimination Laws

The main federal law barring workplace discrimination is Title VII of the federal Civil Rights Act of 1964. Title VII applies to businesses that have 15 or more full-time or part-time employees. It outlaws discrimination in employment based on race, color, religion, gender or national origin. Sexual harassment in the workplace is also prohibited as a variety of illegal gender discrimination.

Other federal laws barring workplace discrimination include:

- the Age Discrimination in Employment Act, which prohibits discrimination in employment on account of age against people who are 40 or more years old and applies to employers with 20 or more employees
- the Pregnancy Discrimination Act, which bars employers from discriminating against employees on account of pregnancy, birth or related conditions and applies to employers with 15 or more employees

- the Immigration Reform and Control Act, which makes it illegal to discriminate against people who aren't U.S. citizens but who have been legally admitted to the United States and applies to all employers
- the Equal Pay Act, which requires employers to provide equal pay and benefits to men and women who do the same job or jobs requiring equal skill, effort and responsibility, and
- the Americans with Disabilities Act, which protects disabled people from employment discrimination and applies to employers with 15 or more employees.

You can find a lot of free information about these employment laws on Nolo's website at www.nolo.com. Click on the Plain-English Law Centers Tab at the top of the home page. Then click on the Employment Law tab on the left side of the page. Under Employers' Rights and Responsibilities, find the heading for Preventing Discrimination in the Workplace. There, you will find an article called *Federal Anti-Discrimination Laws*. For more information about labor and anti-discrimination laws as they apply to employees, refer to the book *Everyday Employment Law: The Basics*. If you want detailed information about these laws, including the text of the laws and government resources, refer to *Federal Employment Laws: A Desk Reference*. Both books are by attorneys Amy DelPo and Lisa Guerin, and both are published by Nolo.

With one very narrow exception (see "Beware of Local Twists," below), none of these anti-discrimination laws applies to ICs. An IC has no legal right to bring a lawsuit against you claiming that you have discriminated in violation of these statutes. And the federal agencies charged with enforcing these laws, such as the Equal Employment Opportunity Commission, have no power to handle claims where ICs are concerned.

But this does not mean that you are off the hook as far as ICs are concerned. There are other federal and state laws that prohibit various forms of discrimination, and these laws may apply to your relationship with the IC. For example, in one recent case, a court held that an IC can sue a hiring company for damages for discrimination under a federal law that bars racial discrimination in private contracts—42 U.S.C. § 1981. In this case, an IC named Benjamin Guiliani, who was a Mexican-American man, operated a company called Danco that maintained parking lots. Danco signed a contract with a Wal-Mart store agreeing to maintain the store's parking lot. After Guiliani began working at the Wal-Mart location, he experienced hostility based on his race. Among other incidents, someone painted the words "white supremacy" on the pavement near where Guiliani unloaded his equipment, and store supervisors made derogatory comments about Latinos in front of him. Guiliani complained about the treatment, and Wal-Mart canceled the contract. Guiliani sued and won a $300,000 judgment. This case established the law in Maine, Massachusetts, New Hampshire, Rhode Island and Puerto Rico. (*Danco, Inc. v. Wal-Mart Stores, Inc.*, 178 F.3d 8 (1st Cir. 1999).) Another court has indicated this rule should also be followed in Alabama, Florida and Georgia. (*Zaklama v. Mt. Sinai Medical Center*, 842 F.2d 291 (11th Cir. 1988). However, courts in some other parts of the country have not extended this federal statute to ICs. For example, a Colorado court held that workers who couldn't bring discrimination claims under Title VII because they were ICs couldn't bring identical claims under Section 1981. (*Lufti v. Brighton Cmty. Hosp. Ass'n*, 85 FEP 1157 (Colo. Ct. App. 2001).)

Workers you've classified as ICs might also be able to sue you for workplace discrimination by claiming that they should have been classified as employees. If such a worker could convince a court he or she was improperly classified, the anti-discrimination laws would then apply. A court or federal agency would likely bend over backwards to find an employment relationship if you have engaged in blatant discrimination.

In addition, an IC might be able to sue you under state anti-discrimination laws and you might be subject to administrative action by a state anti-discrimination agency. Some of these state laws may apply to ICs. (See Section C2.)

BEWARE OF LOCAL TWISTS

Federal courts in some parts of the country—the western United States, for example—have found that in certain situations Title VII can apply to an IC. This is where discrimination against an IC results in damage to the IC's job opportunities.

For example, a doctor was permitted to bring a Title VII action alleging discrimination on the basis of national origin. The doctor, clearly an IC, had submitted a bid to run a hospital's emergency room. The doctor claimed that the bid was rejected because he was Hispanic and that the rejection had adversely affected his job opportunities. (*Gomez v. Alexian Bros. Hosp.*, 698 F.2d 1019 (9th Cir. 1983).)

Until recently, courts almost always used the economic reality test to determine whether a worker was an employee or IC for purposes of federal anti-discrimination statutes. However, many courts are now switching to the common law right of control test. (See Chapter 3 for a discussion of this test.)

2. State Anti-Discrimination Laws

All states except Alabama, Arkansas, Georgia and Mississippi have their own civil rights laws that prohibit discrimination in private employment based on race, color, gender or national origin. Most states also prohibit discrimination based on religion or disability. In addition, many states and localities prohibit forms of discrimination that aren't covered by federal law—for example, discrimination based on marital status.

These laws may be enforced by a special state administrative agency, the state labor department or state attorney general. Covered workers can also bring lawsuits alleging job discrimination against employers in state court.

Most of these state laws apply only to employees, not ICs. Different state courts use both the economic reality and common law tests to determine worker status under these laws. Regardless of what test is used, state agencies and courts often take a very broad view of who qualifies as an employee under these anti-discrimination laws. It's possible, therefore, that a worker might be viewed as an IC under federal anti-discrimination laws but as an employee under a similar state law.

Beware that the civil rights laws of a few states—Louisiana, North Dakota and Vermont, for example—might include ICs as well as employees.

For more information, contact your state labor department. (See Section F for contact details.)

D. Worker Safety Laws

The federal Occupational Safety and Health Act or OSHA (29 U.S.C. §§ 651 to 678) requires employers to keep their workplaces safe and free from recognized hazards that are likely to cause death or serious harm to employees. Employers must also provide safety training to employees, inform them about hazardous chemicals, notify government administrators about serious workplace accidents and keep detailed safety records.

OSHA applies to businesses that affect interstate commerce. The legal definition of interstate commerce is so broad that almost all businesses are covered.

OSHA is enforced by the federal Occupational Safety and Health Administration, or OSHA, a unit of the Department of Labor. OSHA can impose heavy penalties for legal violations and set additional workplace standards.

1. OSHA Coverage of ICs

OSA applies only to employees, not to ICs. OSHA uses the economic reality test to determine if workers are employees or ICs. (See Section A, above, for an in-depth discussion of this test.) OSHA has interpreted the test broadly to bring as many people as possible within the coverage of the law, making a lot of people employees who might not be under other tests—such as applicants for employment. (29 C.F.R. 1977.5(b).)

The training and recordkeeping requirements mentioned above don't apply to ICs. In addition, ICs do not have the legal right to complain to OSHA about safety violations, nor can they refuse to work if such violations persist. However, OSHA regulations requiring employers to notify workers about hazardous chemicals appear to apply to ICs as well as to employees. (29 C.F.R. 1919.1200(c).)

2. Importance of Maintaining a Safe Workplace

Even though OSHA cannot impose penalties against you if you have no employees, it's important for you to maintain a safe workplace. ICs who perform services at your workplace may be able to sue you for negligence and obtain monetary damages if they are injured because of hazardous or unsafe conditions.

E. Immigration Laws

Some workers in the United States are immigrants. And some of these immigrants work illegally—that is, they are not U.S. citizens and don't have a green card or other documentation of their legal status.

All employers must verify that their employees are either U.S. citizens or nationals, or legal aliens authorized to work in the U.S.

You are not required to verify citizenship when you hire an IC. The government uses the common law right of control test to determine whether a worker is an employee or IC for immigration purposes. (See Chapter 3 for an in-depth discussion of the common law test.)

In addition, the verification requirements do not apply to any employees hired before November 7, 1986.

However, although you are not required to verify the immigration status of ICs or others coming within these exceptions, it is still illegal for you to hire any worker whom you know to be an illegal alien. The federal government can impose a fine up to $2,000 for the first offense.

F.   Labor Departments

U.S. Department of Labor
200 Constitution Avenue, NW
Washington, DC 20210
202-219-6666
www.dol.gov

Check government pages of the telephone book for your regional office.

State Labor Departments

Note: Phone numbers are for department headquarters. Check websites for regional office locations and numbers.

Alabama
Department of Industrial Relations
Montgomery, AL
334-242-8990
www.dir.state.al.us

Alaska
Department of Labor and Workforce Development
Juneau, AK
907-465-2700
www.labor.state.ak.us

Arizona
Industrial Commission
Phoenix, AZ
602-542-4411
www.ica.state.az.us

Arkansas
Department of Labor
Little Rock, AR
501-682-4500
www.state.ar.us/labor

California
Department of Industrial Relations
San Francisco, CA
415-703-5070
www.dir.ca.gov

Colorado
Department of Labor and Employment
Denver, CO
303-318-8000
cdle.state.co.us

Connecticut
Department of Labor
Wethersfield, CT
860-263-6000
www.ctdol.state.ct.us

Delaware
Department of Labor
Wilmington, DE
302-761-8000
www.delawareworks.com/DeptLabor

District of Columbia
Department of Employment Services
Washington, DC
202-724-7000
http://does.dc.gov

Florida
Agency for Workforce Innovation
Tallahassee, FL
850-245-7105
www.floridajobs.org

Georgia
Department of Labor
Atlanta, GA
404-656-3045
877-709-8185
www.dol.state.ga.us

Hawaii
Department of Labor and Industrial Relations
Honolulu, HI
808-586-8865
www.state.hi.us/dlir/hiosh

Idaho
Department of Labor
Boise, ID
208-332-3570
www.labor.state.id.us

Illinois
Department of Labor
Chicago, IL
312-793-2800
www.state.il.us/agency/idol

Indiana
Department of Labor
Indianapolis, IN
317-232-2655
www.in.gov/labor

Iowa
Iowa Workforce Development
Des Moines, IA
515-281-5387
800-JOB-IOWA
www.state.ia.us/government/wd/index.htm

Kansas
Department of Human Resources
Office of Employment Standards
Topeka, KS
785-296-4062
www.hr.state.ks.us

Kentucky
Labor Cabinet
Frankfort, KY
502-564-3070
www.labor.ky.gov

STATE LABOR DEPARTMENTS (CONTINUED)

Louisiana
Department of Labor
Baton Rouge, LA
225-342-3111
www.ldol.state.la.us

Maine
Department of Labor
Augusta, ME
207-624-6400
www.state.me.us/labor

Maryland
Department of Labor, Licensing and Regulation
Division of Labor and Industry
Baltimore, MD
410-767-2236
www.dllr.state.md.us/labor

Massachusetts
Department of Labor and Workforce Development
Boston, MA
617-727-6573
www.state.ma.us/dlwd

Michigan
Michigan Consumer and Industry Services
Lansing, MI
517-373-1820
www.cis.state.mi.us

Minnesota
Department of Labor and Industry
St. Paul, MN
651-284-5005
800-342-5354
www.doli.state.mn.us

Mississippi
Employment Security Commission
Jackson, MS
601-354-8711
www.mesc.state.ms.us

Missouri
Department of Labor and Industrial Relations
Jefferson City, MO
573-751-4091
573-751-9691
www.dolir.state.mo.us

Montana
Department of Labor and Industry
Helena, MT 59624
406-444-2840
http://dli.state.mt.us

Nebraska
Department of Labor
Labor and Safety Standards
Lincoln, NE
402-471-2239
Omaha, NE
402-595-3095
www.dol.state.ne.us

Nevada
Division of Industrial Relations
Carson City, NV
775-684-7260
http://dirweb.state.nv.us

New Hampshire
Department of Labor
Concord, NH
603-271-3176
www.state.nh.us/dol

New Jersey
Department of Labor
Labor Standards and Safety Enforcement
Trenton, NJ
609-292-2313
www.state.nj.us/labor

New Mexico
Labor and Industrial Division
Department of Labor
Albuquerque, NM
505-827-6875
www.dol.state.nm.us

New York
Department of Labor
Albany, NY
518-457-9000
www.labor.state.ny.us

North Carolina
Department of Labor
Raleigh, NC
919-807-2796
800-625-2267
www.dol.state.nc.us/DOL

North Dakota
Department of Labor
Bismarck, ND
701-328-2660
800-582-8032
www.state.nd.us/labor

STATE LABOR DEPARTMENTS (CONTINUED)

Ohio
Labor and Worker Safety Division
Department of Commerce
Columbus, OH
614-644-2239
www.com.state.oh.us/ODOC/laws/default.htm

Oklahoma
Department of Labor
Oklahoma City, OK
405-528-1500
888-269-5353
www.oklaosf.state.ok.us/~okdol

Oregon
Bureau of Labor and Industries
Portland, OR
503-731-4200
www.boli.state.or.us

Pennsylvania
Department of Labor and Industry
Harrisburg, PA
717-787-5279
www.dli.state.pa.us

Rhode Island
Department of Labor and Training
Cranston, RI
401-462-8000
www.dlt.state.ri.us

South Carolina
Department of Labor, Licensing and Regulation
Columbia, SC
803-896-4300
www.llr.state.sc.us

South Dakota
Division of Labor and Management
Pierre, SD
605-773-3681
www.state.sd.us/dol/dlm/dlm-home.htm

Tennessee
Department of Labor and Workforce Development
Nashville, TN
615-741-6642
www.state.tn.us/labor-wfd

Texas
Texas Workforce Commission
Austin, TX
512-463-2222
www.twc.state.tx.us

Utah
Labor Commission
Salt Lake City, UT
801-530-6801
800-222-1238
www.labor.state.ut.us

Vermont
Department of Labor and Industry
Montpelier, VT
808-828-2288
www.state.vt.us/labind

Virginia
Department of Labor and Industry
Richmond, VA
804-371-2327
www.dli.state.va.us

Washington
Department of Labor and Industries
Tumwater, WA
360-902-5799
800-547-8367
www.lni.wa.gov

West Virginia
Division of Labor
Charleston, WV
877-558-5134
304-558-7890
www.state.wv.us/labor

Wisconsin
Workforce Development Department
Madison, WI
608-266-1784
www.dwd.state.wi.us

Wyoming
Department of Employment
Cheyenne, WY
307-777-6763
http://wydoe.state.wy.us

Intellectual Property Ownership

This chapter explains the rights and responsibilities of those who hire ICs to help create intellectual property. This includes not only high technology companies and publishers, but any company that has information it wants to keep from its competitors.

A. What Is Intellectual Property?

Intellectual property is a generic term describing products of the human intellect that have economic value. It includes works of authorship such as writings, films and music, inventions and information or know-how not generally known.

Intellectual property is considered property because the law gives the owners of such works legal rights similar to the rights of owners of real estate or tangible personal property such as automobiles. Intellectual property may be owned and bought and sold the same as other personal property.

Despite these similarities, there are some significant ways in which owning intellectual property is quite different from owning a house or car. For example, if you pay an IC to build a house, you own the house. But you can pay an IC to create intellectual property and yet not own the finished product.

B. Laws Protecting Intellectual Property

There are three separate bodies of law that protect most types of intellectual property: copyright, patent and trade secret law.

1. Copyright Law

The federal copyright law (17 U.S.C. §§ 101 and following) protects all original works of authorship. A work of authorship is any work created by a human being that other humans can understand or perceive, either by themselves or with the help of a machine such as a film projector or television. This includes, but is not limited to, all kinds of written works, plays, music, artwork, graphics, photos, films and videos, computer software, architectural blueprints and designs, choreography and pantomimes.

The copyright law gives the owner of a copyright a bundle of exclusive rights over how the work may be used. These include the exclusive right to copy and distribute the protected work, to create derivative works based upon it—updated editions of a book, for example—and to display and perform it. Copyright owners typically profit from their works by selling or licensing all or some of these rights to others—publishers, for example.

For a detailed discussion of copyright, see *The Copyright Handbook: How to Protect & Use Written Works* and *Copyright Your Software*, both by attorney Stephen Fishman (Nolo).

2. Patent Law

The federal patent law (35 U.S.C. §§ 100 and following) protects inventions. To obtain a patent, an inventor must file an application with the U.S. Patent and Trademark Office in Washington, D.C. If the Patent Office determines that the invention meets the legal requirements, it will issue a patent to the inventor. A patent gives an inventor a monopoly to use and commercially profit from the invention for 20 years. Anyone who wants to use or sell the invention must obtain the patent owner's permission. A patent may protect the functional features of a machine, process, manufactured item or composition of matter, or the ornamental design of a non-functional feature. A patent also protects improvements of any such items.

For a detailed discussion of patents, see *Patent It Yourself*, by attorney David Pressman (Nolo).

3. Trade Secret Law

A trade secret is information or know-how that is not generally known by others and that provides its owner with a competitive advantage in the marketplace. The information can be an idea, written words, a formula, process or procedure, technical design, customer list, marketing plan or any other secret that gives the owner an economic advantage.

If a trade secret owner takes reasonable steps to keep the confidential information or know-how secret—for example, does not publish it or otherwise make it freely available to the public—the laws of most states will protect the owner from disclosures of the secret by:

- the owner's employees
- people who agree not to disclose it
- industrial spies, and
- competitors who wrongfully acquire the information.

For detailed information, see *Nondisclosure Agreements: Protect Your Trade Secrets & More*, by attorneys Richard Stim and Stephen Fishman (Nolo).

C. Copyright Ownership

A work of authorship is automatically protected by copyright the moment it is created. At that same moment, someone becomes the owner of the copyright. If you pay an IC to create a copyright-able work on your behalf, you normally want to be the copyright owner. That will give you the exclusive right to copy, distribute and otherwise economically exploit the work. Without these rights, your ability to use the work will be very limited, even though you paid for it.

There are two ownership possibilities. Either:

- the work will be a work made for hire, in which case you will automatically be the copyright owner, or
- the work will not be a work made for hire, in which case the IC will initially own the copyright and you will have no ownership rights unless you specifically obtain them from the IC.

1. Works Made for Hire

When you pay someone to create a work made for hire, you automatically own all the copyright rights in the work. Indeed, you are considered to be the work's author for copyright purposes, even though you didn't create it. The actual creator of a work made for hire has no copyright rights at all. All the creator receives is whatever compensation you give him or her.

As the "author," you're entitled to register the work with the Copyright Office, and you own all the exclusive rights that make up a copyright, such as the right to copy and distribute the work. You can exercise these rights yourself, sell or license them to others or do whatever else you want with them. The person or people you paid to create the work have no say over what you do with your copyright rights in the work.

There are two types of works made for hire. They include:

- works created by employees within the scope of their employment, and
- certain types of specially commissioned works created by ICs.

a. Works by employees

All works of authorship created by your employees within the scope of employment are works made for hire. This means you automatically own all the copyright rights in such works. You aren't legally required to have your employees sign agreements relinquishing their copyright rights in works made for hire. However, costly disputes can develop concerning whether a work is created within the scope of employment. For example, if an employee creates a work partly at home outside working hours, he or she might claim it is not a work for hire because the work was done outside the scope of employment.

For this reason, it is a very good idea to have a written agreement describing the employee's job duties so it will be clear whether a work is created within the scope of employment. It's also wise to include in the agreement a provision assigning or transferring to you the copyright rights in any job-related works that for some reason are not works made for hire.

For sample employment agreements for employees involved in the software industry, see *Web & Software Development: A Legal Guide*, by attorney Stephen Fishman (Nolo).

b. Specially commissioned works by ICs

Certain types of specially commissioned or ordered works created by ICs are also considered to be works made for hire in which the hiring firm automatically owns all copyright rights. However, you and the IC must both sign an agreement stating that the work is made for hire. (See Chapter 13 for more information about agreements with ICs.)

Nine categories of works can be IC-created works made for hire. They are:

- a contribution to a collective work—for example, a work created by more than one author, such as a newspaper, magazine, anthology or encyclopedia
- a part of an audiovisual work—for example, a motion picture screenplay
- a translation
- supplementary works—for example, forewords, afterwords, supplemental pictorial illustrations, maps, charts, editorial notes, bibliographies, appendixes and indexes
- a compilation—for example, an electronic database
- an instructional text
- a test
- answer material for a test, and
- an atlas.

EXAMPLE: The editor of *The Egoist Magazine* asks Gloria, a freelance writer, if she would be interested in writing an article for the magazine on night life in Palm Beach. Gloria agrees and the editor sends Gloria an agreement to sign setting forth such terms as Gloria's compensation, the deadline for the article and its length, and stating that the article "shall be a work made for hire." Gloria signs the agreement, writes the article and is paid by the magazine. Since the article qualifies as a work made for hire, the magazine is the initial owner of all the copyright rights in the article.

Gloria owns no copyright rights in the article. As the copyright owner, the magazine is free to sell reprint rights in the article, to sell film and television rights, translation rights and any other rights anyone wants to buy. Gloria is not entitled to license or sell any rights in the article because she doesn't own any; she gave up all her copyright rights by signing the work-for-hire agreement.

California law provides that a person who commissions a work made for hire is considered to be the employer of the creator of the work for purposes of the workers' compensation, unemployment insurance and unemployment disability insurance laws. (Cal. Labor Code § 3351.5(c); Cal. Unemployment Insurance Code § 621 and § 686.)

No one is sure what impact this has on those who commission works made for hire in California. Neither the California courts nor state agencies have addressed the question. However, it may mean that the hiring firm has to obtain workers' compensation coverage for the person who created the work and might be liable for any injuries sustained in the course of the work. It might also mean that special penalties could be assessed against a hiring firm that does not pay the creator money due after he or she is discharged or resigns.

In addition, it's possible that the IRS could use these California laws as an excuse to classify creators as employees for federal tax purposes. At least one California publisher has had this experience where it paid workers' compensation and unemployment compensation for freelance writers who created specially commissioned works under work-for-hire agreements. This was so even though the writers appeared to qualify as ICs under the common law test. (See Chapter 3 for more information about the common law test.)

These potential requirements and liabilities are good reasons why it might be desirable for those commissioning work in California not to enter into work-for-hire agreements, and instead have the one who created the work assign the desired copyright rights to the hiring firm in advance. (See Section C2.)

2. IC Works That Are Not Made for Hire

Works of authorship created by ICs that do not fall within the list of nine specially commissioned works discussed above can never be works made for hire. This means that the IC, not the hiring firm, initially owns the copyright in such a work. As the copyright owner, the IC has the exclusive right to copy, distribute and create new works based on the work. Even though you paid the IC to create the work, you won't own any of these exclusive rights. You may end up only with a limited right to use the work.

EXAMPLE: Tom hires Jane, a freelance programmer, to create a computer program. Tom and Jane have an oral work agreement and Jane qualifies as an IC. She works at home under her own direction, sets her own hours and uses her own computer. Jane completes her work, delivers her code and Tom pays her.

The program is not a work for hire because Jane is an IC, not Tom's employee, and a computer program does not fall within one of the categories of works created by ICs that can be works made for hire. And, in any event, Jane never signed a work-for-hire agreement. This means that Jane owns all the copyright right in the program. As the copyright owner, Jane has the exclusive right to sell the program to others or permit them to use it. Even though Tom paid Jane to create the program, he doesn't own it and can't sell or license it to others.

Fortunately, it's easy to avoid this unhappy result. Simply require all ICs who create copyrightable works for you to sign written agreements assigning, or transferring, to you the copyright rights you need before they begin work on a project.

An assignment is simply a transfer of copyright ownership. You can obtain all the copyright rights in the work, or part of them. It's up to the IC and you to decide which rights to transfer. As discussed above, a copyright is really a number of rights including the exclusive rights to copy, distribute, perform, display and create derivative works from a work. Each of these rights can be sold or licensed together or separately. They can also be divided and subdivided by geography, time, market segment or any other way you can think up. For example, you could obtain the right to copy and distribute a work in North America for ten years.

An assignment can be made either before or after a work is created, but must be in writing to be valid. (See Chapter 13 for information on creating an assignment.)

> **EXAMPLE:** Tom hires Jane, a freelance programmer, to create a computer program. Before Jane starts work, Tom has her sign an independent contractor agreement providing, among other things, that she transfers all her copyright rights in the program to Tom. Jane completes her work, delivers the program and Tom pays her. Tom owns all the copyright rights in the program.

When you obtain copyright ownership through an assignment, it is legally not the same as owning a work made for hire. When you own a work for hire you are considered to be the work's author, even though you didn't create it. You automatically own all the copyright rights in the work. You are not considered the author when you obtain a copyright through an assignment, and you only acquire those rights covered by the assignment.

However, you'll usually want the assignment to transfer all the IC's copyright rights. When you do this, the only practical difference between an assignment and a work for hire is that the IC or his or her heirs can terminate the assignment 35 to 40 years after it was made. However, in most cases this is meaningless because very few works have a useful economic life of more than 35 years.

FAILING TO OBTAIN COPYRIGHT TRANSFERS FROM ICs

If you fail to obtain a copyright transfer from an IC, the best thing that can happen is that you will be considered a co-author of the work the IC helps create. For this to occur, you or somebody who works for you must actually help the IC to create the work. Giving suggestions or supervision is not enough to be a co-author. If you qualify as a co-author, you and the IC will jointly share copyright ownership in the work. As a co-author, you're entitled to use or let other people use the work without obtaining approval of the other co-author. But any profits you make must be shared with the other co-author or co-authors.

If you don't qualify as a co-author, at most you will have a nonexclusive right to use the work. For example, if you hired an IC to create a computer program, you will be able to use the program without asking the IC for permission. But you won't be allowed to sell or license any copyright rights in the work because you won't own any. The IC will own all the rights and will be able to sell or license them without your permission and without sharing the profits with you.

---

3. Determining Whether Workers Are Employees or ICs

It should be clear by now that it is very important to know whether any person you hire to create a work of authorship qualifies as an employee or IC for copyright ownership purposes. You automatically own the copyright in works created by employees within the scope of employment, but this is emphatically not the case with works created by ICs. The special steps discussed above must be taken to own IC-created works.

The common law right of control test is used to determine whether a worker is an IC or employee for copyright purposes. (See Chapter 13 for an in-depth discussion of the common law test.)

EXAMPLE: Marco, a professional photographer, took photographs for several issues of *Accent Magazine*, a trade journal for the jewelry industry, over a six-month period. Marco had an oral agreement with the magazine and was paid a fee of about $150 per photograph. Marco made no agreement with the magazine concerning copyright ownership of the photos. Marco, who had not signed a work-for-hire agreement, claimed that he owned all the copyright rights in the photos.

The court concluded that Marco was an IC. Marco was an experienced and skilled photographer. He used his own equipment, and worked at his own studio, on days and times of his choosing, without photography assistants hired by the magazine. No income tax was withheld from his payments and he received no employee benefits. He performed discrete assignments for the magazine, rather than hourly or periodic work. Since Marco owned the copyright in the photos, the court held that the magazine had to pay him a licensing fee when it re-used them. (*Marco v. Accent Publishing Co., Inc.*, 969 F.2d 154 (3d Cir. 1992).)

YOU CAN'T HAVE IT BOTH WAYS

Courts don't look favorably upon hiring firms that don't treat workers evenhandedly for copyright ownership purposes. In one case, for example, a federal court held that a part-time programmer employed by a swimming pool retailer was not the company's employee for copyright purposes and the programmer was therefore entitled to ownership of a program he wrote for the company. The court stated that the company's failure to provide the programmer with health, unemployment or life insurance benefits, or to withhold Social Security, federal or state taxes from his pay was a virtual admission that the programmer was an independent contractor. The court stressed that the company could not treat the programmer as an independent contractor for tax purposes and then turn around and claim he was an employee for copyright ownership purposes. (*Aymes v. Bonelli*, 980 F.2d 857 (2d Cir. 1992).)

The moral is that if you treat a worker as an IC for IRS purposes, you had better assume he or she is an IC for copyright ownership purposes as well.

D. Trade Secret and Patent Ownership

The rules for determining ownership of trade secrets and patentable inventions by ICs are essentially the same.

1. Inventions and Trade Secrets Created by Workers

Whenever you hire any worker to create or contribute to the creation of a patentable invention or information or know-how you wish to maintain as a trade secret, it's vital that the worker sign an agreement transferring his or her ownership rights to your company. This is so whether the worker is an employee or IC.

Such an intellectual property ownership transfer is called an assignment. It should be in writing and signed before work begins. It is common practice among high-technology firms and other businesses that create patentable inventions or valuable trade secrets to have creative workers sign such assignments. (See Chapter 13 for information about creating an assignment.)

In the absence of a signed assignment, you can still obtain ownership of any inventions or trade secrets an IC creates on your behalf, but you may be in for a costly legal dispute. You'll have to prove that the worker was hired to develop a specific product or to help create inventions for you.

2. Revealing Trade Secrets to Third Parties

When you hire ICs to perform services for you, it is sometimes necessary for you to reveal to them sensitive business information that you don't want your competitors to know. For example, it may be necessary to reveal highly valuable customer lists to an IC salesperson.

Even in the absence of a written agreement saying so, ICs probably have a duty to keep such information confidential. But just to make sure, it's wise to include a confidentiality clause in an IC agreement providing that the IC has a duty to keep your proprietary information confidential. (See Chapter 13 for information about confidentiality clauses.)

■

Planning to Avoid Trouble

This chapter explains how, with careful planning, you can hire outside workers and lessen your chances of being audited. If you do get audited, these methods will lessen your chances of losing the audit. These methods have been known to legal and employment professionals for years. But you don't have to hire a highly paid expert to use them.

A. Hiring Incorporated Independent Contractors

The single most effective thing you can do to avoid IRS and other government audits is to hire ICs who have formed corporations, rather than those who operate as sole proprietors or partnerships.

To understand why this is so, you need to know a little about the various legal forms a business can take. ICs can legally operate their businesses as:

- sole proprietors
- partnerships
- limited liability companies, or
- corporations.

Find out which category ICs fall into before hiring them, since it could affect the outcome of an IRS or other government audit.

⚠ There Is Nothing in a Name

ICs may call themselves by a variety of names: consultants, independent business people, freelancers, self-employed workers, entrepreneurs and the like. None of these names has any legal significance; ICs can use any of them no matter how their businesses are organized. What's important is whether they're sole proprietors, partnerships, limited liability companies or corporations.

1. Sole Proprietorships

A sole proprietorship is simply a one-owner business. Any person who starts a business and does not incorporate or have one or more partners is automatically a sole proprietor.

A sole proprietor is neither an employee nor an IC of the proprietorship. The owner and the sole proprietorship are treated as a single entity for tax purposes. The business does not pay FICA or FUTA taxes on the owner's income or withhold income tax. Instead, business income and losses are reported on the sole proprietor's individual federal tax return, Form 1040, Schedule C. Sole proprietors must pay all their FICA taxes themselves in the form of self-employment taxes. These taxes are reported on Schedule SE.

> **EXAMPLE:** Imelda operates a computer consulting business as a sole proprietorship. She is the sole owner of the business. For tax purposes, Imelda and her proprietorship are one and the same. All money the business receives is paid to Imelda personally. She must report all the income she receives from her clients on her individual Form 1040, Schedule C. She does not file a separate tax return for her business.

A sole proprietorship is by far the simplest and easiest way to legally operate a business, and it costs virtually nothing to start. For this reason, many ICs are sole proprietors.

Many sole proprietors qualify as ICs. You likely won't have problems having IC status verified if a sole proprietor is clearly running an independent business—for example, offers services to the public, has multiple clients, substantial ongoing business expenses such as workplace rental and insurance, is paid by the project and hires and pays assistants.

But in borderline cases, the fact that a worker is a sole proprietor is never helpful. Sole proprietors who don't hire assistants can look a lot like employees. They're working on their own, just like employees. They're selling their personal services to you, just like employees do. You pay them directly, just as you do employees. They may deposit the money in a personal account, just as employees do. And like employees, they don't have corporate meetings, partnership agreements or other business formalities.

The bottom line is that an IRS or other government auditor is more likely to question the status of a sole proprietor you've hired than a corporation or partnership. Unfortunately, you may not be able to avoid hiring a sole proprietor, because this is how most ICs do business.

2. Partnerships

A partnership is formed automatically whenever two or more people go into business together and do not form a corporation or a limited liability company. This form of business is similar to a sole proprietorship, except there are two or more owners. Like a sole proprietorship, a partnership is legally inseparable from the owners—the partners.

Partners share in profits or losses in the manner in which they've agreed. Partnerships do not themselves pay taxes, although they file an annual tax form. Instead, partnership income and losses are passed through the partnership directly to the partners and reported on the partners' individual federal tax returns, Form 1040, Schedule E.

Partners are neither employees nor ICs of their partnership; they are self-employed business owners. A partnership does not pay FICA and FUTA taxes on the partners' income, nor does it withhold income tax. Like sole proprietors, partners pay their own taxes.

> **EXAMPLE:** Brenda, Dave and Mike start their own computer consulting business. They form a partnership in which all three are partners. For tax purposes, their lives are pretty much the same as if they were sole proprietors. Each partner must pay his or her own FICA and FUTA taxes, and each must report his or her share of partnership income and losses on an individual tax return. Brenda, Dave and Mike are not employees of their partnership; each is a business owner.

Relatively few ICs do business as partnerships. But if you have the choice between hiring a sole proprietor and a partnership, you're usually better off hiring a partnership. Partnerships simply look more like independent businesses than most sole proprietorships. Partnerships involve two or more people in business together, not a single person. Partners' relationships with each other are governed by state partnership laws and partnership agreements, which can be extremely complex and expensive legal documents. Also, partnerships can have their own bank accounts and own property. This means you can pay the partnership for the work, rather than paying the partners directly.

However, even though workers call themselves partners, the IRS can still decide that they are really employees. This is so even if the remuneration is paid to the partnership, rather than directly to the individual partners. (Rev. Rul. 69-183, 1969-1 C.B. 255.)

3. Limited Liability Companies

The limited liability company (LLC) is one of the most popular forms of business in the United States. Indeed, many people believe it will eclipse both the partnership and corporation. Many ICs have formed their own LLCs, although the sole proprietorship remains the most prevalent business form for ICs.

An LLC is essentially a combination of a partnership/sole proprietorship and a corporation. Although the LLC provides the limited liability of a corporation, it is taxed as either a partnership or a sole proprietorship (see below). An LLC is easy to form and to run. For example, unlike a corporation, LLCs do not have to hold regular ownership and management meetings.

Ordinarily, the LLC itself does not pay taxes. Rather, all profits and losses pass through the LLC and get reported on the owners' (or members') individual tax returns. If the LLC has only one member, the IRS treats it as a sole proprietorship for tax purposes. If the LLC has two or more members, the IRS treats it as a partnership for tax purposes. Like a partnership or corporation, an LLC can have its own bank accounts and own title to property.

For a detailed discussion of LLCs, see *Form Your Own Limited Liability Company,* by attorney Anthony Mancuso (Nolo).

To ensure that the worker is an IC rather than an employee, a hiring firm will probably be better off hiring an IC who has formed an LLC than one who works as a sole proprietor. Forming an LLC helps show the IC is in business for himself or herself. However, it is not as advantageous as hiring a corporation. One reason for this is that payments to LLCs must be reported to the IRS on Form 1099-MISC. The only exception is where the LLC elects to be treated as a corporation for tax reporting purposes. But few LLCs do this. Form 1099 is an important audit lead for the IRS—a lead the agency does not have when you hire a corporation because you do not have to file a Form 1099 for a payment to a corporation. (See Chapter 12 for more about paying ICs.)

Another drawback to hiring LLCs, rather than corporations, is that LLC owners ordinarily are not employees of the LLC for tax purposes. They are business owners. The LLC is not required to withhold and pay employment taxes for them. This is not the case with a small corporation, whose owners are usually corporate employees.

Moreover, the informality of an LLC is not helpful to a hiring firm when dealing with the IRS or other government auditor. LLC status does not help to show that the worker is an independent businessperson. In contrast, the need to hold shareholder and board meetings and to keep corporate records impresses a government auditor that the worker is running his or her own business.

4. Corporations

A corporation is created by filing articles of incorporation with the appropriate state agency—usually the secretary of state or corporations commissioner. Once this is done and the appropriate fees paid, the corporation becomes a separate legal entity—distinct from its owners, the shareholders. It can hold title to property, sue and be sued, have bank accounts, borrow money and hire employees and ICs.

a. Corporate officers, directors and shareholders

In theory, corporations consist of three groups:
- those who direct the business—called directors
- those who run the business—called officers, and
- those who invest in it—called shareholders.

In the case of small business corporations, these three groups are often the same person.

All corporate officers—the president, vice president, treasurer and any others—are automatically considered employees for employment tax purposes. Corporate shareholders who are not officers, but who perform full- or part-time services for the corporation, are also employees of the corporation. (Rev. Rul. 71-86, 1971-1 C.B. 285.)

Usually, the owners of a typical incorporated small business are employees of the corporation, either because they serve as officers or perform services for the corporation. The corporation must deduct federal income tax withholding from the owners' wages and pay employment taxes and state payroll taxes as well.

EXAMPLE: Suzy has been operating a one-person sales and marketing business as a sole proprietor. She incorporates the business. Suzy will be the sole shareholder, director and president of Suzy's Sales Services, Inc. After she files articles of incorporation and pays the incorporation fees, she will no longer be self-employed in the eyes of the tax law. Instead, she is a full-time employee of her corporation. As an employee, she earns wages from her corporation, just as if she didn't own the business. The corporation must withhold Suzy's federal income taxes, pay her FUTA and half her FICA taxes and also pay state payroll taxes.

b. Benefits of hiring incorporated outside workers

When you hire incorporated outside workers, you enter into a three-tiered relationship with yourself in the top rung. You pay the worker's corporation, which pays the worker, who is an employee of the corporation. Legally, you have no direct relationship with the worker at all—only with the worker's corporation, which cannot be classified as an employee.

> **EXAMPLE:** Acme Widget Company hires Sam's Sales Services, Inc., to sell widgets. Acme pays no money to Sam directly, even though he is the sole shareholder and president of Sam's Sales Services, Inc., and is the person doing all the work. Instead, Acme pays Sam's corporation, which is Sam's employer. It's the corporation's responsibility to pay state and federal payroll taxes for Sam.

Having a legal entity, the corporation, between you and the worker is the main benefit of hiring an incorporated worker. Legally, the corporation is the worker's employer, not you. It is supposed to pay state and federal payroll taxes and provide workers' compensation insurance, not you. If the corporation fails to pay these taxes, IRS and state auditors will likely concentrate on the corporation and its owners, not you, unless the corporation is a sham. (See Section 3c.)

Even if you're audited, you'll usually have an easier time proving that an incorporated worker is an IC. Forming a corporation is expensive and time-consuming, and operating one can be burdensome as well. Auditors are usually greatly impressed by the fact that a worker has gone to the time and trouble to form and operate a corporation. This is something that only people who are running their own businesses do. And people who are running their own businesses can't be your employees.

Indeed, the IRS audit manual on worker classification provides that an incorporated worker will usually not be treated as an employee of the hiring firm, but as an employee of the worker's corporation.

One case from Idaho shows why many hiring firms prefer to hire corporations rather than sole proprietors. An outpatient surgery center hired two doctors to work as administrators. They both performed the same services. However, one of the doctors had formed a medical corporation of which he was an employee. The surgery center signed a written contract with the corporation, not the doctor personally; it also paid the doctor's corporation, not the doctor personally.

The other doctor was a sole proprietor and had no written contract with the center. The court concluded that the incorporated doctor was not an employee of the surgery center, but the unincorporated doctor was an employee. As a result, the center had to pay substantial back taxes and penalties for the unincorporated doctor, but not for the doctor who was incorporated. (*Idaho Ambucare Center v. U.S.*, 57 F.3d 752 (9th Cir. 1995).)

Another benefit of hiring incorporated outside workers is that you don't have to file a Form 1099-MISC reporting to the IRS payments to corporations—eliminating a very important IRS audit lead. (See Chapter 12 for more about filing IRS forms for ICs.)

c. Problems with corporations

Incorporating is not a panacea. Simply filing articles of incorporation will not magically insulate a hiring firm or worker from the IRS. You're most likely to have problems where an outside worker's corporation fails to pay federal or state payroll taxes. If this is coupled with evidence that the corporation is not being operated as an independent business, it's quite possible that the IRS will disregard the corporation as a sham and determine that the worker is an employee of the hiring firm.

> **EXAMPLE:** Bill, a delivery truck driver, forms a corporation called Bill's Trucking, Inc., with himself as the sole shareholder and president. The corporation has no assets and no employees other than Bill. Acme Press hires Bill's Trucking to make deliveries. Bill is treated just like

an Acme employee; Acme provides him with a truck, gives him health and pension benefits and controls him on the job. Acme pays a monthly check to Bill's Trucking. However, Bill deposits the funds in his personal account and pays no federal or state payroll taxes. It's likely the IRS would conclude that the corporation is a sham and that Bill is Acme's employee.

d. Finding incorporated ICs

Skilled workers such lawyers, doctors and accountants often form their own corporations. You may not have much trouble hiring incorporated workers in these fields.

However, it's unusual for lower skilled and less highly paid workers to be incorporated. For example, it's rare for a trucker or delivery person to be incorporated. So you simply may not be able to find an incorporated worker to perform these types of services.

In addition, you may have to pay more to hire an incorporated worker because operating a corporation is more expensive and burdensome than being a sole proprietor or partner. For example, if there is more than one shareholder, certain formalities must be adhered to such as holding annual meetings and keeping corporate minutes. And in many states, a corporation must pay a minimum annual tax even if it didn't earn any money for the year.

⚠ When to Steer Clear of Incorporators

You should not help a worker form a corporation or pay him or her to do so, since this makes the corporation look like a sham. True ICs who are in business for themselves form their corporations on their own initiative with their own money.

B. Employee Leasing

Instead of hiring workers directly, many companies lease or rent them from outside leasing companies. Such workers may be referred to as temporary employees, temps, contract employees or contingent or casual workers. This chapter refers to them as leased employees.

Using leased employees is sometimes referred to as outsourcing or outside staffing. Whatever the practice is called, leasing employees has become an increasingly popular method for hiring firms to obtain the services of outside workers.

Worker leasing arrangements take a variety of forms. For example, you may lease workers from an employment agency that locates the workers for you or already has them on staff. This is what temporary agencies do. In other cases, the leasing company may hire your employees and lease them back to you for a fee.

Employee leasing can give you many of the benefits that can be obtained by hiring ICs directly. You use them only when needed and then dispense with their services without going through the trauma and expense of laying off your own employees. You do not have to pay and withhold federal and state payroll taxes for leased workers or provide them with workers' compensation or employee benefits.

It can cost more to lease workers through leasing companies than hiring them directly since leasing companies have to pay the leased employees salaries plus earn a profit, but many companies feel it's worth it.

You can obtain the services of highly trained and experienced workers who have been screened and selected by the leasing company. Also, you have reduced exposure to government audits.

Although employee leasing arrangements can work well, there are some serious pitfalls you should be aware of that require careful planning to avoid.

1. Leased Workers' Employment Status

The idea behind worker leasing is that the leased workers are supposed to be the leasing firm's employees, not yours. In the ideal worker leasing arrangement, the leasing firm is responsible for supervising and controlling the worker's job performance, paying the leased workers' salaries and paying and withholding federal and state payroll taxes, paying for unemployment compensation, providing workers' compensation coverage and any employee benefits. Ideally, all you do is pay the leasing firm a fee.

A LOOK AT OTHER ALTERNATIVE WORK ARRANGEMENTS

Besides leasing employees, there are many other alternative work arrangements that don't require full-time year-round work in a hiring firm's workplace. They include:
- hiring part-time workers
- hiring short-term workers
- having workers work at home and communicate with the office via phone and computer—also known as telecommuting, and
- using seasonal workers.

Some hiring firms believe that workers involved in such work arrangements can never be their employees. This is not the case. The fact that workers work part time, short term or at home has relatively little impact on their status. If you have the right to control such workers on the job, they will be your employees.

Whenever you're on the top rung of a three-sided relationship like this, you have much less chance of being audited. As long as the leasing firm pays all applicable taxes, there is little likelihood that you'll have any problems with the IRS.

PROBLEMS WITH RETIREMENT PLANS

If your company leases workers full time for work that used to be performed by employees, the IRS may view the leased workers as company employees for retirement and profit-sharing plan purposes.

The leased workers would be counted in determining whether the nondiscrimination and minimum participation rules governing tax-qualified retirement plans are satisfied. This is important because a minimum number of employees must be included in a retirement plan for it to be tax-qualified—that is, for company contributions to the plan to be deductible by the company and nontaxable to the recipients until retirement.

If any of your plans are found not to comply with the requirements for tax-qualified status, then all previous tax deductions for benefits or contributions to the plan can be thrown out. Your business can lose the deductions, and the benefit recipients will have to pay taxes on the benefits.

There are ways to avoid this problem. But this is a very complex area of the law, so it's best to discuss this issue with a retirement plan administrator, or to seek advice from a retirement plan consultant or an attorney or CPA specializing in this field.

a.   The problem of joint employment

Unfortunately, things don't always work out as described above. If you control a leased worker's performance on the job, you can be considered the worker's employer along with the leasing company. This is called joint employment. If you're a joint employer of a leased employee, you lose all the benefits of employee leasing. You have the same duties and liabilities as if you were the worker's sole employer.

> **EXAMPLE:** The Merrill Lynch securities firm leased the services of Amarnare through an employment agency. Amarnare's pay and benefits were paid by the agency, not Merrill Lynch. Amarnare was fired after two weeks on the job and then sued Merrill Lynch, but not the employment agency, for unlawful discrimination claiming that she was fired because of her sex and race. Merrill Lynch claimed it was not liable because it was not Amarnare's employer, the employment agency was.
>
> The court disagreed. It held that Merrill Lynch was Amarnare's joint employer, along with the employment agency, because it completely controlled Amarnare on the job. Merrill Lynch controlled Amarnare's work assignments, working hours and manner of performance; directly supervised her; and had the right to discharge her and request a replacement if it found her work unsatisfactory. (*Amarnare v. Merrill, Lynch, Pierce, Fenner & Smith, Inc.*, 611 F.Supp. 344 (S.D. N.Y. 1984).)

If you're found to be a joint employer of a leased worker, you'll not only be liable for labor and anti-discrimination law violations, but can have a legal duty to provide the worker with unemployment insurance and workers' compensation. If the leasing company fails to provide them, you'll have to and will be subject to penalties for the leasing company's failure to do so in the first place.

b.   Avoiding joint employer status

To avoid being a joint employer of a leased worker, you must give up all control over the worker. The leasing firm, not you, must control the leased worker's performance on the job.

Carefully follow these guidelines.

- Don't ever deal or negotiate with a leased worker about such matters as time, place and type of work, working conditions or the quality and price of the services to be provided by the worker. The leasing company should handle all these negotiations for you—that is, you tell the leasing company what you want and it tells the worker.
- The leasing company should have the sole right to determine whether to assign or reassign workers to perform needed tasks.
- The leasing company should set the rate of pay for the leased workers.
- The leasing company should pay the leased workers from its own account.
- The leasing company, not you, should have the right to hire or fire the leased workers; if the company fails to provide you with high quality workers, don't fire them. Instead, hire a new leasing company.
- The leasing company should have the authority to assign or reassign a worker to other clients or customers if you feel the worker is not acceptable.

It's also very helpful if the leasing company provides its own supervisor or on-site administrator to manage and supervise the leased workers. This will significantly reduce your control over the workers and reduce the chances that you'll be a joint employer.

If you're unable or unwilling to relinquish all control over leased workers, you can still go ahead with a leasing arrangement. But be aware that you may be considered to be the leased workers' joint employer. As such, you'll need to make certain that the leasing firm is paying all required payroll taxes, providing workers' compensation insurance and not engaging in behavior that could get you sued, such as discriminating against workers on the basis of race or age.

c.   Problems with workers' compensation insurance

Another problem area with which you need to be concerned when you lease workers is workers' compensation insurance. The employee leasing company, not you, is supposed to provide the leased workers with workers' compensation coverage.

In the past, some shady hiring firms saved money on workers' compensation insurance premiums by having equally shady leasing firms hire their employees and lease them back to them. The leasing firm would purchase workers' compensation insurance for the employees at a lower rate than the hiring firm because it was newly in business and few or no workers' compensation claims had been filed against it. Workers' compensation premiums are based in part on how many claims are filed against a company. This factor is called the experience modifier. Companies that have many claims filed by employees pay more than companies that don't. These leasing companies continually changed their names and formed new business entities. Each new entity would have a clean workers' compensation record and so would pay a lower workers' compensation premium.

This scam is no longer possible in most states. Most now require employee leasing companies to use the same experience modifier as their client firms use for similar workers. To make sure that a leasing company is paying the proper workers' compensation premium, ask to see a copy of its workers' compensation policy showing the classifications and experience modifier used. If these are different from those in your own policy, question the leasing company closely.

Also, make sure your agreement with the leasing company requires it to notify you in writing if its workers' compensation insurance is canceled for any reason. You may end up having to pay premiums for leased employees if the leasing firm's insurance is canceled.

2.   Dealing With Established Leasing Companies

It's very important that you deal with a reputable leasing firm that is an established business with its own offices and management. Such a firm is more likely to make all required payroll tax and insurance payments. Remember, if the leasing firm doesn't pay for these items, you may have to pay for them.

Don't take a leasing firm's word it's paying payroll taxes and insurance premiums. Require any leasing firm to provide you with proof that it is withholding and paying federal and state payroll taxes and paying for workers' compensation insurance for your leased employees.

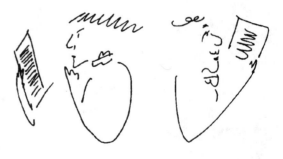

3.   Using Written Agreements

Sign a written lease agreement with a leasing company. Among other things, such an agreement should provide that:

- the leased workers are the leasing company's employees
- the leasing company is responsible for paying the leased workers' wages and withholding and paying all state and federal payroll taxes, including unemployment compensation
- the leasing company will provide the leased workers with workers' compensation insurance, and

- the leasing company will indemnify you—that is, repay you—for all losses you might suffer as a result of its failure to comply with any legal requirements, including the costs of defending against charges of alleged violations. For example, if the leasing company fails to withhold and pay employment taxes, it will pay any IRS assessments and penalties and your legal fees incurred in defending yourself against the IRS.

The agreement should also provide that the leasing company has the sole authority to hire, fire, schedule, supervise and discipline the leased workers. (See Section 1b, above.)

Most leasing companies have their own lease agreements. It's wise to have an attorney review any leasing agreement before you sign it. ■

Procedures for Hiring
Independent Contractors

If you hire ICs, you must assume that, sooner or later, the IRS and other government agencies will audit you and that they will question the status of workers you've classified as ICs. Long before you're audited, you should have in your files all the information and documentation you need to prove that a worker is an IC. Don't wait until you're audited to start thinking about how to prove a worker is an IC; by then it may be too late.

A. Before Hiring an IC

Someone in your company should be in charge of:
- interviewing prospective ICs
- determining whether applicants qualify as ICs
- authorizing workers to be hired as ICs, and
- preparing an IC data file containing the information and documentation you'll need to prove the worker is an IC if you're audited.

This individual, who may be called a Contract Administrator, should be fully trained regarding the laws and rules used to determine a worker's status. If you're running a one-person business, this person is you.

1. Interviewing Prospective ICs

All prospective ICs should fill out the Independent Contractor Questionnaire contained in Appendix 2 and on the CD-ROM, and they should provide the required documentation. Do not have an IC fill out an employment application; this makes the worker look like an employee.

The Contract Administrator should review the questionnaire and documentation with the IC during an initial interview.

QUESTIONS YOU SHOULDN'T ASK

Federal and state laws bar employers from asking certain types of questions in interviews or on employment applications. It's wise to also follow these rules when you interview ICs, even though these laws don't apply to ICs. For example, the Americans with Disabilities Act prohibits most pre-employment questions about a disability. In addition, the Civil Rights Act forbids you to ask about an applicant's race, marital status, gender, birthplace or national origin. There are also restrictions concerning questions about an applicant's age, arrest record, citizenship and affiliations.

2. Required Documentation

Ask any worker you plan to hire as an IC to provide the following documentation:
- copies of the IC's business license if required and any professional licenses the IC has, such as a contractor's license
- certificates showing that the IC has insurance, including general liability insurance and workers' compensation insurance if the IC has employees
- the IC's business cards and stationery
- copies of any advertising the IC has done, such as a Yellow Pages listing
- a copy of the IC's White Pages business phone listing, if there is one
- if the IC is operating under an assumed name, a copy of the fictitious business name statement
- the IC's invoice form used for billing
- a copy of any office lease
- a photograph of the IC's office or workplace
- the IC's unemployment insurance number issued by the state unemployment insurance agency (only ICs with employees will have these)

- copies of 1099 forms issued to the IC by other companies for which the IC has worked
- the names and salaries of all assistants that the IC will use on the job
- the names and salaries of all assistants the IC has used on previous jobs for the past two years and proof that the IC has paid them, such as copies of canceled checks or copies of payroll tax forms
- a list of all the equipment and materials the IC will use in performing the services and how much it costs
- proof that the IC has paid for the equipment, such as copies of canceled checks, is very helpful
- the names and addresses of other clients or customers for whom the IC has performed services during the previous two years (but don't ask for the identities of any clients the IC is required to keep confidential), and

- if the IC is a sole proprietor and will agree to do so, copies of the IC's tax returns for the previous two years showing that the IC has filed a Schedule C, Profit or Loss From a Business.

3. Determining Whether Workers Qualify As ICs

The Contract Administrator must examine the answers the worker provided on the Independent Contractor Questionnaire, the documentation and the task the IC is being hired to perform to see if the worker can qualify as an IC.

This can be difficult because there is no single definition of an IC. Mechanical rules won't work. For example, some firms will hire any worker as an IC so long as he or she is incorporated and works no longer than six months for the firm. While both these factors are very helpful, they are no guarantee that the worker will not be reclassified as an employee by government auditors. All the facts and circumstances must be examined and weighed on a case-by-case basis.

CHECK ON SAFE HARBOR PROTECTIONS

If you can obtain Safe Harbor protection for the worker, you may treat the worker as an IC for employment tax purposes regardless of whether he or she qualifies as such under the normal IRS tests. Safe Harbor protection is available, however, only if you have consistently treated all workers performing similar services as ICs.

One very important question to ask, therefore, is whether your company has ever used employees to perform services similar to those the IC will be asked to do. If you have, you can forget about Safe Harbor protection and you will likely have a harder task dealing with the IRS if you're audited. (See Chapter 4 for more information about Safe Harbor protection.) For this reason, you're much better off keeping the work your employees and ICs do separate.

4. Drafting and Signing an IC Agreement

If you determine that the worker qualifies as an IC, complete and sign an independent contractor agreement before the IC starts work. (See Chapter 13 for guidance on creating an independent contractor agreement.) However, the IC may have his or her own agreement. If so, ask for a copy and use it as your starting point in drafting the agreement. This will show that the agreement is a real negotiated contract, not a standard form you forced the worker to sign. Pay particular attention to whether the IC's agreement contains any provisions that should be deleted or amended, or whether new provisions should be added.

5. Backup Withholding

Sometimes, you may have to withhold money from the IC and give it to the IRS. This is called backup withholding, and you can avoid it if you take the steps that we describe in subsection a, below. If you do find yourself in the position of having to do backup withholding, follow the procedures that we describe in subsection b, below.

a. How to avoid backup withholding

It's very easy to avoid backup withholding. Have the IC fill out and sign IRS Form W-9, Request for Taxpayer Identification Number. Retain it in your IC file. You don't have to file the W-9 with the IRS. This simple form merely requires the IC to list his or her name and address and taxpayer ID number. Corporations, partnerships and sole proprietors must have a federal employer identification number (EIN), which they obtain from the IRS. In the case of sole proprietors without employees, the taxpayer ID number is either the IC's Social Security number or an EIN if the IC has obtained one.

If the IC doesn't already have an EIN, you don't have to backup withhold for 60 days after he or she applies for one. It usually takes several weeks to obtain.

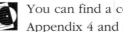 You can find a copy of IRS Form W-9 in Appendix 4 and on the CD-ROM at the back of this book.

WHICH IS BETTER, A SOCIAL SECURITY NUMBER OR EIN?

A sole proprietor IC who doesn't have employees can use either his or her Social Security number or a separate federal employer identification number as the taxpayer ID number. It's better for you if the IC obtains an EIN. This helps show that the IC is running an independent business. Employees don't have EINs. Encourage any sole proprietor IC you hire to obtain an EIN.

Obtaining one is easy and costs nothing. The IC simply files IRS Form SS-4 with the IRS center listed in the instructions on the form. You can find a copy of Form SS-4 in Appendix 4 and on the CD-ROM at the back of this book.

b.   Backup withholding procedure

If you are unable to obtain an IC's taxpayer ID number or the IRS informs you that the number the IC gave you is incorrect, you'll have to do backup withholding. Backup withholding must begin after you pay an IC $600 or more during the year. You need not backup withhold on payments totaling less than $600.

For this procedure, you withhold 31% of the IC's compensation and deposit it every quarter with your bank or other payroll tax depository. You must make these deposits separately from the payroll tax deposits you make for employees.

Report the amounts withheld on IRS Form 945, Annual Return of Withheld Federal Income Tax. This is an annual return you must file by January 31 of the following year. See the instructions to Form 945 for details.

 You can find a copy of IRS Form 945 on the CD-ROM at the back of this book.

6.   Keeping Records

Create a file for each IC you hire. Keep these files separate from the personnel files you use for employees. Each file should contain:

- the signed final IC agreement and copies of any interim drafts
- the IRS W-9 form signed by the IC containing the IC's taxpayer identification number
- all the documentation provided by the IC, such as proof of insurance, business cards and stationery, copies of advertisements, professional licenses, copies of articles of incorporation
- all the invoices the IC submits for billing purposes, and
- copies of all 1099 forms you file reporting your payments to the IC. (See Section C.)

Keep your IC files for at least six years.

B.   During the IC's Work Period

Treat the worker as an IC while he or she works for you—much the way you would the accountant who does your company's taxes or the lawyer who handles your legal work.

There are a number of work habits you must avoid:

- Don't supervise the IC or his or her assistants. The IC should perform the services without your direction. Your control should be limited to accepting or rejecting the final results the IC achieves.
- Don't let the IC work at your offices unless the nature of the services absolutely requires it—for example, where a computer consultant must work on your computers or a carpet installer is hired to lay carpet in your office.
- Don't give the IC employee handbooks or company policy manuals. If you need to provide ICs with orientation materials or suggestions, copies of governmental rules and regulations or similar items, put them all

in a separate folder titled Orientation Materials for Independent Contractors or Suggestions for Independent Contractors.

- Don't establish the IC's working hours.
- Avoid giving ICs so much work or such short deadlines that they have to work full time for you. It's best for ICs to work for others at the same time they work for you.
- Don't provide ongoing instructions or training. If the IC needs special training, he or she should not obtain it in-house and should pay for it himself or herself.
- Don't provide the IC with equipment or materials unless absolutely necessary.
- Don't give an IC business cards or stationery to use that has your company name on them.
- Don't give an IC a title within your company.
- Don't pay the IC's travel or other business expenses. Pay the IC enough to cover these expenses out of his or her own pocket.
- Don't give an IC benefits such as health insurance. Pay ICs enough to provide their own benefits.
- Don't require formal written reports. An occasional phone call inquiring into the work's progress is acceptable. But requiring regular written status reports indicates the worker is an employee.
- Don't invite an IC to employee meetings or functions.
- Don't refer to an IC as an employee, or to your company as the IC's employer, either verbally or in writing.
- Don't pay ICs on a weekly, bi-weekly or monthly basis as you pay employees. Rather, require all ICs to submit invoices to be paid for their work. Pay the invoices at the same time you pay other outside vendors.
- Obey the terms of your IC agreement. Among other things, this means that you can't fire the IC. You can only terminate the IC's contract according to its terms—for example, if the IC's services fail to satisfy the contract specifications.

- Don't give the IC new projects after the original project is completed without signing a new IC agreement.

C. After the IC's Services End

A hiring firm's work is never done. Even after an IC's services end, there is paperwork to complete. Failing to do so may mean severe penalties if you're audited.

1. IRS Form 1099

The single most important thing to do after an unincorporated IC's services end is to provide the worker and IRS with an IRS Form 1099-MISC reporting the compensation you paid the worker. Your failure to do so will result in severe penalties if the IRS later audits you and determines you misclassified the worker:

- you'll be required to pay the IRS twice as much for the misclassification.
- you'll lose the right to Safe Harbor protection for any payments not reported on Form 1099; this means you'll lose one of your most valuable legal rights in defending against the IRS.
- the IRS may impose a $100 fine for each Form 1099 you failed to file.

a. When Form 1099 must be filed

The basic rule is that you must file a Form 1099 whenever you pay an unincorporated IC—that is, an IC who is a sole proprietor or member of a partnership or limited liability company—$600 or more in a year for work done in the course of your trade or business.

EXAMPLE: The Acme Widget Company hires Thomas to install a new computer system. Acme classifies Thomas as an IC and pays him $2,000 during 2003. Thomas is a sole proprietor. Since Acme paid him more than $599, it must file a Form 1099 with the IRS reporting the payment.

In calculating whether the payments made to an IC total $600 or more during a year, you must include payments for parts or materials used by the IC in performing the services.

EXAMPLE: The Old Reliable Insurance Company pays $1,000 to an unincorporated auto repair shop to repair one of its insured's cars. The repair contract states that $300 is for labor and $700 is for parts. Old Reliable must report the entire $1,000 on Form 1099 because the parts were used by the repair shop to perform the car repair services.

b. Services in the course of your trade or business

You only need to file a Form 1099 when an IC performs services that are in the course of your trade or business. A trade or business is an activity carried on for gain or profit. You don't have to file a Form 1099 for payments for non-business related services. This includes payments you make to ICs for personal or household service—for example, payments to babysitters, gardeners and housekeepers. Running your home is not a profit-making activity.

EXAMPLE 1: Eddy owns several homes he rents out to tenants. He is in the business of renting houses. Eddy pays Linda, who operates a painting business as a sole proprietor, $1,750 to paint one of his rental houses. Eddy must report the $1,750 payment to Linda on Form 1099.

EXAMPLE 2: Eddy pays Linda $1,750 to paint his own home. He lives in this home with his wife and family and it is not a part of his home rental business. Eddy need not report this payment on Form 1099 because this work was not done in the course of his business.

Although nonprofit organizations are not engaged in a trade or business, they are still required to report payments made to ICs. Payments to ICs by federal, state or local government agencies must also be reported.

EXAMPLE: Leslie, owner of an unincorporated home repair business, is paid $1,000 for repair work on a church. Even though the church is a tax-exempt nonprofit organization and is not engaged in business, it must report the $1,000 payment to Leslie on Form 1099.

c. Payments exempt from Form 1099 filing requirement

You don't need to report on Form 1099 payments solely for merchandise or inventory. This includes raw materials and supplies that will become a part of merchandise you intend to sell.

EXAMPLE: The Acme Widget Company pays $5,000 to purchase 100 used widgets from Joe's Widgets, a sole proprietorship owned by Joe. Acme intends to fix up and resell the widgets. The payment to Joe need not be reported on Form 1099 because Acme is purchasing merchandise from Joe, not IC services.

In addition, you need not file a Form 1099 when you pay for:
- freight, storage and similar items
- telephone, telegraph and similar services, or
- rent to real estate agents.

You need not file 1099 forms for wages paid to your employees or for payments for their traveling or business expenses. These amounts are reported on Form W-2.

d. No Form 1099 needed for corporations

Subject to only a couple exceptions, you need not file a Form 1099 for payments made to an incorporated IC. This is one of the main advantages of hiring incorporated ICs because the IRS uses Form 1099 as an audit lead.

EXAMPLE: The Acme Sandblasting Company pays $5,000 to Yvonne, a CPA, to perform accounting services. Yvonne has formed her own one-person corporation called Yvonne's Accounting Services, Inc. Acme pays the corporation, not Yvonne personally. Since Acme is paying a corporation, it need not report the payment on Form 1099.

There are two exceptions to this rule:
1. Payments to medical corporations must be reported on Form 1099.

EXAMPLE: The Acme Sandblasting Company pays $2,000 to Dr. Smith to perform physicals for its employees. Smith has formed his own medical corporation, and the $2,000 is paid to the corporation, not to Smith personally. Nevertheless, the payment must be reported on Form 1099 because Smith is operating a medical corporation.

2. In addition, all federal executive agencies must prepare a Form 1099 for services performed by corporations where the corporation is paid $600 or more during the calendar year. This rule took effect in 1997 and only applies to payments made then or later.

Get the Corporation's Full Name and EIN

It's wise to make sure you have an IC corporation's full legal name and federal employer identification number. Without this information, you may not be able to prove to the IRS that the IC was incorporated. An easy way to do this is to have the IC fill out IRS Form W-9, Request for Taxpayer Identification Number, and keep it in your files. This simple form merely requires the IC to provide his or her corporation's name, address and federal EIN. (See Appendix 4 and the CD-ROM for a copy of the form. Look under filename IRSFORMW9.)

e. Payments to lawyers

If you pay $600 or more in one year to an attorney in the course of your trade or business—for example, to represent your company in a lawsuit or to draft contracts for your company—you must report the payment(s) on IRS Form 1099. This is true whether or not the attorney works as a sole proprietor, LLC, member of a partnership or a corporation. You do not have to report payments to attorneys for personal matters—for example, to handle your divorce.

There might be times when you will pay money to an attorney who does not represent your company—for example, an attorney who represents a plaintiff who sues your company. If you give an attorney who does not represent you a lump sum of money, but don't know how much of that money will go to the attorney or how much will go to the attorney's client, you must report the entire amount in box 13 on Form 1099. For example, if you pay $100,000 to an attorney to settle a case but don't know how much of the money will go to the attorney, you must report the entire amount in box 13 of Form 1099. If, on the other hand, you know that the lawyer's fee is $34,000, you would report only that amount in box 7 of Form 1099.

f. Filing procedures

One 1099 form must be filed for each IC to whom you paid $600 or more during the year. You must obtain original 1099 forms from the IRS. You cannot photocopy this form because it is a multi-copy form. Each 1099 form contains three parts and can be used for three different workers. All your 1099s must be submitted together along with one copy of IRS Form 1096, which is a transmittal form—the IRS equivalent of a cover letter. (See below for a sample.) You must obtain an original Form 1096 from the IRS; you cannot submit a photocopy. These forms can be obtained by calling the IRS at: 800-TAX-FORM (829-3676) or by contacting your local IRS office.

Filling out the 1099 form is easy. Follow this step-by-step approach:

- List your name and address in the first box titled "Payer's name."
- Enter your taxpayer identification number in the box entitled "Payer's Federal identification number."

- The IC is called the "Recipient" on this form, meaning the person who received payment from you. You must provide the IC's taxpayer identification number, name and address in the boxes indicated. For sole proprietors, you must list the individual's name first and then may list a different business name, though this is not required. You may not enter only a business name for a sole proprietor.
- You must enter the amount of your payments to the IC in box 7, entitled "Nonemployee compensation." Be sure to fill in the right box or the IRS will deem the 1099 form invalid.
- Finally, if you've done backup withholding for an IC who has not provided you with a taxpayer ID number, enter the amount withheld in box 4.

The 1099-MISC form contains five copies. These must be filed as follows:

- Copy A, the top copy, must be filed with the IRS no later than February 28 of the year af-

IRS Form 1099

ter payment was made to the IC; don't cut or separate this page, even though it has spaces for three workers.

- Copy 1 must be filed with your state taxing authority if your state has a state income tax. The filing deadline is probably February 28, but check with your state tax department to make sure. Your state may have a specific transmittal form you must obtain.
- You must give Copy B and Copy 2 to the worker no later than January 31 of the year after payment was made.
- Copy C is for you to retain for your files.

All the IRS copies of each 1099 form are filed together with Form 1096, a simple transmittal form. You must add up all the payments reported on all the 1099s and list the total in the box indicated on Form 1096. File the forms with the IRS Service Center listed on the reverse of Form 1096.

If you wish, you may file your 1099s electronically instead of by mail. You must first get permission from the IRS to do this by filing IRS Form 4419, Application for Filing Information Magnetically/Electronically. If you file electronically, the deadline for filing 1099s is March 31. For more information, you can visit the IRS website at www.irs.gov. Or call the IRS Information Reporting Program at 304-263-8700.

You may send 1099s to independent contractors via email, but only if the IC agrees. Otherwise, you must deliver the form in person or by mail.

When in Doubt, File a 1099

If you're not sure whether a 1099 form must be filed for a worker, go ahead and file one anyway. You lose nothing by doing so and will save yourself the severe consequences of not filing if you were in fact required to do so.

IRS FORM 1096

Do Not Staple	6969					
Form **1096** Department of the Treasury Internal Revenue Service		**Annual Summary and Transmittal of U.S. Information Returns**			OMB No. 1545-0108	2003

FILER'S name

Street address (including room or suite number)

City, state, and ZIP code

Name of person to contact	Telephone number ( )	**For Official Use Only**
E-mail address	Fax number ( )	

1 Employer identification number	2 Social security number	3 Total number of forms	4 Federal income tax withheld $	5 Total amount reported with this Form 1096 $

Enter an "X" in only one box below to indicate the type of form being filed. | If this is your **final return**, enter an "X" here . . . . ▶ ☐

W-2G 32	1098 81	1098-E 84	1098-T 83	1099-A 80	1099-B 79	1099-C 85	1099-CAP 73	1099-DIV 91	1099-G 86	1099-H 71	1099-INT 92	1099-LTC 93	1099-MISC 95
☐	☐	☐	☐	☐	☐	☐	☐	☐	☐	☐	☐	☐	☐

1099-MSA 94	1099-OID 96	1099-PATR 97	1099-Q 31	1099-R 98	1099-S 75	5498 28	5498-ESA 72	5498-MSA 27					
☐	☐	☐	☐	☐	☐	☐	☐	☐					

OBTAINING AN EXTENSION OF TIME TO FILE 1099S

You can obtain a 30-day extension of the time to file a 1099 form by filing IRS Form 8809, Extension of Time to File Information Returns. The form must be filed with the IRS by February 28. The extension is not granted automatically. You must explain the reason you need it. The IRS will send you a letter of explanation approving or denying your request. See the instructions for Form 8809.

You can find a copy of IRS Form 8809 in Appendix 4 and on the CD-ROM at the back of this book.

2.   IRS Forms 4669 and 4670

If the IRS determines that you intentionally misclassified a worker as an IC, it will impose a 20% income tax assessment, which means you will be required to pay the IRS an amount equal to 20% of all the payments you made to the worker.

However, this assessment will be reduced or eliminated if you can prove the worker reported and paid income taxes on the payments. Such a reduction is called an offset or abatement.

To obtain this abatement, you must file IRS Form 4669, Employee Wage Statement. This form states how much tax the worker paid on the wages in question. The worker must sign the form under penalty of perjury. You must file a Form 4669 for each worker involved along with Form 4670, Request for Relief From Payment of Income Tax Withholding, which is used to summarize and transmit the Form 4669.

Unfortunately, by the time your company is audited, typically one to three years after you hired the worker, it may be impossible for you to locate the worker or persuade him or her to complete and sign a Form 4669. This means you'll be unable to get the abatement.

A better approach is to be proactive and ask workers to sign a Form 4669 as soon as their services end. Retain the signed 4669s in your IC files. This way you'll be sure to be able to obtain an abatement if the worst happens: You're audited by the IRS and it claims you have intentionally misclassified the worker.

By April 15 of the year following the year an IC performed services for you, send him or her a blank Form 4669 to fill out and sign. Your IC agreement should contain a provision obligating the worker to provide the information required in the form. (See Chapter 13 for guidance on creating IC agreements.)

Beginning January 1, 2001, any business that hires an IC in California must notify the California Employment Development Department (EDD) and let it know some basic information about the IC, including how much the IC is being paid. This rule applies to any IC for whom the business must file IRS Form 1099 —in other words, to any IC whom the business pays $600 or more in the course of a year. The EDD and other California state agencies will use this information to aid in the enforcement of child support orders issued against ICs. The information is not supposed to be used for any other purpose—for example, as an audit lead.

A California business that uses an IC does not need to file the EED report at the same time that it files the 1099 form. Rather, the EDD reports must be filed within 20 days after the business:

- enters into an oral or written contract or contracts with an IC in California in which it promises to pay the IC a total of $600 or more for his or her services, or
- actually pays an IC $600 or more; if the business makes multiple payments to the IC, the business must file the form within 20 days after the total payments reach or surpass $600.

Thus, if a business uses many ICs, it will likely have to file EDD reports at various times throughout the year.

The business must give the EDD the following information:

- the IC's full name and Social Security number
- the business's name, address and telephone number
- the business's federal employer identification number, California state employer account number, Social Security number or other identifying number as required by the EDD
- the date the contract was signed, or if there is no contract, the date the payments to the IC reach or surpass $600, and
- the total dollar amount of the contract, if any, and the contract expiration date.

The EDD will retain information until November 1 following the tax year in which the contract is entered into, or if there is no contract, the tax year in which the payments to the IC exceeded $600.

The EDD has created a form for hiring firms to use to comply with these reporting requirements. It is Form DE 542, Report of Independent Contractor(s). You can download a copy from the EDD website at www.edd.cahwnet.gov/txicr.htm. You can also obtain a copy by calling the EDD at 888-745-3886 or by visiting your local employment tax office. Look in the state government section of your telephone book under "Employment Development Department."

Independent Contractor Agreements

This chapter explains why you should use written agreements with independent contractors, describes what such agreements should contain and provides sample language for you to use.

There are a number of ways you can use the suggested text offered here.

- You can draft contracts using the files contained on the CD-ROM. Using the suggested language from the CD gives you the greatest flexibility, as you will be able to pick and choose the clauses that apply to your situation. You can then use your final draft as a starting point of negotiations with the IC and tailor your final agreement to both of your needs.
- If you do not have access to a computer, you can retype the language suggested in this chapter to assemble your final agreement. Again, this will allow you to tailor your document to your specific needs.
- You can complete and use the tear-out sample forms in Appendix 3. While this may be the easiest option available to you, it is the least desirable. This is because IRS examiners and other government officials may be looking into your business matters. They are likely to look askance at a fill-in-the-blanks form, since that implies that you and the IC did not negotiate the agreement, but that you coerced him or her to sign according to your terms.

A. Using Written Agreements

Sign a written agreement with an IC before he or she starts work. An IC agreement serves two main purposes:

- it avoids later disputes by providing a written description of the services the IC is supposed to perform and how much the IC will be paid, and
- it describes the relationship between you and the IC to help make clear that the IC is not your employee.

1. Oral Agreements

Courts are crowded with lawsuits filed by people who entered into oral agreements with one another and later disagreed over what was said. Costly misunderstandings can develop if an IC performs services for you without a writing clearly stating what he or she is supposed to do and what will happen if it isn't done. Such misunderstandings may be innocent; you and the IC may have simply misinterpreted one another. Or they may be purposeful; without a writing to contradict him or her, an IC can claim that you orally agreed to anything.

SOME AGREEMENTS MUST BE IN WRITING

Some types of agreements must be in writing to be legally enforceable. Each state has a law, usually called the Statute of Frauds, listing the types of contracts that must be in writing to be valid.

A typical list includes:

- Any contract that cannot possibly be performed in less than one year. Example: John agrees to perform consulting services for Acme Corp. for the next two years for $2,000 per month. Since the agreement cannot be performed in less than one year, it must be in writing to be legally enforceable.
- Contracts for the sale of goods—that is, tangible personal property such as a computer or car—worth $500 or more.
- A promise to pay someone else's debt. For example, the president of a corporation personally guarantees to pay for the services you sell the corporation. The guarantee must be in writing to be legally enforceable.
- Contracts involving either the sale of real estate or real estate leases lasting more than one year.

Any transfer of copyright ownership must also be in writing to be valid.

Consider a good written IC agreement to be your legal lifeline. If disputes develop, the agreement will provide ways to solve them. If you and the IC end up in court, a written agreement will establish your legal duties to one another.

2.   Establishing IC Status

If your business is audited, an auditor will first ask to see your agreements with all workers you've classified as independent contractors. A well-drafted agreement that indicates that the IC is in business for himself or herself will help make clear to the auditor that the worker is an independent contractor. The document will help demonstrate that you and the worker intended to create an independent contractor relationship. And because written agreements with ICs have become a routine fact of business life, if you don't have one, you will immediately look suspect.

However, a written IC agreement is not a magic legal bullet. It will never by itself make a worker an IC. What really counts is the substance of how you treat a worker. If the agreement is accurate when it says the worker is in business, that will be helpful. But it won't help a bit if, in reality, you treat the worker like an employee.

> **EXAMPLE:** AcmeSoft, Inc., hires Pat to perform computer programming. It requires her to sign a document called an Independent Contractor Agreement. The agreement states that Pat is an IC and that AcmeSoft will exercise no control over Pat on the job. However, in reality Pat is treated just like an AcmeSoft employee: her work is closely supervised, she is paid biweekly, she has set hours of work and she works only for AcmeSoft. Pat is an AcmeSoft employee, despite what the agreement says.

B.   Drafting Agreements

You don't need to hire a lawyer to draft an independent contractor agreement. All you need is a brain and a little common sense. This chapter gives you guidance and suggested language to use as a starting point in fashioning your agreement to meet your needs.

1.   Standard Form Agreements

There are various standard form IC agreements you can obtain from stationery stores and other sources. These forms contain standard one-size-fits-all legalese and are not tailored for any particular occupation.

IRS and state auditors are well aware that hiring firms often have workers sign such generic IC agreements before they start work. The worker may not even bother to read the agreement and certainly makes no changes in it to reflect the real work situation.

The more an IC agreement is custom-tailored for each worker or group of workers performing similar tasks and reflects the true relationship between the hiring firm and workers, the more helpful it will be.

2.   The Drafting Process

Either you or the IC should begin the process of drafting an agreement by offering the other person proposed language to include. Then both of you can negotiate and make changes until you agree on a final version.

a.   Using the IC's agreement

Many ICs have their own agreements they've used in the past. If so, it's often wise to use that agreement as the starting point. This avoids giving government auditors the impression that the agreement is simply a company-drafted standard form the worker was forced to sign.

Read the IC's agreement carefully, because it may contain provisions unduly favorable to the IC and harmful to you. Make sure it contains all the necessary provisions discussed in this chapter. (See Section C.) If not, add them. You may also wish to add some provisions of your own or other optional provisions discussed below. (See Section D.)

Keep copies of the IC's original agreement and all the changes. These will help show auditors that the agreement was negotiated, not a contract you imposed on the IC.

b. Using your own agreement

If the IC does not have an agreement you can use, you'll have to provide one of your own. You can use the general IC agreement provided here and adapt it for almost any kind of work.

A copy of the Independent Contractor Agreement is included in Appendix 3. You can also find it on the CD-ROM under filename GENAGREE. (See Section E.)

Again, feel free to add provisions of your own or other options discussed below. (See Section D.)

In addition, because large numbers of ICs traditionally work in certain occupations, this chapter discusses five different agreements, each tailored for specific types of service providers, including:

- household workers (see Section F1)
- direct sellers (see Section F2)
- real estate salespeople (see Section F3)
- independent consultants (see Section F4), and
- contributors to a work made for hire (see Section F5).

Copies of all of these agreements are on the CD-ROM. You can also find them in Appendix 3.

Generally, independent contractor agreements for the development of computer software must contain a number of complex provisions concerning intellectual property, software testing, source code escrows and other matters outside the scope of this book. For a detailed discussion of software development agreements and sample forms, see *Software Development: A Legal Guide*, by attorney Stephen Fishman (Nolo).

3. Putting the Agreement Together

Make sure your IC agreement is properly signed and put together. This is not difficult if you know what to do. Follow the tips offered below.

a. Signatures

It's best for both you and the IC to sign the agreement. Signatures should be in ink. You and the IC need not be together when you sign, and it isn't necessary for you to sign at the same time. There's no legal requirement that the signatures be located in any specific place in a business contract, but they are customarily placed at the end of the agreement; that helps signify that you both have read and agreed to the entire document.

It's very important that both you and the IC sign the agreement properly. Failure to do so can have drastic consequences. How to sign depends on the legal form of your business and of the IC's business.

- **Sole proprietors.** If you or the IC are sole proprietors, you can simply sign your own names, because a sole proprietorship is not a separate legal entity.

  However, if an IC uses a fictitious business name, it's better for him or her to sign on behalf of the business. This will help show the worker is an IC, not your employee.

  EXAMPLE: You hire Chris Craft, an IC sole proprietor who runs a marketing research business. Instead of using his own name for the business, he calls it AAA Marketing Research. You should have him sign the IC agreement like this:

  AAA Marketing Research

  By: *Chris Craft*
  Chris Craft

- **Partnerships.** If either you or the IC is a partnership, a general partner should sign on the partnership's behalf. Only one partner needs to sign. The signature block for the partnership should state the partnership's name and the name and title of the person signing on the partnership's behalf. If a partner signs only his or her name without mentioning the partnership, the partnership is not bound by the agreement.

EXAMPLE: You hire Chris, the general partner of a partnership called The Chris Partnership, to perform marketing research. He should sign the contract on the partnership's behalf like this:

The Chris Partnership
A California Partnership

By: *Chris Craft*
      Chris Craft, General Partner

If an IC is a partnership and a person who is not a partner signs the agreement, the signature should be accompanied by a partnership resolution stating that the person signing the agreement has the authority to do so. The partnership resolution is a document signed by one or more of the general partners stating that the person named has the authority to sign contracts on the partnership's behalf.

- **Corporations.** If either you or the IC is a corporation, the agreement must be signed by someone who has authority to sign contracts on the corporation's behalf. The corporation's president or chief executive officer (CEO) is presumed to have this authority.

If someone other than the president of an incorporated IC signs—for example, the vice president, treasurer or other corporate officer—ask to see a board of directors' resolution or corporate bylaws authorizing him or her to sign. If the person signing doesn't have authority, the corporation won't be legally bound by the contract.

If you sign personally instead of on your corporation's behalf, you'll be personally liable for the contract.

The signature block for a corporation should state the name of the corporation and indicate by name and title the person signing on the corporation's behalf.

EXAMPLE: You hire Chris, an IC marketing consultant, to perform marketing research. Chris is president of his own corporation called Chris Marketing, Inc. Chris should sign the IC agreement on behalf of his corporation. The signature block should appear in the contract like this:

Chris Marketing, Inc.
A California Corporation

By: *Chris Craft*
      Chris Craft, President

b. Dates

When you sign an agreement, include the date and make sure the IC does, too. You can simply put a date line next to the place where each person signs—for example:

Date: _____, 20___.

You and the IC don't have to sign on the same day. Indeed, you can sign weeks apart.

c. Attachments or exhibits

An easy way to keep the main body of an IC agreement as short as possible is to use attachments, also called exhibits. You can use them to list lengthy details such as performance specifications. This makes the main body of the agreement shorter and easier to read.

If you have more than one attachment or exhibit, they should be numbered or lettered—for example, Attachment 1 or Exhibit A. Be sure to mention that they're included as part of the contract in the main body of the agreement.

d. Last-minute alterations

Sometimes it's necessary to make changes to a contract just before it's signed. If you use a computer to prepare the agreement, it's usually easy to make the changes and print out a new agreement.

However, it's not always necessary to prepare an all new contract. Instead, the changes may be handwritten or typed onto all existing copies of the agreement. The changes should also be initialed by those signing the agreement as close as possible to the place where the change is made. If both people who sign don't initial each change, questions might arise as to whether the change was part of the agreement.

e. Copies of the contract

Prepare at least two originals of your agreement. Make sure that each contains all the needed exhibits and attachments. Both you and the IC should sign both. Both you and the IC should keep one signed original of the agreement.

f. Faxing contracts

It has become very common for hiring firms and ICs to communicate by fax machine. They often send drafts of their proposed agreement back and forth to each other by fax. When a final agreement is reached, one signs a copy of the contract and faxes it to the other who signs it and faxes it back.

A faxed signature is probably legally sufficient if neither you nor the IC dispute that it is a fax of an original signature. However, if an IC claims that a faxed signature was forged, it could be difficult or impossible to prove it's genuine since it is very easy to forge a faxed signature with modern computer technology. Forgery claims are rare, however, so this is usually not a problem. Even so, it's a good practice for you and the IC to follow up the fax with signed originals exchanged by mail or express delivery.

C. Essential Provisions

A number of provisions should be included in most IC agreements. All of these sample clauses are included in the Independent Contractor Agreement. (See Section E for a sample of how an entire agreement might look when assembled.)

The entire text of the following agreement is on the CD-ROM in the back of this book under filename GENAGREE.

This information can be used as:
- a checklist when you review an IC agreement provided by a worker to make sure nothing important has been left out, or
- a starting point to draft your own agreement.

These provisions may be all you need for a simple IC agreement. Or you may need to combine them with some of your own clauses or one or more of the optional clauses discussed here. (See Section D.)

Title of agreement. Deceptively simple things such as what you call an IC agreement and yourself and the IC can have a big impact. You need not have a title for an IC agreement, but if you want one, call it Independent Contractor Agreement or Consulting Agreement. Consulting Agreement may sound a little more high-toned than Independent Contractor Agreement and is often used when contracting with skilled professionals to provide services. For example, IC agreements with computer software experts are often called Consulting Agreements. Do not use Employment Agreement as a title.

SUGGESTED LANGUAGE

INDEPENDENT CONTRACTOR AGREEMENT

 This text is on the CD-ROM under filename TITLE.

Names of IC and hiring firm. Do not refer to an IC as an employee or to yourself as an employer.

Initially, it's best to refer to the IC by his or her full name. If an IC is incorporated, use the corporate name, not the IC's own name—for example: "John Smith, Incorporated" instead of "John Smith." If the IC is unincorporated but is doing business under a fictitious business name, use that name. A fictitious business name or assumed name is a name sole proprietors or partners use to identify their businesses. For example, if consultant Al Brodsky calls his one-person marketing research business "ABC Marketing Research," use that name. This shows you're contracting with a business, not a single individual.

For the sake of brevity, it is usual to identify yourself and the IC by shorter names in the rest of the agreement. You can use an abbreviated version of the IC's full name—for example, ABC for ABC Marketing Research. Or you can refer to the IC simply as Contractor or Consultant.

Refer to yourself initially by your company name and subsequently by a short version of the name or as Client or Firm.

Also include the addresses of the principal places of business of the IC and yourself. If you or the IC have more than one office or workplace, the principal place of business is the main office or workplace.

> **Names of IC and Hiring Firm**
> This Agreement is made between [Your company name] (Client) with a principal place of business at [Your business address] and [IC's name] (Contractor), with a principal place of business at [IC's address].

 The text of this clause is on the CD-ROM under filename NAMES.

1. Term of Agreement

The term of the agreement should be as short as possible. A good outside time limit is six months. A longer term makes the agreement look like an employment agreement, not an IC agreement. If the work is not completed at the end of six months, you can negotiate and sign a new agreement.

The date the agreement begins can be the date you sign it or another date either before or after you sign.

> **Term of Agreement**
> This Agreement will become effective on _____, 20___, and will end no later than _____, 20___.

 The text of this clause is on the CD-ROM under filename TERMAGR.

2. Services to Be Performed

The agreement should describe in as much detail as possible what you expect the IC to do. You must word the description carefully to concentrate on the results you expect him or her to achieve. Don't tell the IC how to achieve the result; that would indicate that you have the right to control how the IC performs the work. Such a right of control is the hallmark of an employment relationship.

EXAMPLE: Jack hires Jill to prepare an index for his multi-volume history of ancient Sparta. Jack describes the results he expects Jill to achieve like this: "Contractor agrees to prepare an index of Client's *History of Sparta* of at least 100 single-spaced pages. Contractor will provide Client with a printout of the finished index and a 3.5 inch computer disk version in ASCII format."

Jack should not tell Jill how to create the index. For example, Jack should not write: "Contractor will prepare an alphabetical three-level index of Client's *History of Sparta*. Contractor will first prepare 3-by-5-inch index cards listing every index entry beginning with Chapter One. After each chapter is completed, Contractor will deliver the index cards to Client for Client's approval. When index cards have been created for all 50 chapters, Contractor will create a computer version of the index using Complex Software Version 7.6. Contractor will then print out and edit the index and deliver it to Client for approval."

It's perfectly okay for you to establish very detailed specifications for the IC's finished work product. But the specs should only describe the end results the IC must achieve, not how to obtain those results.

You can include the description in the main body of the Agreement. Or if it's a lengthy explanation, put it on a separate attachment.

SUGGESTED LANGUAGE: ALTERNATIVE A

Services to Be Performed
Contractor agrees to perform the following services: [Briefly describe services you want performed by IC.]

SUGGESTED LANGUAGE: ALTERNATIVE B

Services to Be Performed
Contractor agrees to perform the services described in Exhibit A, which is attached to this Agreement.

The text of these clauses is on the CD-ROM under filename SERVICES. Choose Alternative A if you include the explanation of services in the contract. Choose Alternative B if the explanation of the services is attached to the main contract.

3. Payment

Independent contractors are usually paid in one of two ways:
- a fixed fee, or
- by unit of time.

a. Fixed fee

Paying an IC a fixed sum for the entire job, rather than an hourly or daily rate, strongly supports a finding of independent contractor status. If paid a fixed sum, the IC risks losing money if the project takes longer than expected, or may earn a substantial profit if the project is completed quickly. Having the opportunity to earn a profit or suffer a loss is a very strong indication of IC status. (See Chapter 3 for information on what makes someone an IC.)

SUGGESTED LANGUAGE: ALTERNATIVE A

Payment
In consideration for the services to be performed by Contractor, Client agrees to pay Contractor $[State amount] according to the terms set out below.

 The text of this clause is on the CD-ROM under filename PAYMENT. Choose Alternative A if you will pay the IC a fixed fee.

b. Unit of time

Paying a worker by the hour or other unit of time usually indicates that the worker is an employee because the worker has no real risk of loss. However, it's customary for ICs in some occupations—for example, lawyers and accountants—to charge by the hour. Government auditors would likely not challenge the IC status of workers in these occupations as long as they are in business for themselves. (See Chapter 3 for information on what makes someone an IC.)

SUGGESTED LANGUAGE: ALTERNATIVE B

> **Payment**
> In consideration for the services to be performed by Contractor, Client agrees to pay Contractor at the rate of $[State amount] per [Hour, day, week or other unit of time] according to the terms of payment set out below.

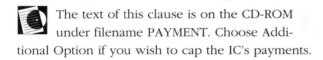 The text of this clause is on the CD-ROM under filename PAYMENT. Choose Alternative B if you will pay the IC by the hour.

If you pay by the hour, you may wish to place a cap on the IC's total compensation. This may be a particularly good idea if you're unsure of the IC's reliability or efficiency.

ADDITIONAL OPTION

> **Payment**
> Unless otherwise agreed in writing, Client's maximum liability for all services performed during the term of this Agreement shall not exceed $[State the top limit on what you will pay].

 The text of this clause is on the CD-ROM under filename PAYMENT. Choose Additional Option if you wish to cap the IC's payments.

4. Terms of Payment

Since an IC is running an independent business, he or she should submit an invoice setting out the amount you have to pay.

a. Fixed fee agreements

The following provision requires you to pay the IC's fixed fee within a reasonable time after the work is completed. If you wish, you can delete "reasonable time" and add a specific time period for payment—for example, 30, 60 or 90 days.

SUGGESTED LANGUAGE: ALTERNATIVE A

> Upon completing Contractor's services under this Agreement, Contractor shall submit an invoice. Client shall pay Contractor the compensation described within a reasonable time after receiving Contractor's invoice.

 The text of this clause is on the CD-ROM under filename TERMPAY. Choose Alternative A if you will pay the IC a fixed fee.

b. Divided payments

You can also opt to pay part of a fixed fee when the agreement is signed and the remainder when the work is finished.

The following provision allows you to pay a specific amount when the IC signs the agreement and then the rest when the work is finished. The amount of the up-front payment is subject to negotiation. It could be as little as 10% or less of the entire fixed fee.

SUGGESTED LANGUAGE: ALTERNATIVE B

> Contractor shall be paid $[State amount] upon signing this Agreement and the rest of the sum described above when the Contractor completes services and submits an invoice.

The text of this clause is on the CD-ROM under filename TERMPAY. Choose Alternative B if you will pay the IC in divided payments.

c. Installment payments

ICs may balk at accepting a fixed fee for complex or long-term projects due to difficulties in accurately estimating how long the job will take. One way to deal with this problem is to break the job into phases or milestones and pay the IC a fixed fee when each phase is completed. If, after one or two phases are completed, it looks like the fixed sum won't be enough to complete the entire project, you can always renegotiate the agreement.

This type of arrangement is far more supportive of an IC relationship than hourly payment, since the IC still has some risk of loss.

To do this, draw up a schedule of installment payments tying each payment to the IC's completion of specific services and attach it to the agreement. The main body of the agreement should simply refer to the attached payment schedule.

SUGGESTED LANGUAGE: ALTERNATIVE C

Terms of Payment

Client shall pay Contractor according to the following schedule of payments

1. $[State sum] when an invoice is submitted and the following services are complete:

    [Describe first stage of services]

2. $[State sum] when an invoice is submitted and the following services are complete:

    [Describe second stage of services]

3. $[State sum] when an invoice is submitted and the following services are complete:

    [Describe third stage of services]

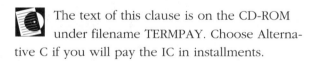 The text of this clause is on the CD-ROM under filename TERMPAY. Choose Alternative C if you will pay the IC in installments.

d.   Payments by unit of time

Even ICs who are paid by the hour or other unit of time should submit invoices. Do not automatically pay an IC weekly or bi-weekly the way you pay employees. It's best to pay ICs no more than once a month, since this is how businesses are normally paid.

SUGGESTED LANGUAGE: ALTERNATIVE D

Terms of Payment

Contractor shall submit an invoice to Client on the last day of each month for the work performed during that month. The invoice should include: an invoice number, the dates covered by the invoice, the hours expended and a summary of the work performed. Client shall pay Contractor's fee within a reasonable time after receiving the invoice.

 The text of this clause is on the CD-ROM under filename TERMPAY. Choose Alternative D if you will pay the IC according to the number of hours worked.

5. Expenses

An IC should usually not be reimbursed for expenses. Instead, compensate the IC well enough so that he or she can pay the expenses directly out of his or her own pocket.

However, it sometimes is customary to pay the expenses of certain types of ICs. For example, attorneys typically charge their clients separately for photocopying charges, deposition fees and travel. Where there is an otherwise clear IC relationship and payment of expenses is customary in the IC's trade or business, you can probably get away with doing it.

SUGGESTED LANGUAGE

Expenses

Contractor shall be responsible for all expenses incurred while performing services under this Agreement. This includes license fees, memberships and dues; automobile and other travel expenses; meals and entertainment; insurance premiums; and all salary, expenses and other compensation paid to employees or contract personnel the Contractor hires to complete the work under this Agreement.

 The text of this clause is on the CD-ROM under filename EXPENSE.

6. Independent Contractor Status

One of the most important functions of an independent contractor agreement is to help establish that the worker is an IC, not your employee. The key to doing this is to make clear that the IC, not the hiring firm, has the right to control how the work will be performed.

You will need to emphasize the factors the IRS and other agencies consider in determining whether an IC controls how the work is done. (See Chapter 3 for information on these factors.)

When you draft your own agreement, include only those provisions that apply to your particular situation. The more that apply, the more likely the worker will be viewed as an IC.

SUGGESTED LANGUAGE

Independent Contractor Status

Contractor is an independent contractor, not Client's employee. Contractor's employees or contract personnel are not Client's employees. Contractor and Client agree to the following rights consistent with an independent contractor relationship.

- Contractor has the right to perform services for others during the term of this Agreement.
- Contractor has the sole right to control and direct the means, manner and method by which the services required by this Agreement will be performed.
- Contractor has the right to perform the services required by this Agreement at any place, location or time.
- Contractor will furnish all equipment and materials used to provide the services required by this Agreement.
- Contractor has the right to hire assistants as subcontractors, or to use employees to provide the services required by this Agreement.
- The Contractor or Contractor's employees or contract personnel shall perform the services required by this Agreement; Client shall not hire, supervise or pay any assistants to help Contractor.
- Neither Contractor nor Contractor's employees or contract personnel shall receive any training from Client in the skills necessary to perform the services required by this Agreement.
- Client shall not require Contractor or Contractor's employees or contract personnel to devote full time to performing the services required by this Agreement.

 The text of this clause is on the CD-ROM under filename STATUS.

To obtain Safe Harbor protection from the IRS, you must have a reasonable basis for classifying the workers involved as ICs. One reasonable basis is that such classification is a longstanding practice of a significant segment of your trade or industry and that you relied on this longstanding practice in making your classification. (See Chapter 4 for more about Safe Harbor protection.)

If you are relying on industry practice, you should say so in your agreement.

SUGGESTED LANGUAGE

> OPTIONAL: Contractor acknowledges that Contractor has been classified as an independent contractor because such classification is a longstanding practice of a significant segment of Client's trade or industry.

 The text of this clause is on the CD-ROM under filename STATUS.

7. Business Permits, Certificates and Licenses

The IC should have all business permits, certificates and licenses needed to perform the work. For example, if you hire an IC to perform construction work, the IC should have a contractor's license if one is required by your state's law. Lack of such licenses and permits makes a worker look like an employee, not an IC in business for himself or herself. The IC should obtain such licenses and permits on his or her own; you should not pay for them.

SUGGESTED LANGUAGE

> **Business Permits, Certificates and Licenses**
> Contractor has complied with all federal, state and local laws requiring business permits, certificates and licenses required to carry out the services to be performed under this Agreement.

 The text of this clause is on the CD-ROM under filename PERMIT.

8. State and Federal Taxes

Do not pay or withhold any taxes on an IC's behalf. Doing so is a very strong indicator that the worker is an employee. Indeed, some courts have held that workers were employees based upon this factor alone.

Include a straightforward provision, such as the one suggested below, to help make sure the IC understands that he or she must pay all applicable taxes.

SUGGESTED LANGUAGE

> **State and Federal Taxes**
> Client will not:
> - withhold FICA (Social Security and Medicare taxes) from Contractor's payments or make FICA payments on Contractor's behalf
> - make state or federal unemployment compensation contributions on Contractor's behalf, or
> - withhold state or federal income tax from Contractor's payments.
>
> Contractor shall pay all taxes incurred while performing services under this Agreement—including all applicable income taxes and, if Contractor is not a corporation, self-employment (Social Security) taxes. Upon demand, Contractor shall provide Client with proof that such payments have been made.

 The text of this clause is on the CD-ROM under filename TAXES.

9.   Fringe Benefits

Do not provide either ICs or their employees with fringe benefits that you provide your own employees such as health insurance, pension benefits, childcare allowances or even the right to use employee facilities such as an exercise room.

Fringe Benefits

Contractor understands that neither Contractor nor Contractor's employees or contract personnel are eligible to participate in any employee pension, health, vacation pay, sick pay or other fringe benefit plan of Client.

 The text of this clause is on the CD-ROM under filename FRINGE.

10.   Workers' Compensation

If a worker qualifies as an IC under your state's workers' compensation law, do not provide the IC with workers' compensation coverage.

If the IC has employees, the IC should provide them with workers' compensation coverage. If an IC's employees lack workers' compensation coverage, it's likely your own workers' compensation insurer will require you to provide coverage under your own policy and pay an additional workers' compensation premium. To avoid this, require ICs to provide you with a certificate of insurance establishing that an IC's employees are covered by workers' compensation insurance. A certificate of insurance is issued by the workers' compensation insurer and is written proof that the IC has a workers' compensation policy.

Whether an IC has employees or not, you may want to require the worker to have his or her own workers' compensation coverage. Self-employed people who have no employees are usually not required to have workers' compensation coverage,

but they usually can obtain it. More and more hiring firms are requiring this because their own workers' compensation insurers may require them to cover ICs who don't have their own workers' compensation insurance. (See Chapter 7 for more about workers' compensation issues and ICs.)

Workers' Compensation

Client shall not obtain workers' compensation insurance on behalf of Contractor or Contractor's employees. If Contractor hires employees to perform any work under this Agreement, Contractor will cover them with workers' compensation insurance and provide Client with a certificate of workers' compensation insurance before the employees begin the work.

 The text of this clause is on the CD-ROM under filename WORKCOMP.

Workers' Compensation

If not operating as a corporation, Contractor shall obtain workers' compensation insurance coverage for Contractor. Contractor shall provide Client with proof that such coverage has been obtained before starting work.

 The text of this clause is on the CD-ROM under filename WORKCOMP. Choose Optional Language if you want the worker to provide his or her own workers' compensation coverage. This clause is best suited to workers who have no employees of their own.

11.   Unemployment Compensation

If the worker qualifies as an IC under your state's unemployment compensation law, do not pay unemployment compensation taxes for him or her.

(See Chapter 6 for more about unemployment issues and ICs.) The IC will not be entitled to receive unemployment compensation benefits when the work is finished or the agreement terminated.

Unemployment Compensation

Client shall make no state or federal unemployment compensation payments on behalf of Contractor or Contractor's employees or contract personnel. Contractor will not be entitled to these benefits in connection with work performed under this Agreement.

 The text of this clause is on the CD-ROM under filename UNEMPL.

12. Insurance

An IC should have his or her own liability insurance policy just like any other business; you need not provide it. This type of coverage insures the IC against personal injury or property damage claims by others. For example, if an IC accidentally injures a bystander while performing services for you, the IC's liability policy will pay the costs of defending a lawsuit and pay damages up to the limits of the policy coverage. This helps eliminate an injured person's motivation to attempt to recover from you as well as the IC for fear the IC won't be able to pay. Also, having insurance helps show that the IC is in business.

The IC should also agree to indemnify—that is, repay—you if somebody he or she injures decides to sue you.

Insurance

Client shall not provide any insurance coverage of any kind for Contractor or Contractor's employees or contract personnel. Contractor agrees to maintain an insurance policy of at least $[State amount] to cover any negligent acts committed by Contractor or Contractor's employees or agents while performing services under this Agreement.

Contractor shall indemnify and hold Client harmless from any loss or liability arising from performing services under this Agreement.

 The text of this clause is on the CD-ROM under filename INSURE.

13. Terminating the Agreement

The circumstances under which you may terminate the agreement are important. You should not retain the right to fire or terminate an IC for any reason or no reason at all as you would with an employee under the generally prevailing employment-at-will doctrine. This type of unfettered termination right strongly indicates an employment relationship. (See Chapter 3 for more about characteristics that make a worker an IC.) Instead, you should be able to terminate the agreement only if you have a reasonable cause to do so.

a. Termination for reasonable cause

You should have the limited right to terminate the IC only if you have a reasonable cause to do so. There are two types of reasonable cause. The first is a serious violation of the agreement by the IC. It would include, for example, the IC's failure to produce results or meet the deadline specified in the agreement.

You can also terminate the agreement if the IC does something to expose you to liability for personal injury or property damage—for example, if the IC's negligence injures your employees, damages your property or damages someone else's property. You don't have to terminate the agreement if this happens, but you have the option of doing so. You may not want to continue dealing with an IC who is extremely careless.

If you fire an IC who performs adequately and otherwise satisfies the terms of the agreement, you'll be liable to him or her for breaking the agreement. The IC can sue you in court and obtain a judgment against you for money damages.

SUGGESTED LANGUAGE: ALTERNATIVE A

Terminating the Agreement

With reasonable cause, either Client or Contractor may terminate this Agreement, effective immediately upon giving written notice.

Reasonable cause includes:

- a material violation of this Agreement, or
- any act exposing the other party to liability to others for personal injury or property damage.

 The text of this clause is on the CD-ROM under filename TERMIN. Choose Alternative A if you wish to allow either you or the worker to end the agreement based on reasonable cause.

b.   Termination with notice

If you just can't live with a restricted termination right, your best approach is to add a provision giving you the right to terminate the agreement for any reason upon written notice. The notice term can be anywhere from a few days to 30 days or more, depending upon the length of the contract term. The longer the term, the more notice you should give.

SUGGESTED LANGUAGE: ALTERNATIVE B

Terminating the Agreement

Either party may terminate this Agreement any time by giving [state term of notice] written notice to the other party of the intent to terminate.

The text of this clause is on the CD-ROM under filename TERMIN. Choose Alternative B if you wish to allow either you or the worker to end the agreement by giving written notice.

14.   Exclusive Agreement

Business contracts normally contain a provision stating that the written agreement is the complete and exclusive agreement between those involved. This reinforces the idea that what is written in the contract is all the agreement entails. Neither you nor the IC can later bring up side letters, oral statements or other material not covered by the contract. A clause such as this avoids later claims that promises not contained in the written contract were made and broken.

Because of this provision, you must make sure that all documents containing any representations made by the IC upon which you are relying are attached to the agreement as exhibits. This may include the IC's proposal or bid, sales literature, side letters and so forth. If they aren't attached, they won't be considered to be part of the agreement.

SUGGESTED LANGUAGE

Exclusive Agreement

This is the entire Agreement between Contractor and Client.

 The text of this clause is on the CD-ROM under filename EXCLUS.

15. Severability

This standard contract provision permits the agreement as a whole to continue even if portions of it are found invalid by a court or arbitrator. For example, if for some reason a court found the provision requiring the IC to obtain workers' compensation coverage to be invalid, the rest of the contract would remain in force.

SUGGESTED LANGUAGE

Severability

If any part of this Agreement is held unenforceable, the rest of the Agreement will continue in effect.

 The text of this clause is on the CD-ROM under filename SEVERAB.

16. Applicable Law

Each state has its own set of laws, and you will have to look to these laws if you and the IC ever have a dispute over the agreement. If you and the IC have offices in the same state, that state's law will apply. But if your offices are in different states, you'll need to decide which state's law should govern the agreement. There is some advantage to having the law of your own state govern, since your local attorney will likely be more familiar with that law.

SUGGESTED LANGUAGE

Applicable Law

This Agreement will be governed by the laws of the state of [Indicate state in which you have main office].

 The text of this clause is on the CD-ROM under filename APPLLAW.

17. Notices

When you want to do something important involving the agreement—terminate it, for example—you need to tell the IC about it. This is called giving notice. The following provision gives you several options for providing the IC with notice: by personal delivery, by mail, or by fax or telex followed by a confirming letter.

If you give notice by mail, it is not effective until three days after it's sent. For example, if you want to end the agreement on 30 days notice and mail your notice of termination to the IC, the agreement will not end until 33 days after you mailed the notice.

SUGGESTED LANGUAGE

Notices

All notices and other communications in connection with this Agreement shall be in writing and shall be considered given as follows:

- when delivered personally to the recipient's address as stated on this Agreement
- three days after being deposited in the United States mail, with postage prepaid to the recipient's address as stated on this Agreement, or
- when sent by fax or telex to the last fax or telex number of the recipient known to the person giving notice. Notice is effective upon receipt provided that a duplicate copy of the notice is promptly given by first class mail, or the recipient delivers a written confirmation of receipt.

 The text of this clause is on the CD-ROM under filename NOTICE.

18. No Partnership

You want to make sure that you and the IC are separate legal entities, not partners or co-venturers. If an IC is viewed as your partner, you'll be liable for his or her debts, and the IC will have the power to make contracts that obligate you to others without your consent.

> **No Partnership**
> This Agreement does not create a partnership relationship. Contractor does not have authority to enter into contracts on Client's behalf.

 The text of this clause is on the CD-ROM under filename NOPART.

19. Assignment

Assignment is a catchall term used to describe two different things: assignment of rights under the contract and delegation of duties. An assignment is the process by which rights or benefits under a contract are transferred to someone else. For example, the IC might assign to someone else the right to be paid the money due for performing services for you. Delegation is the flipside of assignment. Instead of transferring benefits under a contract, the duties are transferred. For example, an IC may delegate to someone else the duty to perform the services for which you've contracted.

Delegation of the IC's duties is the most important issue here. You've hired the IC to do the job, but the IC might try to get someone else to do it in his or her place. Fortunately, the law protects you against an IC who tries to fob off the work on someone else. If the work the IC has agreed to do involves personal services, the IC cannot delegate it to someone else without your consent.

Examples of personal services include those by professionals such as lawyers, physicians or architects. When you hire an architect, he or she can't pass your project to another architectural firm without your consent. Courts consider it unfair for either a client or IC to change horses in midstream. Services by IC writers, artists and musicians are also considered too personal to be delegated without the hiring firm's consent.

Service contracts with ICs involving more mechanical tasks ordinarily are delegable without the hiring firm's consent. For example, a contract to construct or paint a house would ordinarily be delegable. However, even in these cases, the IC can't delegate his or her duties to a person who lacks the skill or experience to complete the work satisfactorily.

Your agreement need not mention assignment and delegation. The work will be assignable or delegable subject to the restrictions noted. This is the best option in most cases.

a.   Assignment allowed

If you absolutely do not care who does the work required by the agreement, choose Alternative A to allow an unrestricted right of assignment and delegation.

This clause can help you if you are challenged on your treatment of the worker as an IC. It is strong evidence of an IC relationship because it shows you're only concerned with results, not who achieves them. It also demonstrates your lack of control over the IC.

Note, however, that if you include this clause in the agreement, the restrictions on assignment and delegation discussed above will not apply—that is, the IC will be able to delegate his or her duties even if they involve personal services.

> **Assignment**
> Either Contractor or Client may assign, delegate or subcontract any rights or obligations under this Agreement.

 The text of this clause is on the CD-ROM under filename ASSIGNM. Choose Alternative A if you wish to allow the IC to assign contractual rights to others.

b. Approval required

There may be some situations in which you really don't want an IC to assign his or her contractual duties without your consent. This is usually where you hire a particular IC because of his or her special expertise, reputation for performance or financial stability.

SUGGESTED LANGUAGE: ALTERNATIVE B

Assignment

Contractor may not assign, delegate or subcontract any rights or obligations under this Agreement without Client's prior written approval.

The text of this clause is on the CD-ROM under filename ASSIGNM. Choose Alternative B if you wish to restrict the IC's right to assign contractual rights to others.

20. Resolving Disputes

If you and the IC get into a dispute—for example, over the price or quality of the IC's services—it is best if the two of you can resolve the matter through informal negotiations. This is by far the easiest and cheapest way to resolve any problem.

Unfortunately, informal negotiations don't always work. If you and the IC reach an impasse, you may need help. This part of the agreement describes how you will handle any disputes you can't resolve on your own. Three alternatives are provided: mediation, arbitration and court. Choose one.

a. Mediation

Choose Alternative A if you want to try mediation before going to court. Mediation, an increasingly popular alternative to going to court, works like this: You and the IC agree on a neutral third person to try to help you settle your dispute. The mediator has no power to impose a decision—but he or she can help you arrive at one. In other words, unless both parties agree with the resolution, there is no resolution.

Insert the place where the mediation meeting will occur. You'll usually want it in the city or county where your office is located. You don't want to have to travel a long distance to attend a mediation.

If the mediation doesn't help resolve the dispute, you still have the option of going to court. If you wish, you may include the optional clause requiring the loser in any court litigation to pay the other person's attorney fees.

SUGGESTED LANGUAGE: ALTERNATIVE A

Resolving Disputes

If a dispute arises under this Agreement, the parties agree to first try to resolve the dispute with the help of a mutually agreed-upon mediator in _____. Any costs and fees other than attorney fees associated with the mediation shall be shared equally by the parties.

If the dispute is not resolved within 30 days after it is referred to the mediator, any party may take the matter to court.

OPTIONAL: If any court action is necessary to enforce this Agreement, the prevailing party shall be entitled to reasonable attorney fees, costs and expenses in addition to any other relief to which he or she may be entitled.

The text of this clause is on the CD-ROM under filename RESOLVE. Choose Alternative A if you wish to require mediation to resolve disputes under the agreement.

b.   Arbitration

Choose Alternative B if you want to avoid court altogether. Under this clause, you and the IC first try to resolve your dispute through mediation. If this doesn't work, you must submit the dispute to binding arbitration. Arbitration is usually like an informal court trial without a jury, but involves arbitrators instead of judges.

You and the IC can agree on anyone to serve as the arbitrator. Arbitrators are often retired judges, lawyers or people with special expertise in the field involved. Businesses often use private dispute resolution services that maintain a roster of arbitrators. The best known of these is the American Arbitration Association, which has offices in most major cities.

You may be represented by a lawyer in the arbitration, but it's not required. The arbitrator's decision is final and binding—that is, you can't go to court and try the dispute again if you don't like the arbitrator's decision, except in unusual cases where the arbitrator was guilty of fraud, misconduct or bias.

By using this provision, then, you give up your right to go to court. The advantage is that arbitration is usually much cheaper and faster than court litigation.

This provision states that the arbitrator's award can be converted into a court judgment. This means that if the losing side doesn't pay the money required by the award, the other party can easily obtain a judgment and enforce it like any other court judgment—for example, have the losing side's bank accounts and property seized to pay the amount due.

The provision leaves it up to the arbitrator to decide who should pay the costs and fees associated with the arbitration.

You must insert the place where the arbitration hearing will occur. For your own convenience, you'll usually want it in the city or county where your office is located.

Resolving Disputes

If a dispute arises under this Agreement, the parties agree to first try to resolve the dispute with the help of a mutually agreed-upon mediator in _____. Any costs and fees other than attorney fees associated with the mediation shall be shared equally by the parties.

If it proves impossible to arrive at a mutually satisfactory solution through mediation, the parties agree to submit the dispute to a mutually agreed-upon arbitrator in _____. Judgment upon the award rendered by the arbitrator may be entered in any court having jurisdiction to do so. Costs of arbitration, including attorney fees, will be allocated by the arbitrator.

The text of this clause is on the CD-ROM under filename RESOLVE. Choose Alternative B if you wish to require arbitration to resolve disputes under the agreement.

For a detailed discussion of mediation and arbitration, see *Mediate Your Dispute*, by Peter Lovenheim (Nolo).

c.   Court litigation

Choose Alternative C if you want to resolve disputes by going to court. This is the traditional way contract disputes are resolved. It is also usually the most expensive and time consuming.

The optional language provides that if either person has to sue the other in court to enforce the agreement and wins, the loser is required by this clause to pay the other person's attorney fees and expenses. Without this clause, each side must pay its own expenses. This can help make filing a lawsuit economically feasible and will give the IC an additional reason to settle if you have a strong case.

However, there may be situations in which you do not want to include an attorney fees provision. An IC who has little or no money won't be able to pay the fees, so the provision is useless as far as you're concerned. What's worse, an attorney fees provision could help the IC convince a lawyer to file a case against you, since the lawyer will be looking to you for his or her fee instead of asking the IC to provide a cash retainer up front. If you have substantially more financial resources than the IC or think it's more likely you'll break the contract than the IC will, an attorney fees provision is not in your interests—and you should not include the optional clause in your agreement.

SUGGESTED LANGUAGE: ALTERNATIVE C

Resolving Disputes

If a dispute arises under this Agreement, any party may take the matter to court.

OPTIONAL: If any court action is necessary to enforce this Agreement, the prevailing party shall be entitled to reasonable attorney fees, costs and expenses in addition to any other relief to which he or she may be entitled.

The text of this clause is on the CD-ROM under filename RESOLVE. Choose Alternative C if you wish to require court action to enforce the agreement. You can also find an attorney fee clause on the CD-ROM under filename FEES.

21. Signatures

The end of the main body of the agreement should contain spaces for you to sign, write in your title and date—and in which the IC can also sign and provide a Taxpayer ID Number.

⚠ The Importance of Numbers

Be sure to obtain the IC's Social Security number or taxpayer ID number if the IC is a corporation or partnership. If you don't, you'll have to withhold federal income taxes from the IC's pay. (See Chapter 12 for more about this issue.)

SUGGESTED LANGUAGE

Signatures

Client: _____
              Name of Client

By: _____
              Signature

_____
Typed or Printed Name

Title: _____

Date: _____

Contractor: _____
              Name of Contractor

By: _____
              Signature

_____
Typed or Printed Name

Title: _____

Taxpayer ID Number: _____

Date: _____

 The text of this clause is on the CD-ROM under filename SIGNS.

SIGNING BY FAX

It is increasingly common to use faxed signatures to finalize contracts. If you use faxed signatures, you should include a specific provision at the end of the agreement.

OPTIONAL LANGUAGE IF FAXED

Signatures

Contractor and Client agree that this Agreement will be considered signed when the signature of a party is delivered by facsimile transmission. Signatures transmitted by facsimile shall have the same effect as original signatures.

The text of this clause is on the CD-ROM under filename SIGNS. Add this clause if you wish to have the parties sign by fax.

D. Optional Provisions

The following provisions are not absolutely necessary to include in every IC agreement, but you may want to include one or more in your agreement depending on the circumstances.

1. Modifying the Agreement

No contract is engraved in stone. You and the IC can always modify or amend your contract if circumstances change. You can even agree to call the whole thing off and cancel your agreement.

EXAMPLE: Barbara, an IC well digger, agrees to dig a 50-foot-deep well on property owned by Kate for $2,000. After digging ten feet, Barbara hits solid rock that no one knew was there. To complete the well, she'll have to lease expensive heavy equipment. To defray the added expense, she asks Kate to pay her $4,000 instead of $2,000 for the work. Kate agrees. Barbara and Kate have amended their original agreement.

Neither you nor the IC is ever obligated to accept a proposed modification to your contract. Either of you can always say no and accept the consequences, which at its most dire, may mean a court battle over breaking the original contract. However, you're usually better off reaching some sort of accommodation with the IC, unless he or she is totally unreasonable.

Unless your contract is one that must be in writing to be legally valid—most commonly, an agreement that can't be performed in less than one year—it can usually be modified by an oral agreement. In other words, you need not write down the changes.

EXAMPLE: Art signs a contract with Zeno to build an addition to his house. Halfway through the project, Art decides that he wants Zeno to do some extra work not covered by their original agreement. Art and Zeno have a telephone conversation in which Zeno agrees to do the extra work for extra money. Although nothing is put in writing, their change to their original agreement is legally enforceable.

In the real world, people make changes to their contracts all the time and never write them down. The flexibility afforded by such an informal approach to contract amendments might be just what you want. However, you should be aware that misunderstandings and disputes can arise from this approach. It's always best to have some sort of writing showing what you've agreed to do. You can do this informally. For example, you can simply send a confirming letter following a telephone call with an IC summarizing the changes you both agreed to make. Be sure to keep a copy for your files. Or if the amendment involves a contract provision that is very important—the IC's payment, for example—you can insist on a written amendment signed by you and the IC.

You may if you wish, however, add a provision to the contract requiring that all amendments be in writing signed by you and the IC before they become effective. You can still negotiate changes by phone or fax, but they won't take effect until you and the IC sign a formal amendment to the agreement. This eliminates even the possibility of orally amending the agreement. This approach requires more time and paperwork, but provides you with the security of knowing that it will be impossible for the IC to legally enforce any claimed oral amendment to the agreement.

SUGGESTED LANGUAGE

Modifying the Agreement

This Agreement may be amended only by a writing signed by both Client and Contractor.

The text of this clause is on the CD-ROM under filename MODIFY.

2. Work at Your Premises

An IC should not work at your office or other premises you maintain unless the nature of the work absolutely requires it. For example, a computer consultant may have to perform work on your computers at your office. In these situations, it's a good idea to add the following provision to the agreement making it clear that the IC is working at your premises because the work requires it.

SUGGESTED LANGUAGE

Work at Your Premises
Because of the nature of the services to be provided by Contractor, Client agrees to furnish space on its premises for Contractor while performing these services.

 The text of this clause is on the CD-ROM under filename PREMISES.

3. Indemnification

If the IRS or another government agency determines that you have misclassified a worker as an IC, you may have to pay back taxes, fines and penalties. This is one of the greatest risks of hiring ICs. Some hiring firms try to shift this risk to the IC's shoulders by including an indemnification clause in their IC agreements. Such a provision requires the IC to repay the hiring firm for any losses it suffers if the IC is reclassified as an employee.

This may sound attractive at first, but there are several reasons why it's usually not a good idea to include such a clause in an IC agreement.

- You are prohibited by law from recovering from a worker any taxes and penalties the IRS assesses against you if it determines that you intentionally misclassified the worker as an IC.
- The clause is practically useless if you're unable to locate the IC when you're audited or the IC has no money to repay you for your losses.
- The clause makes it look as if you're not sure whether the worker is really an IC, and it may also make an auditor doubt whether the worker is an IC.
- Many intelligent ICs will refuse to sign an agreement containing such a clause.
- The Department of Labor does not permit employers to use such clauses to shift liability for failure to pay workers time-and-a-half for overtime.
- Even if you can locate the IC and he or she has the money to repay you for your losses, you'll still have to go to the expense and trouble of going to court to collect if the IC refuses to pay. There is a chance you'll lose because a court might conclude that the indemnification clause goes against public policy and is unenforceable.

4. Intellectual Property Ownership

Where an IC is hired to create intellectual property—for example, writings, music, software programs, designs or inventions—you should include a provision controlling the arrangement. Unless you include a specific provision about the assignment or transfer of intellectual property rights to you by an IC, you can never be sure that you will own the work you pay the IC to create.

You can use the following clause by which the IC assigns to you his or her rights in any intellectual property he or she creates on your behalf. Alternatively, you can use a work-made-for-hire agreement. By using such an agreement, you are considered the author of any copyrightable work the IC creates.

⚠ Work for Hire Is Risky in California

It is not a good idea to use work-for-hire agreements in California because it may cause the worker to be considered your employee for state law purposes. (See Chapter 10 for more on this issue.)

SUGGESTED LANGUAGE

Intellectual Property Ownership

Contractor assigns to Client all patent, copyright and trade secret rights in anything created or developed by Contractor for Client under this Agreement. Contractor shall help prepare any documents Client considers necessary to secure any copyright, patent or other intellectual property rights at no charge to Client. However, Client shall reimburse Contractor for reasonable out-of-pocket expenses.

 The text of this clause is on the CD-ROM under filename INTPROP.

Having paid the IC to create intellectual property for you, you probably won't want the IC to use the material for others without your permission and will probably want to include the following paragraph. However, this is always subject to negotiation.

OPTIONAL LANGUAGE

Intellectual Property Ownership

Contractor agrees not to use any of the intellectual property mentioned above for the benefit of any other party without Client's prior written permission.

The text of this clause is on the CD-ROM under filename INTROP. Add this clause if you wish to require that the worker obtain your written permission before using the intellectual property involved.

5. Confidentiality

If, during the course of his or her work, an IC may have access to your valuable trade secrets—for example, customer lists, business plans, business methods and techniques not known by your competitors—it is reasonable for you to include a nondisclosure provision in the agreement. Such a provision means that the IC may not disclose your trade secrets to others without your permission. (See Chapter 10 for more about ICs and trade secrets.)

SUGGESTED LANGUAGE

Confidentiality

Contractor will not disclose or use, either during or after the term of this Agreement, any proprietary or confidential information of Client without Client's prior written permission except to the extent necessary to perform services on Client's behalf.

Proprietary or confidential information includes:

- the written, printed, graphic or electronically recorded materials furnished by Client for Contractor to use
- business plans, customer lists, operating procedures, trade secrets, design formulas, know-how and processes, computer programs and inventories, discoveries and improvements of any kind, and
- information belonging to customers and suppliers of Client about whom Contractor gained knowledge as a result of Contractor's services to Client.

Contractor shall not be restricted in using any material which is publicly available, already in Contractor's possession or known to Contractor without restriction, or which is rightfully obtained by Contractor from sources other than Client.

Upon termination of Contractor's services to Client, or at Client's request, Contractor shall deliver to Client all materials in Contractor's possession relating to Client's business.

The text of this clause is on the CD-ROM under filename CONFID.

6. Non-Solicitation

If you're concerned about an IC getting to know your clients or customers and perhaps stealing business away from you, you can include the following non-solicitation clause in the agreement.

SUGGESTED LANGUAGE

Non-Solicitation

For a period of [Fill in period from two months to three years] after termination of this Agreement, Contractor agrees not to call on, solicit or take away Client's customers or potential customers of which Contractor became aware as a result of Contractor's services for Client.

 The text of this clause is on the CD-ROM under filename NONSOLIC.

E. Sample IC Agreement

 The text of an Independent Contractor Agreement is on the CD-ROM under filename GENAGREE. You can also find a copy in Appendix 3.

Note that the provisions in the sample agreement below are numbered to coincide with the discussion in Section C. You should be able to craft some form of this agreement to meet your needs if you hire any type of general independent contractor.

INDEPENDENT CONTRACTOR AGREEMENT

This Agreement is made between Acme Widget Co. (Client) with a principal place of business at 123 Main Street, Marred Vista, CA 90000, and ABC Consulting, Inc. (Contractor), with a principal place of business at 456 Grub Street, Santa Longo, CA 90001.

1. Term of Agreement

This Agreement will become effective on May 1, 20XX, and will end no later than June 1, 20XX.

2. Services to Be Performed

Contractor agrees to perform the following services: Install and test Client's DX9-105 widget manufacturing press so that it performs according to the manufacturer's specifications.

3. Payment

In consideration for the services to be performed by Contractor, Client agrees to pay Contractor $20,000 according to the terms set out below.

4. Terms of Payment

Upon completing Contractor's services under this Agreement, Contractor shall submit an invoice. Client shall pay Contractor the compensation described within a reasonable time after receiving Contractor's invoice.

5. Expenses

Contractor shall be responsible for all expenses incurred while performing services under this Agreement. This includes license fees, memberships and dues; automobile and other travel expenses; meals and entertainment; insurance premiums; and all salary, expenses and other compensation paid to employees or contract personnel the Contractor hires to complete the work under this Agreement.

6. Independent Contractor Status

Contractor is an independent contractor, not Client's employee. Contractor's employees or contract personnel are not Client's employees. Contractor and Client agree to the following rights consistent with an independent contractor relationship.

- Contractor has the right to perform services for others during the term of this Agreement.
- Contractor has the sole right to control and direct the means, manner and method by which the services required by this Agreement will be performed.
- Contractor has the right to perform the services required by this Agreement at any place, location or time.
- Contractor will furnish all equipment and materials used to provide the services required by this Agreement.

- Contractor has the right to hire assistants as subcontractors, or to use employees to provide the services required by this Agreement.
- The Contractor or Contractor's employees or contract personnel shall perform the services required by this Agreement; Client shall not hire, supervise or pay any assistants to help Contractor.
- Neither Contractor nor Contractor's employees or contract personnel shall receive any training from Client in the skills necessary to perform the services required by this Agreement.
- Client shall not require Contractor or Contractor's employees or contract personnel to devote full time to performing the services required by this Agreement.

7. Business Permits, Certificates and Licenses

Contractor has complied with all federal, state and local laws requiring business permits, certificates and licenses required to carry out the services to be performed under this Agreement.

8. State and Federal Taxes

Client will not:

- withhold FICA (Social Security and Medicare taxes) from Contractor's payments or make FICA payments on Contractor's behalf
- make state or federal unemployment compensation contributions on Contractor's behalf, or
- withhold state or federal income tax from Contractor's payments.

Contractor shall pay all taxes incurred while performing services under this Agreement—including all applicable income taxes and, if Contractor is not a corporation, self-employment (Social Security) taxes. Upon demand, Contractor shall provide Client with proof that such payments have been made.

9. Fringe Benefits

Contractor understands that neither Contractor nor Contractor's employees or contract personnel are eligible to participate in any employee pension, health, vacation pay, sick pay or other fringe benefit plan of Client.

10. Workers' Compensation

Client shall not obtain workers' compensation insurance on behalf of Contractor or Contractor's employees. If Contractor hires employees to perform any work under this Agreement, Contractor will cover them with workers' compensation insurance and provide Client with a certificate of workers' compensation insurance before the employees begin the work.

11. Unemployment Compensation

Client shall make no state or federal unemployment compensation payments on behalf of Contractor or Contractor's employees or contract personnel. Contractor will not be entitled to these benefits in connection with work performed under this Agreement.

12. Insurance

Client shall not provide any insurance coverage of any kind for Contractor or Contractor's employees or contract personnel. Contractor agrees to maintain an insurance policy of at least $500,000 to cover any negligent acts committed by Contractor or Contractor's employees or agents while performing services under this Agreement.

Contractor shall indemnify and hold Client harmless from any loss or liability arising from performing services under this Agreement.

13. Terminating the Agreement

With reasonable cause, either Client or Contractor may terminate this Agreement, effective immediately upon giving written notice.

Reasonable cause includes:

- a material violation of this Agreement, or
- any act exposing the other party to liability to others for personal injury or property damage.

14. Exclusive Agreement

This is the entire Agreement between Contractor and Client.

15. Severability

If any part of this Agreement is held unenforceable, the rest of the Agreement will continue in effect.

16. Applicable Law

This Agreement will be governed by the laws of the state of California.

17. Notices

All notices and other communications in connection with this Agreement shall be in writing and shall be considered given as follows:

- when delivered personally to the recipient's address as stated on this Agreement
- three days after being deposited in the United States mail, with postage prepaid to the recipient's address as stated on this Agreement, or
- when sent by fax or telex to the last fax or telex number of the recipient known to the person giving notice. Notice is effective upon receipt provided that a duplicate copy of the notice is promptly given by first class mail, or the recipient delivers a written confirmation of receipt.

18. No Partnership

This Agreement does not create a partnership relationship. Contractor does not have authority to enter into contracts on Client's behalf.

19. Assignment

Either Contractor or Client may assign or subcontract any rights or obligations under this Agreement.

20. Signatures

Client:

Acme Widget Co.

By: _Basilio Chew_____
(Signature)

_Basilio Chew_____
(Typed or Printed Name)

Title: _President_____

Date: _April 30, 20XX_____

Contractor:

ABC Consulting, Inc.

By: _George Bailey_____
(Signature)

_George Bailey_____
(Typed or Printed Name)

Title: _President_____

Taxpayer ID Number: _123-45-6789_____

Date: _April 30, 20XX_____

F.   Agreements for Specialized ICs

This book provides five IC agreements that are tailored for specific types of service providers, including:

- household workers (see Section F1)
- direct sellers (see Section F2)
- real estate salespersons (see Section F3)
- independent consultants (see Section F4), and
- contributors to a work made for hire (see Section F5).

1.   Household Workers

 The text of a Household Worker Agreement is on the CD-ROM under filename HOUSEH. You can also find it in Appendix 3.

Household workers are people who perform services in and around your home such as gardeners, housekeepers, cooks and nannies. Part-time gardeners, housecleaners and similar workers can be ICs if they are running their own businesses. However, it's unlikely that a nanny or other in-home child care worker could qualify as an IC. The agreement on the CD-ROM is tailored to use with those household workers who qualify as ICs.

This agreement is as simple and short as possible. It contains a series of boxes for you to check off to indicate exactly what services the worker is required to perform. You can add to these short descriptions if you wish.

The agreement states that the worker will provide all equipment and materials, since this strongly supports IC status. However, if you will be providing any equipment—a lawn mower or vacuum cleaner, for example—delete that reference in the agreement.

Since the worker will be working in and around your home, you need to set up a work schedule. This agreement provides that you and the worker will set up a mutually agreeable schedule. You don't need to set forth the schedule in the agreement. Instead, simply state where the work will be performed.

2.   Direct Sellers

 The text of a Direct Seller's Agreement is on the CD-ROM under filename DIRSELL. You can also find it in Appendix 3.

This agreement is for direct sellers such as traveling salespeople who are paid by commission only. Such salespeople are statutory ICs for IRS purposes if they sign an IC agreement. This means you don't have to withhold or pay employment taxes for them. (See Chapter 4 for more about statutory ICs.)

You need to describe in the agreement what product or merchandise the salesperson will sell. If you give the worker other duties besides selling on commission, the worker will lose his or her statutory IC status.

These salespeople are statutory ICs only if they are paid solely by commission, not on the number of hours worked. The agreement provides for this type of payment.

The agreement also provides that the worker will provide all necessary equipment, but you are permitted to provide sales forms.

Traveling salespeople usually travel by car. This agreement requires the salesperson to have car insurance and to list you as a named insured on the policy. This can make it easier for you to collect if there is an accident. The salesperson also agrees to indemnify you—that is, repay you—if he or she gets into an accident and the victim sues you.

Since salespeople often have to be given access to your valuable customer lists, the agreement requires the salesperson to keep such information confidential.

3. Real Estate Salespeople

The text of a Real Estate Salesperson's Agreement is on the CD-ROM under filename REALEST. You can also find it in Appendix 3.

Real estate salespeople—called real estate agents in some states—who are paid by commission only qualify as statutory ICs if they sign an IC agreement. (See Chapter 4 for more about statutory ICs.)

This agreement provides that the salesperson will be paid by commission only and will be responsible for all expenses incurred in showing and selling real estate including travel and other expenses involved in showing properties.

Most states require that real estate salespeople work for a licensed real estate broker who is responsible for their actions. The broker usually maintains a real estate office and has several salespeople working for him or her. The broker provides clerical and other support staff, while the salespeople are required to be at the office at certain hours to field customer inquiries. The agreement on the CD-ROM provides for this type of arrangement and requires the salesperson to agree upon a schedule of times when the salesperson must be in the office. The schedule doesn't have to be set forth in the agreement.

Real estate salespeople are required to be licensed in most states. Include the state and date of issuance of the salesperson's license on the agreement.

Since real estate salespeople usually travel by car to and from properties, it's important that they have car insurance. This is required in the agreement. The salesperson also agrees to indemnify you—that is, repay you—if he or she gets into an accident and the victim sues you.

4. Consultants

The text of a Consultant's Agreement is on the CD-ROM under filename CONSULT. You can also find it in Appendix 3.

Skilled professionals who provide advice and assistance to businesses are often called consultants. This can include software experts, engineers, marketing, accounting and finance experts and anyone else who calls himself or herself a consultant.

The agreement to be used for consultants is basically the same as the general IC agreement except that provisions regarding intellectual property ownership and confidentiality have been added.

Many consultants are hired to create or contribute to the creation of intellectual property—for example, computer software, important business documents, marketing plans, inventions and trademarks. This agreement provides that the consultant assigns—transfers—all ownership rights in such material to you. This avoids any possible dispute over who owns such material.

In addition, consultants often have access to valuable company trade secrets such as marketing plans, product information and financial information. You probably don't want the consultant to blab about these things to your competitors. This agreement requires the consultant to keep your trade secrets confidential.

5. Works Made for Hire

Don't Use This Agreement in California

Don't use this agreement if the IC is located in California, because it may cause the worker to be considered your employee for workers' compensation, unemployment insurance and disability insurance purposes. (See Chapter 10 for more about this issue.) Instead, use a standard IC agreement including a clause assigning the IC's intellectual property rights to you. (See Section D6.)

The text of a Work-Made-for-Hire Agreement is on the CD-ROM under filename FORHIRE. You can also find it in Appendix 3.

You can use this agreement only when you hire an IC to create or contribute to a work of authorship that falls within one of the following categories:

- a contribution to a collective work—a work created by more than one author, such as a newspaper, magazine, anthology or encyclopedia
- a part of an audiovisual work—for example, a motion picture screenplay
- a translation
- supplementary works such as forewords, afterwords, supplemental pictorial illustrations, maps, charts, editorial notes, bibliographies, appendixes and indexes
- a compilation—for example, an electronic database

- an instructional text
- a test
- answer material for a test, or
- an atlas.

Do not use this agreement for any work that does not fall within one of these categories. (See Chapter 10.)

When an IC signs this agreement, he or she gives up all copyright rights in the work he or she creates. Moreover, you are considered the author of the work for copyright purposes. (See Chapter 10.)

You need to describe in the agreement or on a separate attachment the work the IC will create.

The agreement also provides that the work will be a work made for hire. This means that you, the Client, will be considered the work's author for copyright purposes and own all the copyright rights in the work. However, if for some reason the work fails to qualify as a work made for hire, this agreement contains an assignment from the IC to you of all copyright rights in the work. This will mean you will still own all the copyright rights in the work.

However, in this event, the work won't be a work made for hire and you won't be considered the author. The only practical result of this is that the IC can revoke the assignment 35 years after it's made. There's nothing you can do to prevent this, but in most cases it's meaningless because few works have a useful economic life of more than 35 years. ■

Help Beyond This Book

The legal issues involved in hiring ICs are complex and varied. You may have questions that aren't answered by this book. This chapter provides guidance on how to find and use more specific legal resources including lawyers and other knowledgeable experts. It also explains the basics of doing your own legal research.

A. Finding and Using a Lawyer

An experienced attorney may help answer your questions and allay your fears about working with independent contractors.

1. What Type of Lawyer Do You Need?

Many different areas of law are involved when you hire ICs, including:

- federal tax law
- state tax law
- workers' compensation law
- federal and state employment and anti-discrimination laws, and
- general business law.

Unfortunately, you may find it difficult or impossible to find a single attorney to competently advise you about all these legal issues. For example, an attorney who knows the fine points of tax law may know nothing about your state's workers' compensation and employment laws.

However, there are attorneys who specialize in advising businesses, both large and small. And some of them have experience dealing with the legal issues faced by businesses that hire ICs. These lawyers are a bit like general practitioner doctors: They know a little about a lot of different areas of law.

A lawyer with plenty of experience working with businesses like yours may know enough to answer your questions. For example, if you run a software company, a lawyer who customarily represents software firms may be familiar with the laws as they apply to the software industry and should also know about the legal problems that other software companies that hire ICs have encountered.

But if you can't find a lawyer with this type of experience, you may need to consult more than one attorney or consult other types of experts. For example, a CPA may be able to help you research IRS Rulings, while a business lawyer can help you deal with unemployment compensation, employment and other state laws.

HIRING A TAX ATTORNEY TO HANDLE IRS AUDITS

If you're facing an IRS field audit with the possibility of having to pay several thousands of dollars in assessments or penalties, it makes sense to hire a tax attorney. A tax attorney is a lawyer with either a special tax law degree, an LL.M. in taxation or a tax specialization certification from a state bar association. Tax attorneys specialize in representing taxpayers before the IRS and in court.

2. Finding a Lawyer

When you begin looking for a lawyer, try to find someone with experience representing businesses similar to yours.

Don't start your search by consulting phone books, legal directories or advertisements. Lawyer referral services operated by bar associations are usually equally unhelpful. Often, they simply supply the names of lawyers who have signed onto the service, accepting the lawyer's own word for what types of skills he or she has.

The best way to locate a lawyer who is experienced in advising businesses about hiring ICs is through referrals from other businesses in your community that use ICs. Industry associations and trade groups are also excellent sources of referrals. If you already have or know a lawyer, he or she might also be able to refer you to an experienced person who has the qualifications you need. Other people, such as your banker, accountant or insurance agent may know of good business lawyers.

3. Paying a Lawyer

Whenever you hire a lawyer, insist upon a written explanation of how the fees and costs will be paid.

Most business lawyers charge by the hour. Hourly rates vary, but in most parts of the United States, you can get competent services for your business for $150 to $250 an hour. Comparison shopping among lawyers will help you avoid overpaying. But the cheapest hourly rate isn't necessarily the best. A novice who charges only $80 an hour may take three hours to review a consultant's contract. A more experienced lawyer who charges $200 an hour may do the same job in half an hour and make better suggestions. If a lawyer will be delegating some of the work on your case to a less experienced associate, paralegal or secretary, that work should be billed at a lower hourly rate. Be sure to get this information recorded in your initial written fee agreement.

Sometimes, a lawyer may quote you a flat fee for a specific job. For example, a lawyer may offer to represent you for $3,000 in a dispute with the labor department. You pay the same amount regardless of how much time the lawyer spends. This can be cheaper than paying an hourly fee, but not always.

Alternatively, some businesses hire lawyers on retainer—that is, they pay a flat annual fee in return for the lawyer handling all their routine legal business. However, few small businesses can afford to keep a lawyer on retainer.

4. Using a Lawyer As a Legal Coach

One way to keep your legal costs down is to do as much work as possible yourself and simply use the lawyer as your coach. For example, you can draft your own IC agreements, giving your lawyer the relatively quick and inexpensive task of reviewing them. In an IRS audit or unemployment compensation case, you can assemble needed documents and line up witnesses.

But get a clear understanding about who's going to do what. You don't want to do the work and get billed for it because the lawyer duplicated your efforts. And you certainly don't want any crucial elements to fall through cracks because you each thought the other was attending to the work.

B. Help From Other Experts

Lawyers aren't the only ones who can help you deal with the legal issues involved in hiring ICs. Tax professionals, insurance brokers and trade groups can also be very helpful.

1. Tax Professionals

Attorneys are usually the most expensive, but not always the most knowledgeable, professionals you can go to for advice on tax law. You can get outstanding tax advice at lower cost from many non-attorney tax professionals such as enrolled agents and certified public accountants. These tax professionals can help you research IRS rulings and answer other tax-related questions.

a. Enrolled agents

Enrolled agents are tax advisors and preparers licensed by the IRS. They earn the designation of enrolled agent by either passing a difficult IRS test or working for the IRS for at least five years. An enrolled agent is generally the least expensive of the tax pros and is very adequate for most small business tax advice and reporting.

b. Accountants

Certified public accountants, or CPAs, are licensed and regulated by each state, like attorneys. They perform sophisticated accounting and business-related tax work and prepare tax returns. CPAs shine in giving business tax advice but generally are not as aggressive as tax lawyers when facing IRS personnel. Some states license accountants other than CPAs, such as public accountants. Many of these workers may also be able to give you competent advice on the tax effects of using ICs in your business.

2. Insurance Brokers

Insurance brokers and agents who sell workers' compensation insurance and business liability insurance should be knowledgeable about your state's workers' compensation laws. They can also help you save money when you buy such insurance.

3. Industry and Trade Associations

Business or industry trade associations or similar organizations can be a fount of information on IC issues. Many such groups track federal and state laws, lobby Congress and state legislatures and even help members fight the IRS and other federal and state agencies. Find out if there is such an organization for your business or industry and get in touch with it.

C. Doing Your Own Legal Research

If you decide to investigate the law on your own, your first step should be to obtain a good guide to help you understand legal citations, use the law library and understand what you find there. There are a number of sources that provide a good introduction to legal research, including *Legal Research: How to Find & Understand the Law,* by attorneys Stephen Elias and Susan Levinkind (Nolo). This nontechnical book simply explains how to use all major legal research tools and helps you frame your research questions.

Next, you need to find a law library that's open to the public. Your county should have a public law library, often at the county courthouse. Public law schools often contain especially good collections and generally permit the public to use their libraries. Some private law schools grant access to their libraries—sometimes for a modest fee. The reference department of a major public or university library may have a fairly decent legal research collection. Finally, don't overlook the law library in your own lawyer's office. Most lawyers, on request, will share their books with their clients.

1. Researching Federal Tax Law

Many resources are available to augment and explain the tax information in this book: IRS publications, self-help tax preparation guides, textbooks, court decisions and periodicals. Some are free, and others are reasonably priced. Tax publications for professionals are expensive, but are often available at public or law libraries.

a. IRS booklets

The IRS publishes over 350 free booklets explaining the tax code, and many are clearly written and useful. These booklets, called IRS Publications, range from several pages to several hundred pages in length. The following IRS Publications contain useful information for businesses that hire ICs:

- Publication 15, Circular E, Employer's Tax Guide
- Publication 15A, Employer's Supplemental Tax Guide
- Publication 937, Employment Taxes and Information Returns
- Publication 334, Tax Guide for Small Businesses
- Publication 505, Tax Withholding and Estimated Tax
- Publication 926, Household Employer's Tax Guide
- Publication 51, Circular A, Agricultural Employer's Tax Guide.

These are all available on the CD-ROM at the back of this book. In general, IRS Publications are available in IRS offices, or by calling 800-TAX-FORM (829-3676), or by sending in an order form. (There is no charge, not even for postage.) You can also download these publications from the agency's website at www.irs.gov.

Don't Rely Exclusively on the IRS

IRS publications are useful to obtain information on IRS procedures and to get the IRS's view of the tax law. But keep in mind that they only present the IRS's interpretation of the law, which may be very one-sided and even be contrary to court rulings. So don't rely exclusively on IRS publications for information.

b. The *Internal Revenue Manual*

The *Internal Revenue Manual*, or IRM, is a series of handbooks that serve as internal guides to IRS employees on points of tax law and procedure. The IRM tells IRS employees, such as auditors or collectors, how specific tax code provisions should be enforced. Section 5(10) of the IRM deals with employment tax examinations and provides useful guidance on how IRS auditors handle worker classification questions. It also explains how employment tax audits are conducted. It will be particularly helpful if you're handling an IRS audit yourself.

c. Internal Revenue Code

All federal tax laws are in the Internal Revenue Code, or IRC, which is written by Congress and often referred to as the tax code. The IRC is found in Title 26 of the United States Code, abbreviated as U.S.C. Title simply refers to the place within the massive U.S.C. where the IRC is found. The IRC is divided up into sections, which are subdivided and resubdivided into more parts. A reference to IRC § 3121(d)(3)(C) means that this particular tax law is found in Title 26 of the U.S.C., the Internal Revenue Code, Section 3121, subsection (d), paragraph 3, subparagraph C.

The tax code is extremely long, complex and difficult to understand. Fortunately, you probably don't need to read it. Few sections of the IRC deal with ICs and they have all been summarized in this book.

d.   IRS pronouncements on tax law

The IRS makes written statements of its position on various tax matters. They do not have the force of law, but guide IRS personnel and taxpayers as to how specific tax laws should be interpreted and applied. Over the years, the IRS has issued thousands of rulings on how workers in almost every conceivable occupation should be classified.

Reviewing IRS rulings can help you predict how the IRS is likely to classify a worker if you're audited. However, IRS rulings are not always consistent and may even conflict with each other. Even IRS auditors don't always follow IRS rulings, since they don't have the force of law.

But, if you can find a favorable ruling, it can supply a reasonable basis for classifying a worker as an IC. Such a ruling might enable you to qualify for Safe Harbor protection. (See Chapter 4 for more about Safe Harbor protection.) Unfortunately, the majority of IRS rulings find that the workers involved are employees, not ICs, and will be of little help.

The IRS makes its opinions and legal summaries known in a number of publications.

- *Revenue rulings* (Rev. Rul.) are IRS written statements of how the tax law applies to a specific set of facts. These are published as general guidance to taxpayers. The rulings are reprinted and indexed by IRC section and subject matter. A revenue ruling usually contains a hypothetical set of facts, followed by an explanation of how the tax code applies to those facts. For example: Rev. Rul. 99-41 refers to IRS revenue ruling number 41, issued in 1999.

- *IRS letter rulings* are IRS answers to specific written questions and hypothetical situations posed by taxpayers. There are thousands of IRS letter rulings dealing with how to classify workers. Letter rulings are published in the *Internal Revenue Cumulative Bulletin*, and in private tax service publications found in larger public and law libraries. For example: Ltr. Rul. 992012 refers to a ruling issued in 1999, in the 20th week and which was the 12th letter ruling issued that week.

- *IRS revenue procedures* (Rev. Procs.) are another way the IRS tells taxpayers how to comply with certain tax provisions, although they are primarily written to guide tax professionals and preparers. Revenue procedures often explain when and how to report tax items. They are published in the *Internal Revenue Cumulative Bulletin*, found in larger public and law libraries and widely reprinted in professional tax publications. For example: Rev. Proc. 99-15 refers to a published revenue procedure number 15, issued in 1999.

- *IRS Regulations*, also called Treasury Regulations or Regs, are the IRS's most authoritative statement on how to interpret the IRC. Regs are usually found in a four-volume set, called *Treasury Regulations*, found in most larger libraries and some bookstores. Regulations are somewhat easier to read and comprehend than the tax code However, few Regs concern IC issues.

e.   Tax cases

Federal courts have interpreted the tax law in thousands of court cases, many of which involve worker classification issues. A favorable court decision can also provide you with a reasonable basis for obtaining IRS Safe Harbor protection. (See Chapter 4 for more about Safe Harbor protection.) You may rely on decisions by any federal tax court, federal district court, federal court of appeals or the U.S. Supreme Court.

DIRECTORIES OF IRS RULINGS

Finding an IRS ruling dealing with a situation similar to yours can be very difficult. Fortunately, tax experts have culled through thousands of IRS rulings on worker classification and categorized them by occupation. By using their publications you can find citations to IRS rulings involving workers similar to yours. Look for this type of book at your local law library.

In addition, many state Chambers of Commerce publish guides for companies that hire ICs that list IRS rulings for various occupations. Call your state Chamber of Commerce to see if it publishes such a guide for your state; it probably has an office in your state capitol.

Finally, an industry trade group or association may also be aware of, or even have copies of, helpful IRS rulings and court decisions.

f. Trade association publications

Every business or trade has its own publications and newsletters that closely track tax issues of common interest, including worker classification issues. By reading them, you can learn about recent IRS and court rulings affecting other employers in your industry.

2. Researching Other Areas of Law

Many fields of law other than federal tax law are involved when you hire ICs. These include other federal laws that apply throughout the country and the laws of your particular state.

a. Federal laws

The best starting point for further research into federal employment and anti-discrimination laws that affect your business is *Federal Employment Laws: A Desk Reference,* by attorneys Amy DelPo and Lisa Guerin (Nolo). This guide will likely answer your questions, or at least tell you where to go for more information.

In addition, the U.S. Labor Department publishes a free pamphlet on worker classification for purposes of the federal labor laws called Publication 17, Employee Relationship Under the Fair Labor Standards Act. You can get a copy by calling the Labor Department at: 202-219-6666. You can also log on to the Labor Department's website at www.dol.gov.

b.   State laws

If you have questions about your state workers'
compensation, unemployment compensation, tax
law or employment laws, first contact the
appropriate state agency for more information.
Many of these agencies publish useful information
pamphlets. This book contains contact information
for state workers' compensation agencies (see
Chapter 7), unemployment compensation agencies (see Chapter 6), tax departments (see Chapter
6) and labor departments (see Chapter 9).

More in-depth research into your state law will
require that you review:

- legislation, also called statutes, passed by
  your state legislature; your state unemployment compensation, workers' compensation
  and income tax withholding laws will probably be most important to you
- administrative rules and regulations issued
  by state administrative agencies such as your
  state unemployment compensation agency,
  and
- published decisions of your state courts.

Many states, particularly larger ones, have legal
encyclopedias or treatises that organize the state
case law and some statutes into narrative statements
organized alphabetically by subject. Through citation footnotes, you can locate the full text of the
cases and statutes. These works are a good starting
point for in-depth state law research.

How to Read a Case Citation

To locate a published court decision, you must understand how to read a case citation. A citation provides the names of the people or companies involved on each side of the case, the volume of the legal publication—called a reporter—in which the case can be found, the page number on which it begins and the year in which the case was decided. Here is an example of what a legal citation looks like: *Smith v. Jones Int'l*, 123 F.3d 456 (1995). Smith and Jones are the names of the people having the legal dispute. The case is reported in volume 123 of the Federal Reporter, Third Series, beginning on page 456; the court issued the decision in 1995.

Federal court decisions. There are several different federal courts and the decisions of each are published in a different reporter. Opinions by the federal district courts are in a series called the Federal Supplement, or F.Supp.

Any case decided by a federal court of appeals is found in a series of books called the Federal Reporter. Older cases are contained in the first series of the Federal Reporter, or F. More recent cases are contained in the second or third series of the Federal Reporter, F.2d or F.3d.

Cases decided by the U.S. Supreme Court are found in three publications: United States Reports (identified as U.S.), the Supreme Court Reporter (identified as S.Ct.) and the Supreme Court Reports, Lawyer's Edition (identified as L.Ed.). Supreme Court case citations often refer to all three publications.

There are also federal courts that specialize in handling tax disputes, including the United States Tax Court and United States Claims Court—formerly Court of Claims. Published decisions of the United States Tax Court can be found in the Tax Court Reports, or TC, published by the U.S. Government Printing Office. Tax Court decisions can also be found in a reporter called Tax Court Memorandum Decisions, or TCM, published by Commerce Clearing House, Inc.

Decisions from all federal courts involving taxation can be found in a reporter called U.S. Tax Cases, or USTC, published by Commerce Clearing House, Inc.

State court decisions. Most states publish their own official state reports. All published state court decisions are also included in the West Reporter System. West has divided the country into seven regions—and publishes all the decisions of the supreme and appellate state courts in the region together. These reporters are:

A. and A.2d. Atlantic Reporter (First and Second Series), which includes decisions from Connecticut, Delaware, the District of Columbia, Maine, Maryland, New Hampshire, New Jersey, Pennsylvania, Rhode Island and Vermont.

N.E. and N.E.2d. Northeastern Reporter (First and Second Series), which includes decisions from New York, Illinois, Indiana, Massachusetts and Ohio.

N.W. and N.W.2d. Northwestern Reporter (First and Second Series), which includes decisions from Iowa, Michigan, Minnesota, Nebraska, North Dakota, South Dakota and Wisconsin.

P. and P.2d. Pacific Reporter (First and Second Series), which includes decisions from Alaska, Arizona, California, Colorado, Hawaii, Idaho, Kansas, Montana, Nevada, New Mexico, Oklahoma, Oregon, Utah, Washington and Wyoming.

S.E. and S.E.2d. Southeastern Reporter (First and Second Series), which includes decisions from Georgia, North Carolina, South Carolina, Virginia and West Virginia.

So. and So.2d. Southern Reporter (First and Second Series), which includes decisions from Alabama, Florida, Louisiana and Mississippi.

S.W. and S.W.2d. Southwestern Reporter (First and Second Series), which includes decisions from Arkansas, Kentucky, Missouri, Tennessee and Texas.

All California appellate decisions are published in a separate volume, the California Reporter (Cal. Rptr.) and all decisions from New York appellate courts are published in a separate volume, New York Supplement (N.Y.S.).

3. Online Resources

A vast array of information for small business owners is available on the Internet, a global network of computer networks. To access the Internet, you need a computer and modem, appropriate software and an account with an Internet access provider. Internet access can be obtained for free in many university and some public libraries.

The legal encyclopedia on Nolo's website at www.nolo.com contains much useful information for business people and several articles about independent contractors. Other good websites for small business information include:

- http://smallbusiness.yahoo.com,
- www.allbusiness.com
- www.inc.com, and
- www.entreworld.org.

Somewhat surprisingly, the IRS has perhaps the most useful and colorful Internet site of any government agency. It contains virtually every IRS publication and tax form, IRS announcements and a copy of the *IRS Audit Manual on Independent Contractors*. The Internet address is www.irs.gov.

■

How to Use the CD-ROM

The forms in this book are included on a CD-ROM in the back of the book. This CD-ROM, which can be used with Windows computers, installs files that can be opened, printed and edited using a word processor or other software. It is *not* a stand-alone software program. Please read this Appendix and the README.TXT file included on the CD-ROM for instructions on using the Forms CD.

Note to Mac users: This CD-ROM and its files should also work on Macintosh computers. Please note, however, that Nolo cannot provide technical support for non-Windows users.

HOW TO VIEW THE README FILE

If you do not know how to view the file README.TXT, insert the Forms CD-ROM into your computer's CD-ROM drive and follow these instructions:

- Windows 9x, 2000, Me and XP: (1) On your PC's desktop, double-click the My Computer icon; (2) double-click the icon for the CD-ROM drive into which the Forms CD-ROM was inserted; (3) double-click the file README.TXT.
- Macintosh: (1) On your Mac desktop, double-click the icon for the CD-ROM that you inserted; (2) double-click on the file README.TXT.

While the README file is open, print it out by using the Print command in the File menu.

Two different kinds of forms are contained on the CD-ROM:

- Word processing (RTF) forms that you can open, complete, print and save with your word processing program (see Section B, below), and

- Forms from the IRS (PDF) that can be viewed only with Adobe Acrobat Reader 4.0 or higher. You can install Acrobat Reader from the Forms CD (see Section C below). Some of these forms have "fill-in" text fields, and can be completed using your computer. You will not, however, be able to save the completed forms with the filled-in data. PDF forms without fill-in text fields must be printed out and filled in by hand or with a typewriter.

See Section D, below, for a list of forms, their file names and file formats.

A. Installing the Form Files Onto Your Computer

Before you can do anything with the files on the CD-ROM, you need to install them onto your hard disk. In accordance with U.S. copyright laws, remember that copies of the CD-ROM and its files are for your personal use only.

Insert the forms CD and do the following:

1. Windows 9x, 2000, Me and XP Users

Follow the instructions that appear on the screen. (If nothing happens when you insert the forms CD-ROM, then (1) double-click the My Computer icon; (2) double-click the icon for the CD-ROM drive into which the Forms CD-ROM was inserted; and (3) double-click the file WELCOME.EXE.)

By default, all the files are installed to the \Independent Contractor Forms folder in the \Program Files folder of your computer. A folder called "Independent Contractor Forms" is added to the "Programs" folder of the Start menu.

2. Macintosh Users

Step 1: If the "Independent Contractor CD" window is not open, open it by double-clicking the "Independent Contractor CD" icon.

Step 2: Select the "Independent Contractor Forms" folder icon.

Step 3: Drag and drop the folder icon onto the icon of your hard disk.

B. Using the Word Processing Files to Create Documents

This section concerns the files for forms that can be opened and edited with your word processing program.

All word processing forms come in rich text format. These files have the extension ".RTF." For example, the form for the Workers' Compensation Clause discussed in Chapter 13 is on the file WORKCOMP.RTF. All forms, their file names and file formats are listed in Section D, below.

RTF files can be read by most recent word processing programs including all versions of MS Word for Windows and Macintosh, WordPad for Windows, and recent versions of WordPerfect for Windows and Macintosh.

To use a form from the CD to create your documents you must: (1) open a file in your word processor or text editor; (2) edit the form by filling in the required information; (3) print it out; (4) rename and save your revised file.

The following are general instructions on how to do this. However, each word processor uses different commands to open, format, save and print documents. Please read your word processor's manual for specific instructions on performing these tasks.

Do not call Nolo's technical support if you hve questions on how to use your word processor.

Step 1: Opening a File

There are three ways to open the word processing files included on the CD-ROM after you have installed them onto your computer.

- Windows users can open a file by selecting its "shortcut" as follows: (1) Click the Windows "Start" button; (2) open the "Programs" folder; (3) open the "Independent Contractor Forms" subfolder; (4) open the "RTF" subfolder; and (5) click on the shortcut to the form you want to work with.

- Both Windows and Macintosh users can open a file directly by double-clicking on it. Use My Computer or Windows Explorer (Windows 9x, 2000, Me or XP) or the Finder (Macintosh) to go to the folder you installed or copied the CD-ROM's files to. Then, double-click on the specific file you want to open.

WHERE ARE THE FILES INSTALLED?

Windows Users
- RTF files are installed by default to a folder named \Independent Contractor Forms\RTF in the \Program Files folder of your computer.

Macintosh Users
- RTF files are located in the "RTF" folder within the "Independent Contractor Forms" folder.

- You can also open a file from within your word processor. To do this, you must first start your word processor. Then, go to the File menu and choose the Open command. This opens a dialog box where you will tell the program (1) the type of file you want to open (*.RTF); and (2) the location and name of the file (you will need to navigate through the directory tree to get to the folder on your hard disk where the CD's files have been installed). If these directions are unclear you will need to look through the manual for your word processing program—Nolo's technical support department will *not* be able to help you with the use of your word processing program.

Step 2: Editing Your Document

Fill in the appropriate information according to the instructions and sample agreements in the book. Underlines are used to indicate where you need to enter your information, frequently followed by instructions in brackets. *Be sure to delete the underlines and instructions from your edited document.* If you do not know how to use your word processor to edit a document, you will need

to look through the manual for your word processing program—Nolo's technical support department will *not* be able to help you with the use of your word processing program.

EDITING FORMS THAT HAVE OPTIONAL OR ALTERNATIVE TEXT

Some of the forms have check boxes before text. The check boxes indicate:

- Optional text, where you choose whether to include or exclude the given text.
- Alternative text, where you select one alternative to include and exclude the other alternatives.

If you are using the tear-out forms in the Appendixes, you simply mark the appropriate box to make your choice.

If you are using the Forms CD, however, we recommend that instead of marking the check boxes, you do the following:

Optional text

If you **don't want** to include optional text, just delete it from your document.

If you **do want** to include optional text, just leave it in your document.

In either case, delete the check box itself as well as the italicized instructions that the text is optional.

Alternative text

First delete all the alternatives that you do not want to include.

Then delete the remaining check boxes, as well as the italicized instructions that you need to select one of the alternatives provided.

Step 3: Printing Out the Document

Use your word processor's or text editor's "Print" command to print out your document. If you do not know how to use your word processor to print a document, you will need to look through the manual for your word processing program—Nolo's technical support department will *not* be able to help you with the use of your word processing program.

Step 4: Saving Your Document

After filling in the form, use the "Save As" command to save and rename the file. Because all the files are "read-only," you will not be able to use the "Save" command. This is for your protection. *If you save the file without renaming it, the underlines that indicate where you need to enter your information will be lost and you will not be able to create a new document with this file without re-copying the original file from the CD-ROM.*

If you do not know how to use your word processor to save a document, you will need to look through the manual for your word processing program—Nolo's technical support department will *not* be able to help you with the use of your word processing program.

C. Using the IRS Files

Electronic copies of useful forms from the IRS are included on the CD-ROM in Adobe Acrobat PDF format. You must have the Adobe Acrobat Reader installed on your computer (see below) to use these forms. All forms, their file names and file formats are listed in Section D, below. These files were created by the IRS, not by Nolo.

Some of these forms have fill-in text fields. To create your document using these files, you must: (1) open a file; (2) fill in the text fields using either your mouse or the tab key on your keyboard to navigate from field to field; and (3) print it out.

NOTE: While you can print out your completed form, you will NOT be able to save your completed form to disk.

Forms without fill-in text fields cannot be filled out using your computer. To create your document using these files, you must: (1) open the file; (2) print it out; and (3) complete it by hand or typewriter.

INSTALLING ACROBAT READER

To install the Adobe Acrobat Reader, insert the CD into your computer's CD-ROM drive and follow these instructions:

- **Windows 9x, 2000, Me and XP:** Follow the instructions that appear on screen. (If nothing happens when you insert the Forms CD-ROM, then (1) double-click the My Computer icon; (2) double-click the icon for the CD-ROM drive into which the Forms CD-ROM was inserted; and (3) double click the file WELCOME.EXE.)
- **Macintosh:** (1) If the "Independent Contractor CD" window is not open, open it by double-clicking the "Independent Contractor CD" icon; and (2) double-click on the "Acrobat Reader Installer" icon.

If you do not know how to use Adobe Acrobat to view and print the files, you will need to consult the online documentation that comes with the Acrobat Reader program.

Do *not* call Nolo technical support if you have questions on how to use Acrobat Reader.

Step 1: Opening IRS Forms

PDF files, like the word processing files, can be opened in one of three ways.

- Windows users can open a file by selecting its "shortcut" as follows: (1) Click the Windows "Start" button; (2) open the "Programs" folder; (3) open the "Independent Contractor Forms" subfolder; (4) open the "PDF" folder; and (5) click on the shortcut to the form you want to work with.

- Both Windows and Macintosh users can open a file directly by double-clicking on it. Use My Computer or Windows Explorer (Windows 9x, 2000, Me or XP) or the Finder (Macintosh) to go to the folder you created and copied the CD-ROM's files to. Then, double-click on the specific file you want to open.

- You can also open a PDF file from within Acrobat Reader. To do this, you must first start Reader. Then, go to the File menu and choose the Open command. This opens a dialog box where you will tell the program the location and name of the file (you will need to navigate through the directory tree to get to the folder on your hard disk where the CD's files have been installed). If these directions are unclear, you will need to look through Acrobat Reader's help—Nolo's technical support department will *not* be able to help you with the use of Acrobat Reader.

Step 2: Filling in IRS Forms

Use your mouse or the Tab key on your keyboard to navigate from field to field within these forms. Be sure to have all the information you will need to complete a form on hand, because you will not be able to save a copy of the filled-in form to disk. You can, however, print out a completed version.

NOTE: This step is only applicable to forms that have been created with fill-in text fields. Forms without fill-in fields must be completed by hand or typewriter after you have printed them out.

WHERE ARE THE PDF FILES INSTALLED?

Windows Users
- PDF files are installed by default to a folder named \Independent Contractor Forms\PDF in the \Program Files folder of your computer.

Macintosh Users
- PDF files are located in the "PDF" folder within the "Independent Contractor Forms" folder.

Step 3: Printing IRS Forms

Choose Print from the Acrobat Reader File menu. This will open the Print dialog box. In the "Print Range" section of the Print dialog box, select the appropriate print range, then click OK.

D. Files Provided on the Forms CD-ROM

The following files are included in rich text format (RTF):

Chapter	Form or Clause	File Name
13	*Essential Clauses of Independent Contractor Agreements*	
	Title of Agreement	TITLE.RTF
	Names of IC and Hiring Firm	NAMES.RTF
	Term of Agreement	TERMAGR.RTF
	Services to Be Performed	SERVICES.RTF
	Payment	PAYMENT.RTF
	Terms of Payment	TERMPAY.RTF
	Expenses	EXPENSE.RTF
	Independent Contractor Status	STATUS.RTF
	Business Permits, Certificates and Licenses	PERMIT.RTF
	State and Federal Taxes	TAXES.RTF
	Fringe Benefits	FRINGE.RTF
	Workers' Compensation	WORKCOMP.RTF
	Unemployment Compensation	UNEMPL.RTF
	Insurance	INSURE.RTF
	Terminating the Agreement	TERMIN.RTF
	Exclusive Agreement	EXCLUS.RTF
	Severability	SEVERAB.RTF
	Applicable Law	APPLLAW.RTF
	Notices	NOTICE.RTF
	No Partnership	NOPART.RTF
	Assignment	ASSIGNM.RTF
	Resolving Disputes	RESOLVE.RTF
	Signatures	SIGNS.RTF
13	*Optional Clauses of Independent Contractor Agreements*	
	Modifying the Agreement	MODIFY.RTF
	Work at Your Premises	PREMISES.RTF
	Intellectual Property Ownership	INTPROP.RTF
	Confidentiality	CONFID.RTF
	Non-Solicitation	NONSOLIC.RTF
	Attorney Fees	FEES.RTF
12	Independent Contractor Questionnaire	QUESTION.RTF
App. 2	Documentation Checklist	DOCUMENT.RTF
13	Independent Contractor Agreement	GENAGREE.RTF
8	Independent Contractor Agreement for Household Workers	HOUSEH.RTF

Chapter	Form or Clause	File Name
App. 3	Independent Contractor Agreement for Direct Sellers	DIRSELL.RTF
	Independent Contractor Agreement for Real Estate Salespeople	REALEST.RTF
	Independent Contractor Agreement for Consultants	CONSULT.RTF
	Independent Contractor Agreement for Work Made for Hire	FORHIRE.RTF

The following files are included in Adobe Acrobat PDF format (asterisks indicate forms with fill-in text fields):

Chapter	Form or Publication	File Name
4	IRS Form SS-8*	FSS8.PDF
4	IRS Guidelines for Classifying Workers in the Television Commercial Production and Professional Video Communication Industries	TV-VIDEO.PDF
	IRS Guidelines for Classifying Limo Drivers	LIMO.PDF
	IRS Guidelines for Classifying Van Operators	VAN-OPS.PDF
	IRS Publication 15	P15.PDF
	IRS Publication 15A	P15A.PDF
8	IRS Publication 505	P505.PDF
	IRS Form SS-4*	FSS4.PDF
	IRS Publication 926	P926.PDF
12	IRS Form W-9*	FW9.PDF
	IRS Form 945*	F945.PDF
	IRS Form 8809*	F8809.PDF
14	IRS Publication 334	P334.PDF
	IRS Publication 51	P51.PDF

Contractor's Screening Documents

Independent Contractor Questionnaire

Documentation Checklist

INDEPENDENT CONTRACTOR QUESTIONNAIRE

Name: _____

Fictitious business name (if any): _____

Business address: _____

Business phone and fax #: _____

Employer Identification Number or Social Security Number: _____

Form of business entity (check one): ☐ Corporation ☐ Partnerhsip ☐ Sole Proprietorship

1. Provide the name, address and dates of service of all companies for which you have performed services as an independent contractor for the past two years. But please do not provide any information you have a duty to keep confidential.

2. Have you ever hired employees? If yes, please complete the following:

   Name: _____

   Address: _____

   Title: _____

   Salary: _____

   Dates of Employment: _____

   Workers' compensation carrier and policy number: _____

3. Have you paid federal and state payroll taxes for your employees? ☐ Yes ☐ No

4. Do you hold a professional license? If so, please provide a copy.

5. Do you have a business license? If so, lease provide a copy.

6. Describe the training you have received in your specialty.

   School attended: _____

   Dates of attendance: _____ Degrees received: _____

   School attended: _____

   Dates of attendance: _____ Degrees received: _____

   School attended: _____

   Dates of attendance: _____ Degrees received: _____

7. Do you advertise your services? ☐ Yes ☐ No
   If so, please provide a copy of these advertisements, including a Yellow Pages listing.

8. If you don't advertise, how do you market your services?
   _____
   _____

9. Do you have a White Pages business phone listing? ☐ Yes ☐ No If so, please provide a copy.

10. Do you have a website marketing your services? If yes, please provide a copy of the home page and list the
    URL here: _____

11. Describe the business expenses you have paid in the past, including office or workplace rental, materials
    and equipment expenses, telephone and other expenses: _____
    _____
    _____

12. Describe the business expenses you pay now: _____
    _____
    _____

13. Describe the equipment and facilities you own: _____
    _____
    _____

14. Please describe the tools and materials you will use to perform the services in this job:
    _____
    _____
    _____

    How much do they cost?_____

15. Please list your general liablity insurance carrier: _____
    Policy number: _____

16. Please list your auto insurance carrier: _____
    Policy number: _____

17. Have you ever worked for us before? If so, please complete the following:
    Dates of employment: _____
    Services performed: _____

18. Do you have an independent contractor agreement? If so, please attach a copy.

19. Do you have your own business cards, stationery and invoice forms? If so, provide copies.

20. If you're a sole practitioner, have you paid self-employment taxes on your income and filed a Schedule C
    with your federal tax return? ☐ Yes ☐ No
    If so, will you provide copies of your tax returns for the past two years? ☐ Yes ☐ No

DOCUMENTATION CHECKLIST

Please provide the following documentation:

☐ copies of your business license and any professional licenses you have

☐ certificates showing that you have insurance, including general liability insurance and workers' compensation insurance if you have employees

☐ your business cards and stationery

☐ copies of any advertising you've done, such as a Yellow Pages listing

☐ a copy of your White Pages business phone listing, if there is one

☐ if you're operating under an assumed name, a copy of the fictitious business name statement

☐ a copy of your invoice form to be used for billing purposes

☐ a copy of any office lease and proof that you've paid the rent, such as copies of canceled rental checks

☐ the names and salaries of all assistants that you will use on the job

☐ the names and salaries of all assistants you have used on previous jobs for the past two years and proof that you paid them, such as copies of canceled checks or copies of payroll tax forms

☐ a list of all the equipment and materials you will use in performing the services and how much it costs; proof that you have paid for the equipment, such as copies of canceled checks, is very helpful

☐ the names and addresses of other clients or customers for whom you have performed services during the previous two years; but don't provide any information you have a duty to keep confidential

☐ if you're a sole proprietor and will agree, copies of your tax returns for the previous two years showing that you have filed a Schedule C, Profit or Loss From a Business.

Sample Agreements

Introduction to Sample Agreements

This Appendix contains the full text of six sample agreements, the specifics of which are discussed throughout this book.

Note that the agreements are also available on the CD-ROM—and that additional clauses are available on the CD-ROM so that you may best tailor your independent contractor agreement to meet your situation. (See Chapter 13.)

The following specific agreements are included here.

Independent Contractor Agreement

You should be able to craft some form of this agreement to meet your needs if you hire any type of general independent contractor.

 The text of a General Independent Contractor Agreement is on the CD-ROM under filename GENAGREE.

Independent Contractor Agreement for Household Workers

Household workers—that is, people who perform services in and around your home such as gardeners, housekeepers, cooks and nannies—may or may not qualify as ICs. (See Chapter 8.) The agreement here is tailored to use with those workers who do qualify as ICs.

 The text of the agreement is on the CD-ROM under filename HOUSEH.

Independent Contractor Agreement for Direct Sellers

This agreement is for direct sellers such as traveling salespeople who are paid by commission only. (See Chapter 4, Section B1.)

 The text of this agreement is on the CD-ROM under filename DIRSELL.

Independent Contractor Agreement for Real Estate Salespeople

This agreement is for real estate salespeople—called real estate agents in some states—who are paid by commission only. (See Chapter 4, Section B2.)

 The text of this agreement is on the CD-ROM under filename REALEST.

Independent Contractor Agreement for Consultants

This agreement can be used for almost any type of independent consultant—that is, an IC you hire to give you expert professional advice.

 The text of this agreement is on the CD-ROM under filename CONSULT.

Independent Contractor Agreement for Work Made for Hire

This agreement is a work-made-for-hire agreement. You can use this agreement only when you hire an IC to create or contribute to a work of authorship that falls within one of the following categories:

- a contribution to a collective work—a work created by more than one author, such as a newspaper, magazine, anthology or encyclopedia
- a part of an audiovisual work—for example, a motion picture screenplay
- a translation
- supplementary works such as forewords, afterwords, supplemental pictorial illustrations, maps, charts, editorial notes, bibliographies, appendixes and indexes

- a compilation—for example, an electronic database
- an instructional text
- a test
- answer material for a test, or
- an atlas.

Do not use this agreement for any work that does not fall within one of these categories.

 The text of this agreement is on the CD-ROM under filename FORHIRE.

■

INDEPENDENT CONTRACTOR AGREEMENT

This Agreement is made between _____ (Client)
with a principal place of business at _____
and _____ (Contractor), with a
principal place of business at _____.

This Agreement will become effective on _____, 20_____, and will end no later than
_____, 20_____.

Services to Be Performed

(Check and complete applicable provision.)

☐ Contractor agrees to perform the following services:

_____

_____

OR

☐ Contractor agrees to perform the services described in Exhibit A, which is attached to this Agreement.

_____

_____

Payment

(Check and complete applicable provision.)

☐ In consideration for the services to be performed by Contractor, Client agrees to pay Contractor
$_____ according to the terms set out below.

OR

☐ In consideration for the services to be performed by Contractor, Client agrees to pay Contractor at the rate of
$_____ per _____ according to the terms of payment set out below.

Additional Option

(Check and complete if applicable.)

☐ Unless otherwise agreed in writing, Client's maximum liability for all services performed during the term of this
Agreement shall not exceed $_____ .

Terms of Payment

(Check and complete applicable provision.)

☐ Upon completing Contractor's services under this Agreement, Contractor shall submit an invoice. Client shall
pay Contractor the compensation described within a reasonable time after receiving Contractor's invoice.

OR

☐ Contractor shall be paid $_____ upon signing this Agreement and the rest of the sum described
above when the Contractor completes services and submits an invoice.

OR

☐ Client shall pay Contractor according to the following schedule of payments.

1. $_____ when an invoice is submitted and the following services are complete:

_____

2. $_____ when an invoice is submitted and the following services are complete:

3. $_____ when an invoice is submitted and the following services are complete:

_____

OR

☐ Contractor shall submit an invoice to Client on the last day of each month for the work performed during that month. The invoice should include: an invoice number, the dates covered by the invoice, the hours expended and a summary of the work performed. Client shall pay Contractor's fee within a reasonable time after receiving the invoice.

Expenses

Contractor shall be responsible for all expenses incurred while performing services under this Agreement. This includes license fees, memberships and dues; automobile and other travel expenses; meals and entertainment; insurance premiums; and all salary, expenses and other compensation paid to employees or contract personnel the Contractor hires to complete the work under this Agreement.

Independent Contractor Status

Contractor is an independent contractor, not Client's employee. Contractor's employees or contract personnel are not Client's employees. Contractor and Client agree to the following rights consistent with an independent contractor relationship.

- Contractor has the right to perform services for others during the term of this Agreement.
- Contractor has the sole right to control and direct the means, manner and method by which the services required by this Agreement will be performed.
- Contractor has the right to perform the services required by this Agreement at any place, location or time.
- Contractor will furnish all equipment and materials used to provide the services required by this Agreement.
- Contractor has the right to hire assistants as subcontractors, or to use employees to provide the services required by this Agreement.
- The Contractor or Contractor's employees or contract personnel shall perform the services required by this Agreement; Client shall not hire, supervise or pay any assistants to help Contractor.
- Neither Contractor nor Contractor's employees or contract personnel shall receive any training from Client in the skills necessary to perform the services required by this Agreement.
- Client shall not require Contractor or Contractor's employees or contract personnel to devote full time to performing the services required by this Agreement.

Business Permits, Certificates and Licenses

Contractor has complied with all federal, state and local laws requiring business permits, certificates and licenses required to carry out the services to be performed under this Agreement.

State and Federal Taxes

Client will not:

- withhold FICA (Social Security and Medicare taxes) from Contractor's payments or make FICA payments on Contractor's behalf
- make state or federal unemployment compensation contributions on Contractor's behalf, or
- withhold state or federal income tax from Contractor's payments.

Contractor shall pay all taxes incurred while performing services under this Agreement—including all applicable income taxes and, if Contractor is not a corporation, self-employment (Social Security) taxes. Upon demand, Contractor shall provide Client with proof that such payments have been made.

Fringe Benefits

Contractor understands that neither Contractor nor Contractor's employees or contract personnel are eligible to participate in any employee pension, health, vacation pay, sick pay or other fringe benefit plan of Client.

Workers' Compensation

Client shall not obtain workers' compensation insurance on behalf of Contractor or Contractor's employees. If Contractor hires employees to perform any work under this Agreement, Contractor will cover them with workers' compensation insurance and provide Client with a certificate of workers' compensation insurance before the employees begin the work.

Additional Option

(Check if applicable.)

☐ If not operating as a corporation, Contractor shall obtain workers' compensation insurance coverage for Contractor. Contractor shall provide Client with proof that such coverage has been obtained before starting work.

Unemployment Compensation

Client shall make no state or federal unemployment compensation payments on behalf of Contractor or Contractor's employees or contract personnel. Contractor will not be entitled to these benefits in connection with work performed under this Agreement.

Insurance

Client shall not provide any insurance coverage of any kind for Contractor or Contractor's employees or contract personnel. Contractor agrees to maintain an insurance policy of at least $_____ to cover any negligent acts committed by Contractor or Contractor's employees or agents while performing services under this Agreement.

Contractor shall indemnify and hold Client harmless from any loss or liability arising from performing services under this Agreement.

Terminating the Agreement

(Check applicable provision.)

☐ With reasonable cause, either Client or Contractor may terminate this Agreement, effective immediately upon giving written notice.

Reasonable cause includes:

- a material violation of this Agreement, or
- any act exposing the other party to liability to others for personal injury or property damage.

OR

☐ Either party may terminate this Agreement any time by giving thirty days written notice to the other party of the intent to terminate.

Exclusive Agreement

This is the entire Agreement between Contractor and Client.

Severability

If any part of this Agreement is held unenforceable, the rest of the Agreement will continue in effect.

Applicable Law

This Agreement will be governed by the laws of the state of _____.

Notices

All notices and other communications in connection with this Agreement shall be in writing and shall be considered given as follows:

- when delivered personally to the recipient's address as stated on this Agreement
- three days after being deposited in the United States mail, with postage prepaid to the recipient's address as stated on this Agreement, or
- when sent by fax or telex to the last fax or telex number of the recipient known to the person giving notice. Notice is effective upon receipt provided that a duplicate copy of the notice is promptly given by first class mail, or the recipient delivers a written confirmation of receipt.

No Partnership

This Agreement does not create a partnership relationship. Contractor does not have authority to enter into contracts on Client's behalf.

Resolving Disputes

(Check applicable provision.)

Alternative A

☐ If a dispute arises under this Agreement, any party may take the matter to court.

Additional Option

(Check if applicable.)

☐ If any court action is necessary to enforce this Agreement, the prevailing party shall be entitled to reasonable attorney fees, costs and expenses in addition to any other relief to which he or she may be entitled.

Alternative B

☐ If a dispute arises under this Agreement, the parties agree to first try to resolve the dispute with the help of a mutually agreed upon mediator in _____. Any costs and fees other than attorney fees associated with the mediation shall be shared equally by the parties.

If the dispute is not resolved within 30 days after it is referred to the mediator, any party may take the matter to court.

Alternative C

☐ If a dispute arises under this Agreement, the parties agree to first try to resolve the dispute with the help of a mutually agreed upon mediator in _____. Any costs and fees other than attorney fees associated with the mediation shall be shared equally by the parties.

If it proves impossible to arrive at a mutually satisfactory solution through mediation, the parties agree to submit the dispute to a mutually agreed upon arbitrator in _____. Judgment upon the award rendered by the arbitrator may be entered in any court having jurisdiction to do so. Costs of arbitration, including attorney fees, will be allocated by the arbitrator.

Signatures

Client: _____

Name of Client

By: _____

Signature

_____

Typed or Printed Name

Title: _____

Date: _____

Contractor: _____

Name of Contractor

By: _____

Signature

_____

Typed or Printed Name

Title: _____

Taxpayer ID Number: _____

Date: _____

If Agreement Is Faxed:

Contractor and Client agree that this Agreement will be considered signed when the signature of a party is delivered by facsimile transmission. Signatures transmitted by facsimile shall have the same effect as original signatures.

INDEPENDENT CONTRACTOR AGREEMENT
FOR HOUSEHOLD WORKERS

This Agreement is made between _____ (Client)

with a principal place of business at _____

and _____ (Contractor), with a

principal place of business at _____.

This Agreement will become effective on _____, 20_____, and will end no later

than _____, 20_____.

Services to Be Performed

Contractor agrees to perform the following services.

a. Cleaning Interior

   Contractor will clean the following rooms and areas:

   _____

   _____

   _____

   _____

b. Cleaning Exterior

   Contractor will clean the following:

   ☐ Front porch or deck: _____

   _____

   _____

   ☐ Back porch or deck: _____

   _____

   _____

   ☐ Garage: _____

   _____

   _____

   ☐ Pool, hot tub or sauna: _____

   _____

   _____

   ☐ Other exterior areas: _____

   _____

   _____

   _____

c. Gardening

Contractor will perform the following gardening services:

_____

_____

d. Other Responsibilities

_____

_____

_____

_____

_____

_____

_____

_____

_____

_____

_____

_____

_____

_____

Payment

In consideration for the services to be performed by Contractor, Client agrees to pay Contractor at the rate of $_____ per [☐ hour, ☐ day, ☐ week, ☐ month] according to the terms of payment set forth below.

Terms of Payment

Upon completing Contractor's services under this Agreement, Contractor shall submit an invoice. Client shall pay Contractor the compensation described within a reasonable time after receiving Contractor's invoice.

Expenses

Contractor shall be responsible for all expenses incurred while performing services under this Agreement. This includes license fees, memberships and dues; automobile and other travel expenses; meals and entertainment; insurance premiums; and all salary, expenses and other compensation paid to employees or contract personnel the Contractor hires to complete the work under this Agreement.

Independent Contractor Status

Contractor is an independent contractor, not Client's employee. Contractor's employees or contract personnel are not Client's employees. Contractor and Client agree to the following rights consistent with an independent contractor relationship.

- Contractor has the right to perform services for others during the term of this Agreement.
- Contractor has the sole right to control and direct the means, manner and method by which the services required by this Agreement will be performed.
- Contractor will furnish all equipment and materials used to provide the services required by this Agreement except for _____
  _____.
- Contractor has the right to hire assistants as subcontractors, or to use employees to provide the services required by this Agreement.
- The Contractor or Contractor's employees or contract personnel shall perform the services required by this Agreement; Client shall not hire, supervise or pay any assistants to help Contractor.
- Neither Contractor nor Contractor's employees or contract personnel shall receive any training from Client in the skills necessary to perform the services required by this Agreement.
- Client shall not require Contractor or Contractor's employees or contract personnel to devote full time to performing the services required by this Agreement.

Time and Place of Performance

Contractor shall perform the services at _____
_____ during reasonable hours on a schedule to be mutually agreed upon by Client and Contractor based upon Client's needs and Contractor's availability to perform such services.

Business Permits, Certificates and Licenses

Contractor has complied with all federal, state and local laws requiring business permits, certificates and licenses required to carry out the services to be performed under this Agreement.

State and Federal Taxes

Client will not:

- withhold FICA (Social Security and Medicare taxes) from Contractor's payments or make FICA payments on Contractor's behalf
- make state or federal unemployment compensation contributions on Contractor's behalf, or
- withhold state or federal income tax from Contractor's payments.

Contractor shall pay all taxes incurred while performing services under this Agreement—including all applicable income taxes and, if Contractor is not a corporation, self-employment (Social Security) taxes. Upon demand, Contractor shall provide Client with proof that such payments have been made.

Workers' Compensation

Client shall not obtain workers' compensation insurance on behalf of Contractor or Contractor's employees. If Contractor hires employees to perform any work under this Agreement, Contractor will cover them with workers' compensation insurance and provide Client with a certificate of workers' compensation insurance before the employees begin the work.

Unemployment Compensation

Client shall make no state or federal unemployment compensation payments on behalf of Contractor or Contractor's employees or contract personnel. Contractor will not be entitled to these benefits in connection with work performed under this Agreement.

Terminating the Agreement

(Check applicable provision.)

☐ With reasonable cause, either Client or Contractor may terminate this Agreement, effective immediately upon giving written notice.

   Reasonable cause includes:

   • a material violation of this Agreement, or

   • any act exposing the other party to liability to others for personal injury or property damage.

                                  OR

☐ Either party may terminate this Agreement any time by giving thirty days written notice to the other party of the intent to terminate.

Signatures

Client: _____
                                Name of Client

By: _____
                                  Signature

_____
                            Typed or Printed Name

Title: _____

Date: _____

Contractor: _____
                             Name of Contractor

By: _____
                                  Signature

_____
                            Typed or Printed Name

Title: _____

Taxpayer ID Number: _____

Date: _____

INDEPENDENT CONTRACTOR AGREEMENT
FOR DIRECT SELLERS

This Agreement is made between _____ (Client)
with a principal place of business at _____
and _____ (Contractor), with a
principal place of business at _____.

This Agreement will become effective on _____, 20_____, and will end no later
than _____, 20_____.

Services to Be Performed

Contractor agrees to sell the following product or merchandise for owner: _____
(Check if applicable)

☐ Contractor shall seek sales of the product in the homes of various individuals.

This work will be done by Contractor as an independent contractor, and not as an employee. Contractor shall
have no obligation to perform any services other than the sale of the product described here.

Compensation

In consideration for the services to be performed by Contractor, Client agrees to pay Contractor a commission
on completed sales as follows: _____

Contractor acknowledges that no other compensation is payable by Client, and that all of Contractor's
compensation will depend on sales made by Contractor. None of Contractor's compensation shall be based on
the number of hours worked by Contractor.

Expenses

Contractor shall be responsible for all expenses incurred while performing services under this Agreement. This
includes license fees, memberships and dues; automobile and other travel expenses; meals and entertainment;
insurance premiums; and all salary, expenses and other compensation paid to employees or contract personnel
the Contractor hires to complete the work under this Agreement.

Independent Contractor Status

Contractor is an independent contractor, not Client's employee. Contractor's employees or contract personnel
are not Client's employees. Contractor and Client agree to the following rights consistent with an independent
contractor relationship.

- Contractor has the right to perform services for others during the term of this Agreement.
- Contractor has the sole right to control and direct the means, manner and method by which the services
  required by this Agreement will be performed.

  Consistent with this freedom from Client's control, Contractor:

  —does not have to pursue or report on leads furnished by Client

  —is not required to attend sales meetings organized by Client

  —does not have to obtain Client's pre-approval for orders, and

  —shall adopt and carry out its own sales strategy.

- Subject to any restrictions on Contractor's sales territory contained in this Agreement, Contractor has the
  right to perform the services required by this Agreement at any location or time.

- Contractor will furnish all equipment and materials used to provide the services required by this Agreement.
- Contractor has the right to hire assistants as subcontractors, or to use employees to provide the services required by this Agreement, except that Client may supply Contractor with sales forms.
- The Contractor or Contractor's employees or contract personnel shall perform the services required by this Agreement; Client shall not hire, supervise or pay any assistants to help Contractor.
- Neither Contractor nor Contractor's employees or contract personnel shall receive any training from Client in the skills necessary to perform the services required by this Agreement.
- Client shall not require Contractor or Contractor's employees or contract personnel to devote full time to performing the services required by this Agreement.

Business Permits, Certificates and Licenses

Contractor has complied with all federal, state and local laws requiring business permits, certificates and licenses required to carry out the services to be performed under this Agreement.

State and Federal Taxes

Client will not:

- withhold FICA (Social Security and Medicare taxes) from Contractor's payments or make FICA payments on Contractor's behalf
- make state or federal unemployment compensation contributions on Contractor's behalf, or
- withhold state or federal income tax from Contractor's payments.

Contractor shall pay all taxes incurred while performing services under this Agreement—including all applicable income taxes and, if Contractor is not a corporation, self-employment (Social Security) taxes. Upon demand, Contractor shall provide Client with proof that such payments have been made.

Fringe Benefits

Contractor understands that neither Contractor nor Contractor's employees or contract personnel are eligible to participate in any employee pension, health, vacation pay, sick pay or other fringe benefit plan of Client.

Workers' Compensation

Client shall not obtain workers' compensation insurance on behalf of Contractor or Contractor's employees. If Contractor hires employees to perform any work under this Agreement, Contractor will cover them with workers' compensation insurance and provide Client with a certificate of workers' compensation insurance before the employees begin the work.

Optional Language

(Check if provision is applicable.)

☐ If not operating as a corporation, Contractor shall obtain workers' compensation insurance coverage for Contractor. Contractor shall provide Client with proof that such coverage has been obtained before starting work.

Unemployment Compensation

Client shall make no state or federal unemployment compensation payments on behalf of Contractor or Contractor's employees or contract personnel. Contractor will not be entitled to these benefits in connection with work performed under this Agreement.

Insurance

Client shall not provide any insurance coverage of any kind for Contractor or Contractor's employees or contract personnel. Contractor agrees to maintain an insurance policy of at least $_____ to cover any negligent acts committed by Contractor or Contractor's employees or agents while performing services under this Agreement.

Contractor warrants and represents that Contractor now carries automobile liability insurance for injuries to person and property. Contractor shall include Client's name as one of the named insureds under this policy and deliver a certificate of that policy.

Contractor shall indemnify and hold Client harmless from any loss or liability arising from performing services under this Agreement, including any claim for injuries or damages caused by Contractor while traveling in Contractor's automobile and performing services under this Agreement.

Confidentiality

Contractor will not disclose or use, either during or after the term of this Agreement, any proprietary or confidential information of Client without Client's prior written permission except to the extent necessary to perform services on Client's behalf.

Proprietary or confidential information includes:

- the written, printed, graphic or electronically recorded materials furnished by Client for Contractor to use
- business plans, customer lists, operating procedures, trade secrets, design formulas, know-how and processes, computer programs and inventories, discoveries and improvements of any kind, and
- information belonging to customers and suppliers of Client about whom Contractor gained knowledge as a result of Contractor's services to Client.

Contractor shall not be restricted in using any material which is publicly available, already in Contractor's possession or known to Contractor without restriction, or which is rightfully obtained by Contractor from sources other than Client.

Upon termination of Contractor's services to Client, or at Client's request, Contractor shall deliver to Client all materials in Contractor's possession relating to Client's business.

Terminating the Agreement

(Check applicable provision.)

☐ With reasonable cause, either Client or Contractor may terminate this Agreement, effective immediately upon giving written notice.

Reasonable cause includes:

- a material violation of this Agreement, or
- any act exposing the other party to liability to others for personal injury or property damage.

OR

☐ Either party may terminate this Agreement any time by giving thirty days written notice to the other party of the intent to terminate.

Exclusive Agreement

This is the entire Agreement between Contractor and Client.

Severability

If any part of this Agreement is held unenforceable, the rest of the Agreement will continue in effect.

Applicable Law

This Agreement will be governed by the laws of the state of _____.

Notices

All notices and other communications in connection with this Agreement shall be in writing and shall be considered given as follows:

- when delivered personally to the recipient's address as stated on this Agreement
- three days after being deposited in the United States mail, with postage prepaid to the recipient's address as stated on this Agreement, or
- when sent by fax or telex to the last fax or telex number of the recipient known to the person giving notice. Notice is effective upon receipt provided that a duplicate copy of the notice is promptly given by first class mail, or the recipient delivers a written confirmation of receipt.

No Partnership

This Agreement does not create a partnership relationship. Contractor does not have authority to enter into contracts on Client's behalf.

Resolving Disputes
(Check applicable provisions.)

Alternative A

☐ If a dispute arises under this Agreement, any party may take the matter to court.

Additional Option
(Check if applicable.)

☐ If any court action is necessary to enforce this Agreement, the prevailing party shall be entitled to reasonable attorney fees, costs and expenses in addition to any other relief to which he or she may be entitled.

Alternative B

☐ If a dispute arises under this Agreement, the parties agree to first try to resolve the dispute with the help of a mutually agreed upon mediator in _____. Any costs and fees other than attorney fees associated with the mediation shall be shared equally by the parties.

If the dispute is not resolved within 30 days after it is referred to the mediator, any party may take the matter to court.

Alternative C

☐ If a dispute arises under this Agreement, the parties agree to first try to resolve the dispute with the help of a mutually agreed upon mediator in _____. Any costs and fees other than attorney fees associated with the mediation shall be shared equally by the parties.

If it proves impossible to arrive at a mutually satisfactory solution through mediation, the parties agree to submit the dispute to a mutually agreed upon arbitrator in _____. Judgment upon the award rendered by the arbitrator may be entered in any court having jurisdiction to do so. Costs of arbitration, including attorney fees, will be allocated by the arbitrator.

Signatures

Client: _____

Name of Client

By: _____

Signature

_____

Typed or Printed Name

Title: _____

Date: _____

Contractor: _____

Name of Contractor

By: _____

Signature

_____

Typed or Printed Name

Title: _____

Taxpayer ID Number: _____

Date: _____

If Agreement Is Faxed:

Contractor and Client agree that this Agreement will be considered signed when the signature of a party is delivered by facsimile transmission. Signatures transmitted by facsimile shall have the same effect as original signatures.

INDEPENDENT CONTRACTOR AGREEMENT
FOR REAL ESTATE SALESPEOPLE

This Agreement is made between _____ (Broker)

with a principal place of business at _____

and _____ (Salesperson),

with a principal place of business at _____ .

Services to Be Performed

Salesperson agrees to sell, lease or rent real estate listed with Broker. Salesperson will not be treated as an employee with respect to the services performed by salesperson as a real estate agent for federal tax purposes.

Compensation

In consideration for the services to be performed by Salesperson, Broker agrees to pay Salesperson a commission on completed sales by Salesperson as follows: _____

_____

_____ .

Salesperson shall have no right to compensation based on the number of hours worked.

Expenses

Salesperson shall be responsible for all expenses incurred while performing services under this Agreement. This includes license fees, memberships and dues; automobile and other travel expenses; meals and entertainment; insurance premiums; and all salary, expenses and other compensation paid to employees or contract personnel the Salesperson hires to complete the work under this Agreement.

Broker's Sales Office

Broker agrees to provide Salesperson with the use, equally with other Salespersons, of all the facilities of the sales office operated by Broker at _____ [address of Broker's real estate office to be used by salesperson].

Independent Contractor Status

Salesperson is an independent contractor, not Broker's employee. Salesperson's employees or contract personnel are not Broker's employees. Salesperson and Broker agree to the following rights consistent with an independent contractor relationship.

- Salesperson has the right to perform services for others during the term of this Agreement.
- Salesperson has the sole right to control and direct the means, manner and method by which the services required by this Agreement will be performed.
- Subject to any restrictions on Contractor's sales territory contained in this Agreement, Salesperson has the right to perform the services required by this Agreement at any location or time.
- Salesperson has the right to hire assistants as subcontractors, or to use employees to provide the services required by this Agreement.

Business Permits, Certificates and Licenses

Salesperson has complied with all federal, state and local laws requiring business permits, certificates and licenses required to carry out the services to be performed under this Agreement.

Salesperson represents and warrants that Salesperson is a licensed real estate salesperson in good standing, having been licensed by _____ on _____ , 20_____ .

State and Federal Taxes

Broker will not:

- withhold FICA (Social Security and Medicare taxes) from Salesperson's payments or make FICA payments on Salesperson's behalf;
- make state or federal unemployment compensation contributions on Salesperson's behalf; or
- withhold state or federal income tax from Salesperson's payments.

Salesperson shall pay all taxes incurred while performing services under this Agreement—including all applicable income taxes and, if Salesperson is not a corporation, self-employment (Social Security) taxes. Upon demand, Salesperson shall provide Broker with proof that such payments have been made.

Fringe Benefits

Salesperson understands that neither Salesperson nor Salesperson's employees or contract personnel are eligible to participate in any employee pension, health, vacation pay, sick pay or other fringe benefit plan of Broker.

Workers' Compensation

Broker shall not obtain workers' compensation insurance on behalf of Salesperson or Salesperson's employees. If Salesperson hires employees to perform any work under this Agreement, Salesperson will cover them with workers' compensation insurance to the extent required by law and provide Broker with a certificate of workers' compensation insurance before the employees begin the work.

Optional Language

(Check if provision is applicable.)

☐ Salesperson shall obtain workers' compensation insurance coverage for Salesperson. Salesperson shall pro-vide Broker with proof that such coverage has been obtained before starting work.

Unemployment Compensation

Broker shall make no state or federal unemployment compensation payments on behalf of Salesperson or Salesperson's employees or contract personnel. Salesperson will not be entitled to these benefits in connection with work performed under this Agreement.

Insurance

Broker shall not provide any insurance coverage of any kind for Salesperson or Salesperson's employees or contract personnel. Salesperson agrees to maintain an insurance policy in an adequate amount to cover any negligent acts committed by Salesperson or Salesperson's employees or agents while performing services under this Agreement.

Salesperson shall indemnify and hold Broker harmless from any loss or liability arising from performing services under this Agreement.

This includes any claim for injuries or damages caused by Salesperson while traveling in Salesperson's automobile and performing sevices under this Agreement.

Terminating the Agreement

(Check applicable provision.)

☐ With reasonable cause, either Broker or Salesperson may terminate this Agreement, effective immediately upon giving written notice. Reasonable cause includes:

- a material violation of this Agreement, or
- any act exposing the other party to liability to others for personal injury or property damage.

OR

☐ Either party may terminate this Agreement any time by giving thirty days written notice to the other party of the intent to terminate.

Exclusive Agreement

This is the entire Agreement between Salesperson and Broker.

Resolving Disputes

(Check applicable provisions.)

☐ If a dispute arises under this Agreement, any party may take the matter to court.

Additional Option

(Check if applicable.)

Alternative A

☐ If any court action is necessary to enforce this Agreement, the prevailing party shall be entitled to reasonable attorney fees, costs and expenses in addition to any other relief to which he or she may be entitled.

Alternative B

☐ If a dispute arises under this Agreement, the parties agree to first try to resolve the dispute with the help of a mutually agreed upon mediator in _____. Any costs and fees other than attorney fees associated with the mediation shall be shared equally by the parties.

If the dispute is not resolved within 30 days after it is referred to the mediator, any party may take the matter to court.

Alternative C

☐ If a dispute arises under this Agreement, the parties agree to first try to resolve the dispute with the help of a mutually agreed upon mediator in _____. Any costs and fees other than attorney fees associated with the mediation shall be shared equally by the parties.

If it proves impossible to arrive at a mutually satisfactory solution through mediation, the parties agree to submit the displute to a mutually agreed upon arbitrator in _____. Judgment upon the award rendered by the arbitrator may be entered in any court having jurisdiction to do so. Costs of arbitration, including attorney fees, will be allocated by the arbitrator.

Applicable Law

This Agreement will be governed by the laws of the state of _____.

Notices

All notices and other communications in connection with this Agreement shall be in writing and shall be considered given as follows:

- when delivered personally to the recipient's address as stated on this Agreement
- three days after being deposited in the United States mail, with postage prepaid to the recipient's address as stated on this Agreement, or
- when sent by fax or telex to the last fax or telex number of the recipient known to the person giving notice. Notice is effective upon receipt provided that a duplicate copy of the notice is promptly given by first class mail, or the recipient delivers a written confirmation of receipt.

No Partnership

This Agreement does not create a partnership relationship. Salesperson does not have authority to enter into contracts on Broker's behalf.

Signatures

Client:

Name of Broker:

_____

By: _____
Signature

_____
Typed or Printed Name

Title: _____

Date: _____

Contractor:

Name of Salesperson: _____

By: _____
Signature

_____
Typed or Printed Name

Taxpayer ID Number: _____

Date: _____

INDEPENDENT CONTRACTOR AGREEMENT
FOR CONSULTANTS

This Agreement is made between _____ (Client)

with a principal place of business at _____

and _____ (Contractor),

with a principal place of business at _____ .

This Agreement will become effective on _____ , 20_____ , and will end no later

than _____ , 20_____ .

Services to Be Performed

Consultant agrees to perform the following consulting services on Client's behalf:

_____

_____

_____

_____

Payment

(Check and complete applicable provision.)

☐ In consideration for the services to be performed by Consultant, Client agrees to pay Consultant
$_____ according to the terms set out below.

OR

☐ In consideration for the services to be performed by Consultant, Client agrees to pay Consultant at the rate of
$_____ per _____ according to the terms of payment set out below.

Additional Option

(Check and complete if applicable.)

☐ Unless otherwise agreed in writing, Client's maximum liability for all services performed during the term of
this Agreement shall not exceed $_____ .

Terms of Payment

(Check applicable provision.)

☐ Upon completing Consultant's services under this Agreement, Consultant shall submit an invoice. Client shall
pay Consultant the compensation described within a reasonable time after receiving Consultant's invoice.

OR

☐ Consultant shall be paid $_____ upon signing this Agreement and the rest of the sum described
above when the Consultant completes services and submits an invoice.

OR

☐ Client shall pay Consultant according to the following schedule of payments.

1. $_____ when an invoice is submitted and the following services are complete:

_____

2. $_____ when an invoice is submitted and the following services are complete:

_____

3. $_____ when an invoice is submitted and the following services are complete:

_____

OR

☐ If paid hourly, Consultant shall submit an invoice to Client on the last day of each month for the work performed during that month. The invoice should include: an invoice number, the dates covered by the invoice, the hours expended and a summary of the work performed. Client shall pay Consultant's fee within a reasonable time after receiving the invoice.

Expenses

Consultant shall be responsible for all expenses incurred while performing services under this Agreement. This includes license fees, memberships and dues; automobile and other travel expenses; meals and entertainment; insurance premiums; and all salary, expenses and other compensation paid to employees or contract personnel the Consultant hires to complete the work under this Agreement.

Independent Contractor Status

Consultant is an independent contractor, not Client's employee. Consultant's employees or contract personnel are not Client's employees. Consultant and Client agree to the following rights consistent with an independent contractor relationship.

- Consultant has the right to perform services for others during the term of this Agreement.
- Consultant has the sole right to control and direct the means, manner and method by which the services required by this Agreement will be performed.
- Consultant has the right to perform the services required by this Agreement at any place, location or time.
- Consultant will furnish all equipment and materials used to provide the services required by this Agreement.
- Consultant has the right to hire assistants as subcontractors, or to use employees to provide the services required by this Agreement.
- The Consultant or Consultant's employees or contract personnel shall perform the services required by this Agreement; Client shall not hire, supervise or pay any assistants to help Consultant.
- Neither Consultant nor Consultant's employees or contract personnel shall receive any training from Client in the skills necessary to perform the services required by this Agreement.
- Client shall not require Consultant or Consultant's employees or contract personnel to devote full time to performing the services required by this Agreement.

Intellectual Property Ownership

Consultant assigns to Client all rights in all designs, creations, improvements, original works of authorship, formulas, processes, know-how, techniques, inventions and all other information or items created by Consultant during the term of this Agreement. The rights assigned include title and interest in all patent, copyright, trade secret, trademark and other proprietary rights.

Consultant shall help prepare any papers that Client considers necessary to secure any patents, copyrights, trademarks or other proprietary rights at no charge to Client. However, Client shall reimburse Consultant for reasonable out-of-pocket expenses incurred.

Consultant must obtain written assurances from Consultant's employees and contract personnel that they agree with this assignment.

Optional Addition

(Check if applicable.)

☐ Consultant agrees not to use any of the intellectual property mentioned above for the benefit of any other party without Client's prior written permission.

Confidentiality

Consultant will not disclose or use, either during or after the term of this Agreement, any proprietary or confidential information of Client without Client's prior written permission except to the extent necessary to perform services on Client's behalf.

Proprietary or confidential information includes:

- the written, printed, graphic or electronically recorded materials furnished by Client for Consultant to use
- business plans, customer lists, operating procedures, trade secrets, design formulas, know-how and processes, computer programs and inventories, discoveries and improvements of any kind, and
- information belonging to customers and suppliers of Client about whom Consultant gained knowledge as a result of Contractor's services to Client.

Consultant shall not be restricted in using any material which is publicly available, already in Consultant's possession or known to Consultant without restriction, or which is rightfully obtained by Consultant from sources other than Client.

Upon termination of Consultant's services to Client, or at Client's request, Consultant shall deliver to Client all materials in Consultant's possession relating to Client's business.

Business Permits, Certificates and Licenses

Consultant has complied with all federal, state and local laws requiring business permits, certificates and licenses required to carry out the services to be performed under this Agreement.

State and Federal Taxes

Client will not:

- withhold FICA (Social Security and Medicare taxes) from Consultant's payments or make FICA payments on Consultant's behalf
- make state or federal unemployment compensation contributions on Consultant's behalf, or
- withhold state or federal income tax from Consultant's payments.

Consultant shall pay all taxes incurred while performing services under this Agreement—including all applicable income taxes and, if Consultant is not a corporation, self-employment (Social Security) taxes. Upon demand, Consultant shall provide Client with proof that such payments have been made.

Fringe Benefits

Consultant understands that neither Consultant nor Consultant's employees or contract personnel are eligible to participate in any employee pension, health, vacation pay, sick pay or other fringe benefit plan of Client.

Workers' Compensation

Client shall not obtain workers' compensation insurance on behalf of Consultant or Consultant's employees. If Consultant hires employees to perform any work under this Agreement, Consultant will cover them with workers' compensation insurance and provide Client with a certificate of workers' compensation insurance before the employees begin the work.

Optional Language

(Check if provision is applicable.)

If not operating as a corporation, Consultant shall obtain workers' compensation insurance coverage for Consultant. Consultant shall provide Client with proof that such coverage has been obtained before starting work.

Unemployment Compensation

Client shall make no state or federal unemployment compensation payments on behalf of Consultant or Consultant's employees or contract personnel. Consultant will not be entitled to these benefits in connection with work performed under this Agreement.

Insurance

Client shall not provide any insurance coverage of any kind for Consultant or Consultant's employees or contract personnel. Consultant agrees to maintain an insurance policy of at least $_____ to cover any negligent acts committed by Consultant or Consultant's employees or agents while performing services under this Agreement.

Consultant shall indemnify and hold Client harmless from any loss or liability arising from performing services under this Agreement.

Terminating the Agreement

(Check applicable provision.)

☐ With reasonable cause, either Client or Consultant may terminate this Agreement, effective immediately upon giving written notice.

Reasonable cause includes:

- a material violation of this Agreement, or
- any act exposing the other party to liability to others for personal injury or property damage.

OR

☐ Either party may terminate this Agreement any time by giving thirty days written notice to the other party of the intent to terminate.

Exclusive Agreement

This is the entire Agreement between Consultant and Client.

Severability

If any part of this Agreement is held unenforceable, the rest of the Agreement will continue in effect.

Applicable Law

This Agreement will be governed by the laws of the state of _____.

Notices

All notices and other communications in connection with this Agreement shall be in writing and shall be considered given as follows:

- when delivered personally to the recipient's address as stated on this Agreement
- three days after being deposited in the United States mail, with postage prepaid to the recipient's address as stated on this Agreement, or

- when sent by fax or telex to the last fax or telex number of the recipient known to the person giving notice. Notice is effective upon receipt provided that a duplicate copy of the notice is promptly given by first class mail, or the recipient delivers a written confirmation of receipt.

No Partnership

This Agreement does not create a partnership relationship. Consultant does not have authority to enter into contracts on Client's behalf.

Resolving Disputes

(Check applicable provisions.)

☐ If a dispute arises under this Agreement, any party may take the matter to court.

Additional Option

(Check if applicable.)

Alternative A

☐ If any court action is necessary to enforce this Agreement, the prevailing party shall be entitled to reasonable attorney fees, costs and expenses in addition to any other relief to which he or she may be entitled.

Alternative B

☐ If a dispute arises under this Agreement, the parties agree to first try to resolve the dispute with the help of a mutually agreed upon mediator in _____. Any costs and fees other than attorney fees associated with the mediation shall be shared equally by the parties.

If the dispute is not resolved within 30 days after it is referred to the mediator, any party may take the matter to court.

Alternative C

☐ If a dispute arises under this Agreement, the parties agree to first try to resolve the dispute with the help of a mutually agreed upon mediator in _____. Any costs and fees other than attorney fees associated with the mediation shall be shared equally by the parties.

If it proves impossible to arrive at a mutually satisfactory solution through mediation, the parties agree to submit the dispute to a mutually agreed upon arbitrator in _____. Judgment upon the award rendered by the arbitrator may be entered in any court having jurisdiction to do so. Costs of arbitration, including attorney fees, will be allocated by the arbitrator.

Signatures

Client: _____
Name of Client

By: _____
Signature

_____
Typed or Printed Name

Title: _____

Date: _____

Contractor: _____
Name of Contractor

By: _____
Signature

_____
Typed or Printed Name

Title: _____

Taxpayer ID Number: _____

Date: _____

If Agreement Is Faxed:

Consultant and Client agree that this Agreement will be considered signed when the signature of a party is delivered by facsimile transmission. Signatures transmitted by facsimile shall have the same effect as original signatures.

INDEPENDENT CONTRACTOR
AGREEMENT FOR WORK MADE FOR HIRE

This Agreement is made between _____ (Client)

with a principal place of business at _____

and _____ (Contractor), with a

principal place of business at _____.

    This Agreement will become effective on _____, 20_____, and will end no later

than _____, 20_____.

Services to Be Performed

(Check and complete applicable provision.)

☐ Contractor agrees to perform the following services:

_____

_____

OR

☐ Contractor agrees to perform the services described in Exhibit A, which is attached to this Agreement.

Payment

(Check and complete applicable provision.)

☐ In consideration for the services to be performed by Contractor, Client agrees to pay Contractor

    $_____ according to the terms set out below.

OR

☐ In consideration for the services to be performed by Contractor, Client agrees to pay Contractor at the rate of

    $_____ per _____ according to the terms of payment set out below.

Additional Option

(Check and complete applicable provision.)

☐ Unless otherwise agreed in writing, Client's maximum liability for all services performed during the term of

    this Agreement shall not exceed $_____.

Terms of Payment

(Check applicable provision.)

☐ Upon completing Contractor's services under this Agreement, Contractor shall submit an invoice. Client shall

    pay Contractor the compensation described within a reasonable time after receiving Contractor's invoice.

OR

☐ Contractor shall be paid $_____ upon signing this Agreement and the rest of the sum described

    above when the Contractor completes services and submits an invoice.

OR

☐ Client shall pay Contractor according to the following schedule of payments.

    1. $_____ when an invoice is submitted and the following services are complete:

_____

_____

    2. $_____ when an invoice is submitted and the following services are complete:

_____

3. $_____ when an invoice is submitted and the following services are complete:

_____

_____

OR

☐ Contractor shall submit an invoice to Client on the last day of each month for the work performed during that month. The invoice should include: an invoice number, the dates covered by the invoice, the hours expended and a summary of the work performed. Client shall pay Contractor's fee within a reasonable time after receiving the invoice.

Expenses

Contractor shall be responsible for all expenses incurred while performing services under this Agreement. This includes license fees, memberships and dues; automobile and other travel expenses; meals and entertainment; insurance premiums; and all salary, expenses and other compensation paid to employees or contract personnel the Contractor hires to complete the work under this Agreement.

Independent Contractor Status

Contractor is an independent contractor, not Client's employee. Contractor's employees or contract personnel are not Client's employees. Contractor and Client agree to the following rights consistent with an independent contractor relationship.

- Contractor has the right to perform services for others during the term of this Agreement.
- Contractor has the sole right to control and direct the means, manner and method by which the services required by this Agreement will be performed.
- Contractor has the right to perform the services required by this Agreement at any place, location or time.
- Contractor will furnish all equipment and materials used to provide the services required by this Agreement.
- Contractor has the right to hire assistants as subcontractors, or to use employees to provide the services required by this Agreement.
- The Contractor or Contractor's employees or contract personnel shall perform the services required by this Agreement; Client shall not hire, supervise or pay any assistants to help Contractor.
- Neither Contractor nor Contractor's employees or contract personnel shall receive any training from Client in the skills necessary to perform the services required by this Agreement.
- Client shall not require Contractor or Contractor's employees or contract personnel to devote full time to performing the services required by this Agreement.

Intellectual Property Ownership

To the extent that the work performed by Contractor under this Agreement (Contractor's Work) includes any work of authorship entitled to protection under the copyright laws, the parties agree to the following provisions.

- Contractor's Work has been specially ordered and commissioned by Client as a contribution to a collective work, a supplementary work or other category of work eligible to be treated as a work made for hire under the United States Copyright Act.
- Contractor's Work shall be deemed a commissioned work and a work made for hire to the greatest extent permitted by law.

- Client shall be the sole author of Contractor's Work and any work embodying the Contractor's Work according to the United States Copyright Act.
- To the extent that Contractor's Work is not properly characterized as a work made for hire, Contractor grants to Client all right, title and interest in Contractor's Work, including all copyright rights, in perpetuity and throughout the world.
- Contractor shall help prepare any papers Client considers necessary to secure any copyrights, patents, trademarks or intellectual property rights at no charge to Client. However, Client shall reimburse Contractor for reasonable out-of-pocket expenses incurred.
- Contractor agrees to require any employees or contract personnel Contractor uses to perform services under this Agreement to assign in writing to Contractor all copyright and other intellectual property rights they may have in their work product. Contractor shall provide Client with a signed copy of each such assignment.

Optional Addition

(Check if applicable.)

☐ Contractor agrees not to use any of the intellectual property mentioned above for the benefit of any other party without Client's prior written permission.

Confidentiality

Contractor will not disclose or use, either during or after the term of this Agreement, any proprietary or confidential information of Client without Client's prior written permission except to the extent necessary to perform services on Client's behalf.

Proprietary or confidential information includes:

- the written, printed, graphic or electronically recorded materials furnished by Client for Contractor to use
- business plans, customer lists, operating procedures, trade secrets, design formulas, know-how and processes, computer programs and inventories, discoveries and improvements of any kind, and
- information belonging to customers and suppliers of Client about whom Contractor gained knowledge as a result of Contractor's services to Client.

Contractor shall not be restricted in using any material which is publicly available, already in Contractor's possession or known to Contractor without restriction, or which is rightfully obtained by Contractor from sources other than Client.

Upon termination of Contractor's services to Client, or at Client's request, Contractor shall deliver to Client all materials in Contractor's possession relating to Client's business.

State and Federal Taxes

Client will not:

- withhold FICA (Social Security and Medicare taxes) from Contractor's payments or make FICA payments on Contractor's behalf
- make state or federal unemployment compensation contributions on Contractor's behalf, or
- withhold state or federal income tax from Contractor's payments.

Contractor shall pay all taxes incurred while performing services under this Agreement—including all applicable income taxes and, if Contractor is not a corporation, self-employment (Social Security) taxes. Upon demand, Contractor shall provide Client with proof that such payments have been made.

Fringe Benefits

Contractor understands that neither Contractor nor Contractor's employees or contract personnel are eligible to participate in any employee pension, health, vacation pay, sick pay or other fringe benefit plan of Client.

Workers' Compensation

Client shall not obtain workers' compensation insurance on behalf of Contractor or Contractor's employees. If Contractor hires employees to perform any work under this Agreement, Contractor will cover them with workers' compensation insurance and provide Client with a certificate of workers' compensation insurance before the employees begin the work.

Optional Addition

(Check if provision is applicable.)

☐ If not operating as a corporation, Contractor shall obtain workers' compensation insurance coverage for Contractor. Contractor shall provide Client with proof that such coverage has been obtained before starting work.

Unemployment Compensation

Client shall make no state or federal unemployment compensation payments on behalf of Contractor or Contractor's employees or contract personnel. Contractor will not be entitled to these benefits in connection with work performed under this Agreement.

Insurance

Client shall not provide any insurance coverage of any kind for Contractor or Contractor's employees or contract personnel. Contractor agrees to maintain an insurance policy of at least $_____ to cover any negligent acts committed by Contractor or Contractor's employees or agents while performing services under this Agreement.

Contractor shall indemnify and hold Client harmless from any loss or liability arising from performing services under this Agreement.

Terminating the Agreement

(Check applicable provision.)

☐ With reasonable cause, either Client or Contractor may terminate this Agreement, effective immediately upon giving written notice.

Reasonable cause includes:

- a material violation of this Agreement, or
- any act exposing the other party to liability to others for personal injury or property damage.

OR

☐ Either party may terminate this Agreement any time by giving thirty days written notice to the other party of the intent to terminate.

Exclusive Agreement

This is the entire Agreement between Contractor and Client.

Severability

If any part of this Agreement is held unenforceable, the rest of the Agreement will continue in effect.

Applicable Law

This Agreement will be governed by the laws of the state of _____.

Notices

All notices and other communications in connection with this Agreement shall be in writing and shall be considered given as follows:

- when delivered personally to the recipient's address as stated on this Agreement
- three days after being deposited in the United States mail, with postage prepaid to the recipient's address as stated on this Agreement, or
- when sent by fax or telex to the last fax or telex number of the recipient known to the person giving notice. Notice is effective upon receipt provided that a duplicate copy of the notice is promptly given by first class mail, or the recipient delivers a written confirmation of receipt.

No Partnership

This Agreement does not create a partnership relationship. Contractor does not have authority to enter into contracts on Client's behalf.

Resolving Disputes

(Check applicable provisions.)

Alternative A

☐ If a dispute arises under this Agreement, any party may take the matter to court.

Additional Option

(Check if applicable.)

☐ If any court action is necessary to enforce this Agreement, the prevailing party shall be entitled to reasonable attorney fees, costs and expenses in addition to any other relief to which he or she may be entitled.

Alternative B

☐ If a dispute arises under this Agreement, the parties agree to first try to resolve the dispute with the help of a mutually agreed upon mediator in _____. Any costs and fees other than attorney fees associated with the mediation shall be shared equally by the parties.

If the dispute is not resolved within 30 days after it is referred to the mediator, any party may take the matter to court.

Alternative C

☐ If a dispute arises under this Agreement, the parties agree to first try to resolve the dispute with the help of a mutually agreed upon mediator in _____. Any costs and fees other than attorney fees associated with the mediation shall be shared equally by the parties.

If it proves impossible to arrive at a mutually satisfactory solution through mediation, the parties agree to submit the dispute to a mutually agreed upon arbitrator in _____. Judgment upon the award rendered by the arbitrator may be entered in any court having jurisdiction to do so. Costs of arbitration, including attorney fees, will be allocated by the arbitrator.

Signatures

Client: _____
                                    Name of Client

By: _____
                                    Signature

_____
                                    Typed or Printed Name

Title: _____

Date: _____

Contractor: _____
                                    Name of Contractor

By: _____
                                    Signature

_____
                                    Typed or Printed Name

Title: _____

Taxpayer ID Number: _____

Date: _____

If Agreement Is Faxed:

Contractor and Client agree that this Agreement will be considered signed when the signature of a party is delivered by facsimile transmission. Signatures transmitted by facsimile shall have the same effect as original signatures.

Blank IRS Forms

Claim for Refund and Request for Abatement

▶ See separate instructions.

OMB No. 1545-0024

Use Form 843 only if your claim involves (a) one of the taxes shown on line 3a or (b) a refund or abatement of interest, penalties, or additions to tax on line 4a.

Do not *use Form 843 if your claim is for—*

- *An overpayment of income taxes;*
- *A refund for nontaxable use (or sales) of fuel; or*
- *An overpayment of excise taxes reported on Form(s) 11-C, 720, 730, or 2290.*

Name of claimant	Your SSN or ITIN
Address (number, street, and room or suite no.)	Spouse's SSN or ITIN
City or town, state, and ZIP code	Employer identification number (EIN)
Name and address shown on return if different from above	Daytime telephone number ( )

(Type or print)

1 Period. Prepare a separate Form 843 for each tax period
From   /   /   to   /   /

2 Amount to be refunded or abated
$

3a Type of tax, penalty, or addition to tax:
☐ Employment   ☐ Estate   ☐ Gift   ☐ Excise (see instructions)
☐ Penalty—IRC section ▶ _____

b Type of return filed (see instructions):
☐ 706   ☐ 709   ☐ 940   ☐ 941   ☐ 943   ☐ 945   ☐ 990-PF   ☐ 4720   ☐ Other (specify)

4a Request for abatement or refund of:
☐ Interest as a result of IRS errors or delays.
☐ A penalty or addition to tax as a result of erroneous advice from the IRS.

b Dates of payment ▶

5 **Explanation and additional claims.** Explain why you believe this claim should be allowed, and show computation of tax refund or abatement of interest, penalty, or addition to tax. If you need more space, attach additional sheets.

Signature. If you are filing Form 843 to request a refund or abatement relating to a joint return, both you and your spouse must sign the claim. Claims filed by corporations must be signed by a corporate officer authorized to sign, and the signature must be accompanied by the officer's title.

Under penalties of perjury, I declare that I have examined this claim, including accompanying schedules and statements, and, to the best of my knowledge and belief, it is true, correct, and complete.

Signature (Title, if applicable. Claims by corporations must be signed by an officer.)   Date

Signature   Date

For Privacy Act and Paperwork Reduction Act Notice, see separate instructions.   Cat. No. 10180R   Form **843** (Rev. 11-2002)

Form **8809**

(Rev. May 2002)

Department of the Treasury
Internal Revenue Service

Request for Extension of Time To File Information Returns

(For Forms W-2 series, W-2G, 1042-S, 1098 series, 1099 series, 5498 series, and 8027)

▶ **Send to IRS–Martinsburg Computing Center.** See **Where to file** on page 2.

OMB No. 1545-1081

Extension Requested for Tax Year 20_____

(Enter one year only.)

1 Filer or transmitter information. **Type or print clearly in black ink.**

Filer/Transmitter Name _____

Address _____

City _____ State _____ ZIP Code _____

Contact Name _____ Telephone number (_____) _____

E-mail address _____

2 Taxpayer identification number (Enter your nine-digit number. Do not enter hyphens.)

3 Transmitter Control Code (TCC)

4 Check your method of filing information returns (check only one box). Use a separate Form 8809 for each method.

☐ electronic   ☐ magnetic media   ☐ paper

5 If you are requesting an extension for more than one filer, enter the total number of filers and attach a list of names and taxpayer identification numbers. Requests for more than 50 filers must be filed electronically or magnetically. See **How to file** below for details. ▶

6 Electronic/magnetic media requests only. Enter the total number of records in your file. **Do not** attach a list.

▶ _____

7 Check this box only if you received an extension and you now need an additional extension. See instructions. ▶ ☐

8 Caution: *Do not use this form to request an extension of time to (1) provide statements to recipients, (2) file Form 1042 (instead use Form 2758), or (3) file Form 1040 (instead use Form 4868).*

Check the box(es) that apply. **Do not** enter the number of returns.

Form	✓ **here**	Form	✓ **here**	Form	✓ **here**
W-2 series		5498		8027	
1098 series, 1099 series, W-2G		5498-ESA		REMIC	
1042-S		5498-MSA			

9 State **in detail** why you need an extension of time. You must give a reason or your request will be denied. If you need more space, attach additional sheets.

Under penalties of perjury, I declare that I have examined this form, including any accompanying statements, and, to the best of my knowledge and belief, it is true, correct, and complete.

Signature ▶   Title ▶   Date ▶

General Instructions

Purpose of form. Use this form to request an extension of time to file any form shown in line 8.

Who may file. Filers of returns submitted on paper, on magnetic media, or electronically may request an extension of time to file on this form.

How to file. When you request extensions of time to file for **more than 50 filers** for the forms shown in line 8, except Form 8027, you **must** submit the extension requests magnetically or electronically.

For **10–50 filers,** you are encouraged to submit the extension request magnetically or electronically.

If filing on paper with **50 or less filers,** you must attach a list of the filers' names and taxpayer identification numbers. If you are filing the extension request magnetically or electronically, you do not have to provide a list.

For more information, see **Pub. 1220,** Specifications for Filing Forms 1098, 1099, 5498, and W-2G Electronically or Magnetically and **Pub. 1187,** Specifications for Filing Form 1042-S, Foreign Person's U.S. Source Income Subject to Withholding, Magnetically or Electronically.

Note: *Specifications for filing **Forms W-2,** Wage and Tax Statements, magnetically or electronically, are only available from the Social Security Administration (SSA). Call 1-800-SSA-6270 for more information.*

For Privacy Act and Paperwork Reduction Act Notice, see back of form.   Cat. No. 10322N   Form **8809** (Rev. 5-2002)

When to file. File Form 8809 as soon as you know an extension of time to file is necessary. However, Form 8809 **must** be filed by the due date of the returns. See the chart below that shows the due dates for filing this form on paper, magnetically, or electronically. IRS will respond in writing beginning in January.

If you are requesting an extension of time to file several types of forms, you may use one Form 8809, but you must file Form 8809 by the earliest due date. For example, if you are requesting an extension of time to file both **Forms 1099-INT,** Interest Income, and **Forms 1099-DIV,** Dividend Income, you must file Form 8809 by February 28 (March 31 if you file electronically). You may complete more than one Form 8809 to avoid this problem. **An extension cannot be granted if a request is filed after the due date of the original returns.**

The due dates for filing Form 8809 are shown below.

IF you file Form . . .	MAGNETICALLY or on PAPER, then the due date is . . .	ELECTRONICALLY, then the due date is . . .
W-2 Series	Last day of February	March 31
W-2G	February 28	March 31
1042-S	March 15	March 15
1098 Series	February 28	March 31
1099 Series	February 28	March 31
5498 Series	May 31	May 31
8027	Last day of February	March 31

If any due date falls on a Saturday, Sunday, or legal holiday, file by the next business day.

Caution: *You do not have to wait for a response before filing your returns. File your returns as soon as they are ready. For all forms shown in line 8, except Form 8027, if you have received a response, **do not** send a copy of the letter or Form 8809 with your returns. If you have not received a response by the end of the extension period, file your returns. When filing Form 8027 on paper **only,** attach a copy of your approval letter. If an approval letter has not been received, attach a copy of your timely filed Form 8809.*

Where to file. Send Form 8809 to IRS-Martinsburg Computing Center, Information Reporting Program, Attn: Extension of Time Coordinator, 240 Murall Dr., Kearneysville, WV 25430.

Extension period. If the IRS approves your extension request, you will be granted an extension of 30 days from the original due date.

Additional extension. Although rarely granted, you may request an additional 30-day extension by submitting another Form 8809 before the end of the first extension period.

Approval or denial of request. Requests for extensions of time to file information returns are not automatically granted. Approval or denial is based on administrative criteria and guidelines. The IRS will send you a letter of explanation approving or denying your request.

Note: *If your extension request is approved, it will only extend the due date for filing the returns. It will not extend the due date for providing statements to recipients.*

Penalty. If you file required information returns late and you have not applied for and received an approved extension of time to file, you may be subject to a late filing penalty. The amount of the penalty is based on when you file the correct information return. For more information on penalties, see the **General Instructions for Forms 1099, 1098, 5498, and W-2G.**

Specific Instructions

Tax year. You may request an extension for only 1 tax year on this form. If no tax year is shown, the IRS will assume you are requesting an extension for the returns currently due to be filed.

Line 1. Enter the name and complete mailing address, including room or suite number of the filer or transmitter requesting the extension of time. Use the name and address

where you want the response sent. For example, if you are a preparer and want to receive the response, enter your client's complete name, care of (c/o) your firm, and your complete mailing address. Enter the name of someone who is familiar with this request whom the IRS can contact if additional information is required. Please provide your telephone number and e-mail address. If you act as transmitter for a group of filers, enter your name and address here, and see **How to file** on page 1.

Note: *Approval or denial notification will be sent only to the person who requested the extension (filer or transmitter).*

Line 2. Enter your nine-digit employer identification number (EIN) or qualified intermediary employer identification number (QI-EIN). If you are not required to have an EIN or QI-EIN, enter your social security number. Do not enter hyphens. Failure to provide this number, and the list of numbers if you are acting as a transmitter as explained under **Line 1,** will result in automatic denial of the extension request.

Line 3. For electronic or magnetic media only. If you filed **Form 4419,** Application for Filing Information Returns Magnetically/Electronically, to file Forms 1042-S, 1098, 1099, 5498, W-2G, or 8027, and it was approved, the IRS-Martinsburg Computing Center assigned you a five-character Transmitter Control Code (TCC). Enter that TCC here. Leave this line blank if you **(1)** are requesting an extension to file any Forms W-2, **(2)** are requesting an extension to file forms on paper, or **(3)** have not yet received your TCC.

Line 7. Check this box **if** you have already received at least one extension, but you need an additional extension for the same year and for the same forms. Do not check this box unless you received an original extension.

Signature. Form 8809 must be signed by you or a person who is duly authorized to sign a return, statement, or other document.

Privacy Act and Paperwork Reduction Act Notice. We ask for the information on this form to carry out the Internal Revenue laws of the United States. Form 8809 is provided by the IRS to request an extension of time to file information returns. Regulations section 1.6081-1 requires you to provide the requested information if you desire an extension of time for filing an information return. If you do not provide the requested information, an extension of time for filing an information return may not be granted. Section 6109 requires you to provide your taxpayer identification number (TIN). Routine uses of this information include giving it to the Department of Justice for civil and criminal litigation, and cities, states, and the District of Columbia for use in administering their tax laws. We may also disclose this information to Federal, state, or local agencies that investigate or respond to acts or threats of terrorism or participate in intelligence or counterintelligence activities concerning terrorism. If you fail to provide this information in a timely manner, you may be liable for penalties and interest.

You are not required to provide the information requested on a form that is subject to the Paperwork Reduction Act unless the form displays a valid OMB control number. Books or records relating to a form or its instructions must be retained as long as their contents may become material in the administration of any Internal Revenue law. Generally, tax returns and return information are confidential, as required by Code section 6103.

The time needed to complete and file this form will vary depending on individual circumstances. The estimated average time is: **Recordkeeping,** 2 hrs., 10 min.; **Learning about the law or the form,** 27 min.; **Preparing and sending the form to the IRS,** 28 min.

If you have comments concerning the accuracy of these time estimates or suggestions for making this form simpler, we would be happy to hear from you. You can write to the Tax Forms Committee, Western Area Distribution Center, Rancho Cordova, CA 95743-0001. **Do not** send the form to this address. Instead, see **Where to file** above.

Form **SS-4**

(Rev. December 2001)

Department of the Treasury
Internal Revenue Service

Application for Employer Identification Number

(For use by employers, corporations, partnerships, trusts, estates, churches,
government agencies, Indian tribal entities, certain individuals, and others.)

▶ See separate instructions for each line.   ▶ Keep a copy for your records.

EIN

OMB No. 1545-0003

Type or print clearly.

1 Legal name of entity (or individual) for whom the EIN is being requested

2 Trade name of business (if different from name on line 1)

3 Executor, trustee, "care of" name

4a Mailing address (room, apt., suite no. and street, or P.O. box)

5a Street address (if different) (Do not enter a P.O. box.)

4b City, state, and ZIP code

5b City, state, and ZIP code

6 County and state where principal business is located

7a Name of principal officer, general partner, grantor, owner, or trustor

7b SSN, ITIN, or EIN

8a **Type of entity** (check only one box)

☐ Sole proprietor (SSN) _____

☐ Partnership

☐ Corporation (enter form number to be filed) ▶ _____

☐ Personal service corp.

☐ Church or church-controlled organization

☐ Other nonprofit organization (specify) ▶ _____

☐ Other (specify) ▶

☐ Estate (SSN of decedent) _____

☐ Plan administrator (SSN) _____

☐ Trust (SSN of grantor) _____

☐ National Guard   ☐ State/local government

☐ Farmers' cooperative   ☐ Federal government/military

☐ REMIC   ☐ Indian tribal governments/enterprises

Group Exemption Number (GEN) ▶ _____

8b If a corporation, name the state or foreign country (if applicable) where incorporated

State

Foreign country

9 **Reason for applying** (check only one box)

☐ Started new business (specify type) ▶ _____

☐ Hired employees (Check the box and see line 12.)

☐ Compliance with IRS withholding regulations

☐ Other (specify) ▶

☐ Banking purpose (specify purpose) ▶ _____

☐ Changed type of organization (specify new type) ▶ _____

☐ Purchased going business

☐ Created a trust (specify type) ▶ _____

☐ Created a pension plan (specify type) ▶ _____

10 Date business started or acquired (month, day, year)

11 Closing month of accounting year

12 First date wages or annuities were paid or will be paid (month, day, year). **Note:** *If applicant is a withholding agent, enter date income will first be paid to nonresident alien. (month, day, year)* . . . . ▶

13 Highest number of employees expected in the next 12 months. **Note:** *If the applicant does not expect to have any employees during the period, enter "-0-."* . . . . ▶

Agricultural	Household	Other

14 Check **one** box that best describes the principal activity of your business.

☐ Construction   ☐ Rental & leasing   ☐ Transportation & warehousing

☐ Real estate   ☐ Manufacturing   ☐ Finance & insurance

☐ Health care & social assistance   ☐ Wholesale–agent/broker

☐ Accommodation & food service   ☐ Wholesale–other   ☐ Retail

☐ Other (specify) ▶

15 Indicate principal line of merchandise sold; specific construction work done; products produced; or services provided.

16a Has the applicant ever applied for an employer identification number for this or any other business? . . . . . ☐ **Yes**   ☐ **No**

Note: *If "Yes," please complete lines 16b and 16c.*

16b If you checked "Yes" on line 16a, give applicant's legal name and trade name shown on prior application if different from line 1 or 2 above.

Legal name ▶   Trade name ▶

16c Approximate date when, and city and state where, the application was filed. Enter previous employer identification number if known.

Approximate date when filed (mo., day, year)   City and state where filed   Previous EIN

Third Party Designee

Complete this section **only** if you want to authorize the named individual to receive the entity's EIN and answer questions about the completion of this form.

Designee's name

Designee's telephone number (include area code)

(   )

Address and ZIP code

Designee's fax number (include area code)

(   )

Under penalties of perjury, I declare that I have examined this application, and to the best of my knowledge and belief, it is true, correct, and complete.

Applicant's telephone number (include area code)

(   )

Name and title (type or print clearly) ▶

Applicant's fax number (include area code)

Signature ▶   Date ▶

(   )

For Privacy Act and Paperwork Reduction Act Notice, see separate instructions.   Cat. No. 16055N   Form **SS-4** (Rev. 12-2001)

Do I Need an EIN?

File Form SS-4 if the applicant entity does not already have an EIN but is required to show an EIN on any return, statement, or other document.[1] **See also the separate instructions for each line on Form SS-4.**

IF the applicant...	AND...	THEN...
Started a new business	Does not currently have (nor expect to have) employees	Complete lines 1, 2, 4a-6, 8a, and 9-16c.
Hired (or will hire) employees, including household employees	Does not already have an EIN	Complete lines 1, 2, 4a-6, 7a-b (if applicable), 8a, 8b (if applicable), and 9-16c.
Opened a bank account	Needs an EIN for banking purposes only	Complete lines 1-5b, 7a-b (if applicable), 8a, 9, and 16a-c.
Changed type of organization	Either the legal character of the organization or its ownership changed (e.g., you incorporate a sole proprietorship or form a partnership)[2]	Complete lines 1-16c (as applicable).
Purchased a going business[3]	Does not already have an EIN	Complete lines 1-16c (as applicable).
Created a trust	The trust is other than a grantor trust or an IRA trust[4]	Complete lines 1-16c (as applicable).
Created a pension plan as a plan administrator[5]	Needs an EIN for reporting purposes	Complete lines 1, 2, 4a-6, 8a, 9, and 16a-c.
Is a foreign person needing an EIN to comply with IRS withholding regulations	Needs an EIN to complete a Form W-8 (other than Form W-8ECI), avoid withholding on portfolio assets, or claim tax treaty benefits[6]	Complete lines 1-5b, 7a-b (SSN or ITIN optional), 8a-9, and 16a-c.
Is administering an estate	Needs an EIN to report estate income on Form 1041	Complete lines 1, 3, 4a-b, 8a, 9, and 16a-c.
Is a withholding agent for taxes on non-wage income paid to an alien (i.e., individual, corporation, or partnership, etc.)	Is an agent, broker, fiduciary, manager, tenant, or spouse who is required to file **Form 1042,** Annual Withholding Tax Return for U.S. Source Income of Foreign Persons	Complete lines 1, 2, 3 (if applicable), 4a-5b, 7a-b (if applicable), 8a, 9, and 16a-c.
Is a state or local agency	Serves as a tax reporting agent for public assistance recipients under Rev. Proc. 80-4, 1980-1 C.B. 581[7]	Complete lines 1, 2, 4a-5b, 8a, 9, and 16a-c.
Is a single-member LLC	Needs an EIN to file **Form 8832,** Classification Election, for filing employment tax returns, **or** for state reporting purposes[8]	Complete lines 1-16c (as applicable).
Is an S corporation	Needs an EIN to file **Form 2553,** Election by a Small Business Corporation[9]	Complete lines 1-16c (as applicable).

[1] For example, a sole proprietorship or self-employed farmer who establishes a qualified retirement plan, or is required to file excise, employment, alcohol, tobacco, or firearms returns, must have an EIN. **A partnership, corporation, REMIC (real estate mortgage investment conduit), nonprofit organization (church, club, etc.), or farmers' cooperative must use an EIN for any tax-related purpose even if the entity does not have employees.**

[2] However, **do not** apply for a new EIN if the existing entity only **(a)** changed its business name, **(b)** elected on Form 8832 to change the way it is taxed (or is covered by the default rules), or **(c)** terminated its partnership status because at least 50% of the total interests in partnership capital and profits were sold or exchanged within a 12-month period. (The EIN of the terminated partnership should continue to be used. See Regulations section 301.6109-1(d)(2)(iii).)

[3] Do not use the EIN of the prior business unless you became the "owner" of a corporation by acquiring its stock.

[4] However, IRA trusts that are required to file **Form 990-T,** Exempt Organization Business Income Tax Return, must have an EIN.

[5] A plan administrator is the person or group of persons specified as the administrator by the instrument under which the plan is operated.

[6] Entities applying to be a Qualified Intermediary (QI) need a QI-EIN even if they already have an EIN. **See Rev. Proc. 2000-12.**

[7] See also *Household employer* on page 4. (**Note:** State or local agencies may need an EIN for other reasons, e.g., hired employees.)

[8] Most LLCs **do not** need to file Form 8832. See **Limited liability company (LLC)** on page 4 for details on completing Form SS-4 for an LLC.

[9] An existing corporation that is electing or revoking S corporation status should use its previously-assigned EIN.

Form **SS-8**

(Rev. January 2001)

Department of the Treasury
Internal Revenue Service

Determination of Worker Status
for Purposes of Federal Employment Taxes
and Income Tax Withholding

OMB No. 1545-0004

Name of firm (or person) for whom the worker performed services	Worker's name	
Firm's address (include street address, apt. or suite no., city, state, and ZIP code)	Worker's address (include street address, apt. or suite no., city, state, and ZIP code)	
Trade name	Telephone number (include area code) ( )	Worker's social security number
Telephone number (include area code) ( )	Firm's employer identification number	Worker's employer identification number (if any)

Important Information Needed To Process Your Request

If this form is being completed by the worker, the IRS must have your permission to disclose your name to the firm. Do you object to disclosing your name and the information on this form to the firm? . . . . ☐ **Yes** ☐ **No**
If you answered "Yes" or did not check a box, stop here. The IRS cannot act on your request and a determination will not be issued.

You must answer ALL items OR mark them "Unknown" or "Does not apply." If you need more space, attach another sheet.

A This form is being completed by: ☐ Firm ☐ Worker; for services performed _____ to _____ .
  (beginning date)   (ending date)

B Explain your reason(s) for filing this form (e.g., you received a bill from the IRS, you believe you received a Form 1099 or Form W-2 erroneously, you are unable to get worker's compensation benefits, you were audited or are being audited by the IRS). ---------------------------
----

C Total number of workers who performed or are performing the same or similar services _____ .

D How did the worker obtain the job? ☐ Application ☐ Bid ☐ Employment Agency ☐ Other (specify) _____

E Attach copies of all supporting documentation (contracts, invoices, memos, Forms W-2, Forms 1099, IRS closing agreements, IRS rulings, etc.). In addition, please inform us of any current or past litigation concerning the worker's status. If no income reporting forms (Form 1099-MISC or W-2) were furnished to the worker, enter the amount of income earned for the year(s) at issue $ _____ .

F Describe the firm's business. --

G Describe the work done by the worker and provide the worker's job title. ---
----

H Explain why you believe the worker is an employee or an independent contractor. ------------------------------------
----

I Did the worker perform services for the firm before getting this position? . . . . ☐ **Yes** ☐ **No** ☐ **N/A**
If "Yes," what were the dates of the prior service? --
If "Yes," explain the differences, if any, between the current and prior service. ---------------------------------------
----

J If the work is done under a written agreement between the firm and the worker, attach a copy (preferably signed by both parties). Describe the terms and conditions of the work arrangement. --
----

Part I   Behavioral Control

1   What specific training and/or instruction is the worker given by the firm? ....

2   How does the worker receive work assignments? ....

3   Who determines the methods by which the assignments are performed? ....

4   Who is the worker required to contact if problems or complaints arise and who is responsible for their resolution? ....

5   What types of reports are required from the worker? Attach examples. ....

6   Describe the worker's daily routine (i.e., schedule, hours, etc.). ....

7   At what location(s) does the worker perform services (e.g., firm's premises, own shop or office, home, customer's location, etc.)? ....

8   Describe any meetings the worker is required to attend and any penalties for not attending (e.g., sales meetings, monthly meetings, staff meetings, etc.). ....

9   Is the worker required to provide the services personally? . . . . ☐ **Yes**   ☐ **No**

10 If substitutes or helpers are needed, who hires them? ....

11 If the worker hires the substitutes or helpers, is approval required? . . . . ☐ **Yes**   ☐ **No**
    If "Yes," by whom? ....

12 Who pays the substitutes or helpers? ....

13 Is the worker reimbursed if the worker pays the substitutes or helpers? . . . . ☐ **Yes**   ☐ **No**
    If "Yes," by whom? ....

Part II   Financial Control

1   List the supplies, equipment, materials, and property provided by each party:
    The firm ....
    The worker ....
    Other party ....

2   Does the worker lease equipment? . . . . ☐ **Yes**   ☐ **No**
    If "Yes," what are the terms of the lease? (Attach a copy or explanatory statement.) ....

3   What expenses are incurred by the worker in the performance of services for the firm? ....

4   Specify which, if any, expenses are reimbursed by:
    The firm ....
    Other party ....

5   Type of pay the worker receives: ☐ Salary   ☐ Commission   ☐ Hourly Wage   ☐ Piece Work
    ☐ Lump Sum   ☐ Other (specify) ....
    If type of pay is commission, and the firm guarantees a minimum amount of pay, specify amount $ _____ .

6   If the worker is paid by a firm other than the one listed on this form for these services, enter name, address, and employer identification number of the payer. ....

7   Is the worker allowed a drawing account for advances? . . . . ☐ **Yes**   ☐ **No**
    If "Yes," how often? ....
    Specify any restrictions. ....

8   Whom does the customer pay? . . . . ☐ Firm   ☐ Worker
    If worker, does the worker pay the total amount to the firm? ☐ **Yes**   ☐ **No**   If "No," explain. ....

9   Does the firm carry worker's compensation insurance on the worker? . . . . ☐ **Yes**   ☐ **No**

10 What economic loss or financial risk, if any, can the worker incur beyond the normal loss of salary (e.g., loss or damage of equipment, material, etc.)? ....

Part III Relationship of the Worker and Firm

1 List the benefits available to the worker (e.g., paid vacations, sick pay, pensions, bonuses). _____

2 Can the relationship be terminated by either party without incurring liability or penalty? ☐ **Yes** ☐ **No**
If "No," explain your answer. _____

3 Does the worker perform similar services for others? ☐ **Yes** ☐ **No**
If "Yes," is the worker required to get approval from the firm? ☐ **Yes** ☐ **No**

4 Describe any agreements prohibiting competition between the worker and the firm while the worker is performing services or during any later period. Attach any available documentation. _____

5 Is the worker a member of a union? ☐ **Yes** ☐ **No**

6 What type of advertising, if any, does the worker do (e.g., a business listing in a directory, business cards, etc.)? Provide copies, if applicable.

7 If the worker assembles or processes a product at home, who provides the materials and instructions or pattern? _____

8 What does the worker do with the finished product (e.g., return it to the firm, provide it to another party, or sell it)? _____

9 How does the firm represent the worker to its customers (e.g., employee, partner, representative, or contractor)? _____

10 If the worker no longer performs services for the firm, how did the relationship end? _____

Part IV For Service Providers or Salespersons- Complete this part if the worker provided a service directly to customers or is a salesperson.

1 What are the worker's responsibilities in soliciting new customers? _____

2 Who provides the worker with leads to prospective customers? _____

3 Describe any reporting requirements pertaining to the leads. _____

4 What terms and conditions of sale, if any, are required by the firm? _____

5 Are orders submitted to and subject to approval by the firm? ☐ **Yes** ☐ **No**

6 Who determines the worker's territory? _____

7 Did the worker pay for the privilege of serving customers on the route or in the territory? ☐ **Yes** ☐ **No**
If "Yes," whom did the worker pay? _____
If "Yes," how much did the worker pay? $ _____

8 Where does the worker sell the product (e.g., in a home, retail establishment, etc.)? _____

9 List the product and/or services distributed by the worker (e.g., meat, vegetables, fruit, bakery products, beverages, or laundry or dry cleaning services). If more than one type of product and/or service is distributed, specify the principal one. _____

10 Does the worker sell life insurance full time? ☐ **Yes** ☐ **No**

11 Does the worker sell other types of insurance for the firm? ☐ **Yes** ☐ **No**
If "Yes," enter the percentage of the worker's total working time spent in selling other types of insurance. _____%

12 If the worker solicits orders from wholesalers, retailers, contractors, or operators of hotels, restaurants, or other similar establishments, enter the percentage of the worker's time spent in the solicitation. _____%

13 Is the merchandise purchased by the customers for resale or use in their business operations? ☐ **Yes** ☐ **No**
Describe the merchandise and state whether it is equipment installed on the customers' premises. _____

Part V Signature (see page 4)

Under penalties of perjury, I declare that I have examined this request, including accompanying documents, and to the best of my knowledge and belief, the facts presented are true, correct, and complete.

Signature ▶ _____ Title ▶ _____ Date ▶ _____
(Type or print name below)

Form **W-9**

(Rev. January 2003)

Department of the Treasury
Internal Revenue Service

Request for Taxpayer
Identification Number and Certification

Give form to the requester. Do not send to the IRS.

Print or type — See Specific Instructions on page 2.

Name

Business name, if different from above

Check appropriate box: ☐ Individual/ Sole proprietor ☐ Corporation ☐ Partnership ☐ Other ▶ .... ☐ Exempt from backup withholding

Address (number, street, and apt. or suite no.)

Requester's name and address (optional)

City, state, and ZIP code

List account number(s) here (optional)

Part I — Taxpayer Identification Number (TIN)

Enter your TIN in the appropriate box. For individuals, this is your social security number (SSN). **However, for a resident alien, sole proprietor, or disregarded entity, see the Part I instructions on page 3.** For other entities, it is your employer identification number (EIN). If you do not have a number, see **How to get a TIN** on page 3.

Note: *If the account is in more than one name, see the chart on page 4 for guidelines on whose number to enter.*

Social security number

or

Employer identification number

Part II — Certification

Under penalties of perjury, I certify that:

1. The number shown on this form is my correct taxpayer identification number (or I am waiting for a number to be issued to me), **and**

2. I am not subject to backup withholding because: **(a)** I am exempt from backup withholding, or **(b)** I have not been notified by the Internal Revenue Service (IRS) that I am subject to backup withholding as a result of a failure to report all interest or dividends, or **(c)** the IRS has notified me that I am no longer subject to backup withholding, **and**

3. I am a U.S. person (including a U.S. resident alien).

Certification instructions. You must cross out item **2** above if you have been notified by the IRS that you are currently subject to backup withholding because you have failed to report all interest and dividends on your tax return. For real estate transactions, item **2** does not apply. For mortgage interest paid, acquisition or abandonment of secured property, cancellation of debt, contributions to an individual retirement arrangement (IRA), and generally, payments other than interest and dividends, you are not required to sign the Certification, but you must provide your correct TIN. (See the instructions on page 4.)

Sign Here

Signature of U.S. person ▶

Date ▶

Purpose of Form

A person who is required to file an information return with the IRS, must obtain your correct taxpayer identification number (TIN) to report, for example, income paid to you, real estate transactions, mortgage interest you paid, acquisition or abandonment of secured property, cancellation of debt, or contributions you made to an IRA.

U.S. person. Use Form W-9 only if you are a U.S. person (including a resident alien), to provide your correct TIN to the person requesting it (the requester) and, when applicable, to:

  1. Certify that the TIN you are giving is correct (or you are waiting for a number to be issued),

  2. Certify that you are not subject to backup withholding, or

  3. Claim exemption from backup withholding if you are a U.S. exempt payee.

  Note: *If a requester gives you a form other than Form W-9 to request your TIN, you must use the requester's form if it is substantially similar to this Form W-9.*

Foreign person. If you are a foreign person, use the appropriate Form W-8 (see **Pub. 515,** Withholding of Tax on Nonresident Aliens and Foreign Entities).

Nonresident alien who becomes a resident alien. Generally, only a nonresident alien individual may use the terms of a tax treaty to reduce or eliminate U.S. tax on certain types of income. However, most tax treaties contain a provision known as a "saving clause." Exceptions specified in the saving clause may permit an exemption from tax to continue for certain types of income even after the recipient has otherwise become a U.S. resident alien for tax purposes.

If you are a U.S. resident alien who is relying on an exception contained in the saving clause of a tax treaty to claim an exemption from U.S. tax on certain types of income, you must attach a statement that specifies the following five items:

  1. The treaty country. Generally, this must be the same treaty under which you claimed exemption from tax as a nonresident alien.

  2. The treaty article addressing the income.

  3. The article number (or location) in the tax treaty that contains the saving clause and its exceptions.

  4. The type and amount of income that qualifies for the exemption from tax.

  5. Sufficient facts to justify the exemption from tax under the terms of the treaty article.

Cat. No. 10231X

Form **W-9** (Rev. 1-2003)

Example. Article 20 of the U.S.-China income tax treaty allows an exemption from tax for scholarship income received by a Chinese student temporarily present in the United States. Under U.S. law, this student will become a resident alien for tax purposes if his or her stay in the United States exceeds 5 calendar years. However, paragraph 2 of the first Protocol to the U.S.-China treaty (dated April 30, 1984) allows the provisions of Article 20 to continue to apply even after the Chinese student becomes a resident alien of the United States. A Chinese student who qualifies for this exception (under paragraph 2 of the first protocol) and is relying on this exception to claim an exemption from tax on his or her scholarship or fellowship income would attach to Form W-9 a statement that includes the information described above to support that exemption.

If you are a **nonresident alien or a foreign entity** not subject to backup withholding, give the requester the appropriate completed Form W-8.

What is backup withholding? Persons making certain payments to you must under certain conditions withhold and pay to the IRS 30% of such payments (29% **after** December 31, 2003; 28% **after** December 31, 2005). This is called "backup withholding." Payments that may be subject to backup withholding include interest, dividends, broker and barter exchange transactions, rents, royalties, nonemployee pay, and certain payments from fishing boat operators. Real estate transactions are not subject to backup withholding.

You will **not** be subject to backup withholding on payments you receive if you give the requester your correct TIN, make the proper certifications, and report all your taxable interest and dividends on your tax return.

Payments you receive will be subject to backup withholding if:

1. You do not furnish your TIN to the requester, or

2. You do not certify your TIN when required (see the Part II instructions on page 4 for details), or

3. The IRS tells the requester that you furnished an incorrect TIN, or

4. The IRS tells you that you are subject to backup withholding because you did not report all your interest and dividends on your tax return (for reportable interest and dividends only), or

5. You do not certify to the requester that you are not subject to backup withholding under **4** above (for reportable interest and dividend accounts opened after 1983 only).

Certain payees and payments are exempt from backup withholding. See the instructions below and the separate **Instructions for the Requester of Form W-9.**

Penalties

Failure to furnish TIN. If you fail to furnish your correct TIN to a requester, you are subject to a penalty of $50 for each such failure unless your failure is due to reasonable cause and not to willful neglect.

Civil penalty for false information with respect to withholding. If you make a false statement with no reasonable basis that results in no backup withholding, you are subject to a $500 penalty.

Criminal penalty for falsifying information. Willfully falsifying certifications or affirmations may subject you to criminal penalties including fines and/or imprisonment.

Misuse of TINs. If the requester discloses or uses TINs in violation of Federal law, the requester may be subject to civil and criminal penalties.

Specific Instructions

Name

If you are an individual, you must generally enter the name shown on your social security card. However, if you have changed your last name, for instance, due to marriage without informing the Social Security Administration of the name change, enter your first name, the last name shown on your social security card, and your new last name.

If the account is in joint names, list first, and then circle, the name of the person or entity whose number you entered in Part I of the form.

Sole proprietor. Enter your **individual** name as shown on your social security card on the "Name" line. You may enter your business, trade, or "doing business as (DBA)" name on the "Business name" line.

Limited liability company (LLC). If you are a single-member LLC (including a foreign LLC with a domestic owner) that is disregarded as an entity separate from its owner under Treasury regulations section 301.7701-3, **enter the owner's name on the "Name" line.** Enter the LLC's name on the "Business name" line.

Other entities. Enter your business name as shown on required Federal tax documents on the "Name" line. This name should match the name shown on the charter or other legal document creating the entity. You may enter any business, trade, or DBA name on the "Business name" line.

Note: *You are requested to check the appropriate box for your status (individual/sole proprietor, corporation, etc.).*

Exempt From Backup Withholding

If you are exempt, enter your name as described above and check the appropriate box for your status, then check the "Exempt from backup withholding" box in the line following the business name, sign and date the form.

Generally, individuals (including sole proprietors) are not exempt from backup withholding. Corporations are exempt from backup withholding for certain payments, such as interest and dividends.

Note: *If you are exempt from backup withholding, you should still complete this form to avoid possible erroneous backup withholding.*

Exempt payees. Backup withholding is **not required** on any payments made to the following payees:

1. An organization exempt from tax under section 501(a), any IRA, or a custodial account under section 403(b)(7) if the account satisfies the requirements of section 401(f)(2);

2. The United States or any of its agencies or instrumentalities;

3. A state, the District of Columbia, a possession of the United States, or any of their political subdivisions or instrumentalities;

4. A foreign government or any of its political subdivisions, agencies, or instrumentalities; or

5. An international organization or any of its agencies or instrumentalities.

Other payees that **may be exempt** from backup withholding include:

6. A corporation;

7. A foreign central bank of issue;

8. A dealer in securities or commodities required to register in the United States, the District of Columbia, or a possession of the United States;

9. A futures commission merchant registered with the Commodity Futures Trading Commission;

10. A real estate investment trust;

11. An entity registered at all times during the tax year under the Investment Company Act of 1940;

12. A common trust fund operated by a bank under section 584(a);

13. A financial institution;

14. A middleman known in the investment community as a nominee or custodian; or

15. A trust exempt from tax under section 664 or described in section 4947.

The chart below shows types of payments that may be exempt from backup withholding. The chart applies to the exempt recipients listed above, **1** through **15**.

If the payment is for . . .	THEN the payment is exempt for . . .
Interest and dividend payments	All exempt recipients except for **9**
Broker transactions	Exempt recipients **1** through **13**. Also, a person registered under the Investment Advisers Act of 1940 who regularly acts as a broker
Barter exchange transactions and patronage dividends	Exempt recipients **1** through **5**
Payments over $600 required to be reported and direct sales over $5,000 [1]	Generally, exempt recipients **1** through **7** [2]

[1] See **Form 1099-MISC**, Miscellaneous Income, and its instructions.

[2] However, the following payments made to a corporation (including gross proceeds paid to an attorney under section 6045(f), even if the attorney is a corporation) and reportable on Form 1099-MISC are **not exempt** from backup withholding: medical and health care payments, attorneys' fees; and payments for services paid by a Federal executive agency.

Part I. Taxpayer Identification Number (TIN)

Enter your TIN in the appropriate box. If you are a **resident alien** and you do not have and are not eligible to get an SSN, your TIN is your IRS individual taxpayer identification number (ITIN). Enter it in the social security number box. If you do not have an ITIN, see **How to get a TIN** below.

If you are a **sole proprietor** and you have an EIN, you may enter either your SSN or EIN. However, the IRS prefers that you use your SSN.

If you are a single-owner **LLC** that is disregarded as an entity separate from its owner (see **Limited liability company (LLC)** on page 2), enter your SSN (or EIN, if you have one). If the LLC is a corporation, partnership, etc., enter the entity's EIN.

Note: *See the chart on page 4 for further clarification of name and TIN combinations.*

How to get a TIN. If you do not have a TIN, apply for one immediately. To apply for an SSN, get **Form SS-5,** Application for a Social Security Card, from your local Social Security Administration office or get this form on-line at **www.ssa.gov/online/ss5.html**. You may also get this form by calling 1-800-772-1213. Use **Form W-7,** Application for IRS Individual Taxpayer Identification Number, to apply for an ITIN, or **Form SS-4,** Application for Employer Identification Number, to apply for an EIN. You can get Forms W-7 and SS-4 from the IRS by calling 1-800-TAX-FORM (1-800-829-3676) or from the IRS Web Site at **www.irs.gov**.

If you are asked to complete Form W-9 but do not have a TIN, write "Applied For" in the space for the TIN, sign and date the form, and give it to the requester. For interest and dividend payments, and certain payments made with respect to readily tradable instruments, generally you will have 60 days to get a TIN and give it to the requester before you are subject to backup withholding on payments. The 60-day rule does not apply to other types of payments. You will be subject to backup withholding on all such payments until you provide your TIN to the requester.

Note: *Writing "Applied For" means that you have already applied for a TIN **or** that you intend to apply for one soon.*

Caution: *A disregarded domestic entity that has a foreign owner must use the appropriate Form W-8.*

Part II. Certification

To establish to the withholding agent that you are a U.S. person, or resident alien, sign Form W-9. You may be requested to sign by the withholding agent even if items 1, 3, and 5 below indicate otherwise.

For a joint account, only the person whose TIN is shown in Part I should sign (when required). Exempt recipients, see **Exempt from backup withholding** on page 2.

Signature requirements. Complete the certification as indicated in **1** through **5** below.

1. Interest, dividend, and barter exchange accounts opened before 1984 and broker accounts considered active during 1983. You must give your correct TIN, but you do not have to sign the certification.

2. Interest, dividend, broker, and barter exchange accounts opened after 1983 and broker accounts considered inactive during 1983. You must sign the certification or backup withholding will apply. If you are subject to backup withholding and you are merely providing your correct TIN to the requester, you must cross out item **2** in the certification before signing the form.

3. Real estate transactions. You must sign the certification. You may cross out item **2** of the certification.

4. Other payments. You must give your correct TIN, but you do not have to sign the certification unless you have been notified that you have previously given an incorrect TIN. "Other payments" include payments made in the course of the requester's trade or business for rents, royalties, goods (other than bills for merchandise), medical and health care services (including payments to corporations), payments to a nonemployee for services, payments to certain fishing boat crew members and fishermen, and gross proceeds paid to attorneys (including payments to corporations).

5. Mortgage interest paid by you, acquisition or abandonment of secured property, cancellation of debt, qualified tuition program payments (under section 529), IRA or Archer MSA contributions or distributions, and pension distributions. You must give your correct TIN, but you do not have to sign the certification.

What Name and Number To Give the Requester

For this type of account:	Give name and SSN of:
1. Individual	The individual
2. Two or more individuals (joint account)	The actual owner of the account or, if combined funds, the first individual on the account [1]
3. Custodian account of a minor (Uniform Gift to Minors Act)	The minor [2]
4. a. The usual revocable savings trust (grantor is also trustee)	The grantor-trustee [1]
b. So-called trust account that is not a legal or valid trust under state law	The actual owner [1]
5. Sole proprietorship or single-owner LLC	The owner [3]

For this type of account:	Give name and EIN of:
6. Sole proprietorship or single-owner LLC	The owner [3]
7. A valid trust, estate, or pension trust	Legal entity [4]
8. Corporate or LLC electing corporate status on Form 8832	The corporation
9. Association, club, religious, charitable, educational, or other tax-exempt organization	The organization
10. Partnership or multi-member LLC	The partnership
11. A broker or registered nominee	The broker or nominee
12. Account with the Department of Agriculture in the name of a public entity (such as a state or local government, school district, or prison) that receives agricultural program payments	The public entity

[1] List first and circle the name of the person whose number you furnish. If only one person on a joint account has an SSN, that person's number must be furnished.

[2] Circle the minor's name and furnish the minor's SSN.

[3] **You must show your individual name,** but you may also enter your business or "DBA" name. You may use either your SSN or EIN (if you have one).

[4] List first and circle the name of the legal trust, estate, or pension trust. (Do not furnish the TIN of the personal representative or trustee unless the legal entity itself is not designated in the account title.)

Note: *If no name is circled when more than one name is listed, the number will be considered to be that of the first name listed.*

Privacy Act Notice

Section 6109 of the Internal Revenue Code requires you to provide your correct TIN to persons who must file information returns with the IRS to report interest, dividends, and certain other income paid to you, mortgage interest you paid, the acquisition or abandonment of secured property, cancellation of debt, or contributions you made to an IRA or Archer MSA. The IRS uses the numbers for identification purposes and to help verify the accuracy of your tax return. The IRS may also provide this information to the Department of Justice for civil and criminal litigation, and to cities, states, and the District of Columbia to carry out their tax laws. We may also disclose this information to other countries under a tax treaty, or to Federal and state agencies to enforce Federal nontax criminal laws and to combat terrorism.

You must provide your TIN whether or not you are required to file a tax return. Payers must generally withhold 30% of taxable interest, dividend, and certain other payments to a payee who does not give a TIN to a payer. Certain penalties may also apply.

Index

■

Remember:

Little publishers have big ears.
We really listen to you.

Take 2 Minutes & Give Us Your 2 cents

Your comments make a big difference in the development and revision of Nolo books and software. Please take a few minutes and register your Nolo product—and your comments—with us. Not only will your input make a difference, you'll receive special offers available only to registered owners of Nolo products on our newest books and software. Register now by:

PHONE
1-800-728-3555

FAX
1-800-645-0895

EMAIL
cs@nolo.com

or **MAIL** us
this registration card

fold here

- -

NOLO **Registration Card**

NAME _____ DATE _____

ADDRESS _____

_____

CITY _____ STATE _____ ZIP _____

PHONE _____ E-MAIL _____

WHERE DID YOU HEAR ABOUT THIS PRODUCT? _____

WHERE DID YOU PURCHASE THIS PRODUCT? _____

DID YOU CONSULT A LAWYER? (PLEASE CIRCLE ONE)   YES   NO   NOT APPLICABLE

DID YOU FIND THIS BOOK HELPFUL?   (VERY)   5   4   3   2   1   (NOT AT ALL)

COMMENTS _____

_____

_____

WAS IT EASY TO USE?   (VERY EASY)   5   4   3   2   1   (VERY DIFFICULT)

We occasionally make our mailing list available to carefully selected companies whose products may be of interest to you.

❑ If you do not wish to receive mailings from these companies, please check this box.

❑ You can quote me in future Nolo promotional materials.
    Daytime phone number _____.

HICI 4.0

Nolo in the NEWS

"Nolo helps lay people perform legal tasks without the aid—or fees—of lawyers."

—USA TODAY

Nolo books are ..."written in plain language, free of legal mumbo jumbo, and spiced with witty personal observations."

—ASSOCIATED PRESS

"...Nolo publications...guide people simply through the how, when, where and why of law."

—WASHINGTON POST

"Increasingly, people who are not lawyers are performing tasks usually regarded as legal work... And consumers, using books like Nolo's, do routine legal work themselves."

—NEW YORK TIMES

"...All of [Nolo's] books are easy-to-understand, are updated regularly, provide pull-out forms...and are often quite moving in their sense of compassion for the struggles of the lay reader."

—SAN FRANCISCO CHRONICLE

fold here

- -

Place
stamp here

Nolo
950 Parker Street
Berkeley, CA 94710-9867

Attn: HICI 4.0